BEYOND KNOWLEDGE

Extracognitive Aspects
of Developing High Ability

The Educational Psychology Series
Robert J. Sternberg and Wendy M. Williams, Series Editors

Marton/Booth • *Learning and Awareness*

Hacker/Dunlovsky/Graesser, Eds. • *Metacognition in Educational Theory and Practice*

Smith/Pourchot, Eds. • *Adult Learning and Development: Perspectives From Educational Psychology*

Sternberg/Williams, Eds. • *Intelligence, Instruction, and Assessment: Theory Into Practice*

Martinez • *Education as the Cultivation of Intelligence*

Torff/Sternberg, Eds. • *Understanding and Teaching the Intuitive Mind: Student and Teacher Learning*

Sternberg/Zhang, Eds. • *Perspectives on Cognitive, Learning, and Thinking Styles*

Ferrari, Ed. • *The Pursuit of Excellence Through Education*

Corno, Cronbach, Kupermintz, Lohman, Mandinach, Porteus, Albert/The Stanford Aptitude Seminar • *Remaking the Concept of Aptitude: Extending the Legacy of Richard E. Snow*

Dominowski • *Teaching Undergraduates*

Valdés • *Expanding Definitions of Giftedness: The Case of Young Interpreters From Immigrant Communities*

Shavinina/Ferrari, Eds. • *Beyond Knowledge: Extracognitive Aspects of Developing High Ability*

BEYOND KNOWLEDGE

Extracognitive Aspects
of Developing High Ability

Edited by

Larisa V. Shavinina
*Département des Sciences Administratives,
Université du Québec en Outaouais, Canada*

Michel Ferrari
*Ontario Institute for Studies in Education,
University of Toronto, Canada*

LAWRENCE ERLBAUM ASSOCIATES, PUBLISHERS
2004   Mahwah, New Jersey   London

Copyright © 2004 by Lawrence Erlbaum Associates, Inc.
All rights reserved. No part of this book may be reproduced in
any form, by photostat, microform, retrieval system, or any other
means, without the prior written permission of the publisher.

Lawrence Erlbaum Associates, Inc., Publishers
10 Industrial Avenue
Mahwah, New Jersey 07430

Cover design by Kathryn Houghtaling Lacey

Library of Congress Cataloging-in-Publication Data

Beyond knowledge : extracognitive aspects of developing high ability / edited by Larisa V. Shavinina, Michel Ferrari.
 p. cm. — (The educational psychology series)
 Includes bibliographical references and indexes.
 ISBN 0-8058-3991-7 (cloth : alk. paper) — ISBN 0-8058-3992-5 (pbk. : alk. paper)
 1. Genius. 2. Gifted persons. 3. Creative ability. 4. Creative thinking. I. Shavinina, Larisa V., PhD. II. Ferrari, Michel, Ph. D. III. Series.

BF412.B44 2003
153.9—dc21
2003056135
CIP

Books published by Lawrence Erlbaum Associates are printed on acid-free paper, and their bindings are chosen for strength and durability.

Printed in the United States of America
10 9 8 7 6 5 4 3 2 1

*This book is dedicated to the memory of Michael Howe,
a great scholar who devoted his professional life
to the study of high abilities.
He is deeply missed by all who knew him.*

Contents

Preface ix

I INTRODUCTION 1

1 Extracognitive Facets of Developing High Ability: Introduction to Some Important Issues 3
Larisa V. Shavinina and Michel Ferrari

II EXTRACOGNITIVE ASPECTS OF EXCEPTIONAL CREATIVE ACHIEVEMENTS 15

2 Creativity as an Extracognitive Phenomenon 17
Mark A. Runco

3 The Role of Unconscious Processes in the Evolvement of Creativity 27
Gudmund J. W. Smith

4 Exceptional Creativity and Chance: Creative Thought as a Stochastic Combinatorial Process 39
Dean Keith Simonton

5 Extracognitive Phenomena in the Intellectual Functioning of Gifted, Creative, and Talented Individuals 73
Larisa V. Shavinina and Kavita L. Seeratan

III DEVELOPING EXTRACOGNITIVE ASPECTS OF EXCEPTIONAL ABILITIES 103

6 Some Insights of Geniuses Into the Causes of Exceptional Achievement 105
Michael J. A. Howe

7 The Development of Talent in Different Domains 119
Deborah A. Greenspan, Becca Solomon, and Howard Gardner

8 Transforming Elite Musicians Into Professional Artists: A View of the Talent Development Process at the Juilliard School 137
Rena Subotnik

IV EXTRACOGNITIVE ASPECTS OF HIGH ABILITY AND THE IDEAL ENDS OF DEVELOPMENT 167

9 Wisdom and Giftedness 169
Robert J. Sternberg

10 High Abilities and Excellence: A Cultural Perspective 181
Jin Li

V CONCLUSION 209

11 Educating Selves to Be Creative and Wise 211
Michel Ferrari

Author Index 239

Subject Index 247

Preface

As psychologists delve further into the essence of giftedness and creativity, they discover many phenomena that help us to better understand the nature of high ability. Clearly, some facets of high ability cannot be explained by cognitive, developmental, personality, or social approaches considered in isolation. There is something at the intersection of these approaches—something deeply hidden, and at the same time very important. These are the extracognitive facets of high ability and they are what this volume is all about.

We have wanted to see this book published for many years and are in special debt to two people without whom this book would not have been possible. Marina A. Kholodnaya initially introduced Larisa Shavinina to the fascinating topic of extracognitive facets of high ability, showing her their undoubted importance. Robert J. Sternberg was also well aware of the importance of extracognitive aspects of giftedness and creativity and supported the idea of this book from the beginning, inviting us to publish it in this series he edits for Lawrence Erlbaum Associates.

Finally, a very grateful thanks to the contributors for their interesting chapters and the effort that they invested in preparing them.

—*Larisa V. Shavinina*
—*Michel Ferrari*
Toronto, May 2002

INTRODUCTION

Chapter 1

Extracognitive Facets of Developing High Ability: Introduction to Some Important Issues

Larisa V. Shavinina
Département des Sciences Administratives,
Université du Québec en Outaouais, Canada

Michel Ferrari
Ontario Institute for Studies in Education,
University of Toronto, Canada

One way to understand the history of human civilization is via its inventions and discoveries. All human cultural development builds on the amazing technological, scientific, educational, and moral achievements of the human mind. People of exceptionally high ability thus remain an extremely important source of cultural innovation and renewal. By "high ability," we mean exceptional human abilities referred to by terms like *giftedness, talent, creativity, genius, child prodigies, innovation,* and *wisdom*. Despite the evident social importance of highly able people, the phenomenon of high ability is far from well understood.

Extracognitive facets play an essential role in the development and expression of exceptional achievement. Extracognitive facets are those that go beyond cognition. In other words, they concern those facets of intelligence that are not captured by many traditional accounts of giftedness or expertise. These include various feelings (e.g., feeling of beauty), temperament, and institutional and cultural influences critical to developing high ability. These facets lie at the intersection of many branches of psychology (e.g., personality, cognitive, and developmental psychology) and of many subdisciplines of the psychology of high ability (e.g., psychology of giftedness, creativity, and wisdom).

The history of psychology has at least two long-established research traditions that aim to study extracognitive facets in high ability: the study of *personality traits* associated with high ability (the so-called personality trait approach[1] in the psychology of giftedness and creativity) and the investigation of *social factors* facilitating the development of human talents. We review them briefly here to allow readers to situate our book with regard to these traditions.

STUDIES OF EXCEPTIONAL ABILITY

Personality Traits Associated With High Ability

Even a brief look at studies conducted within the personality trait approach demonstrates that this approach is one of the earliest, most traditional, and popular approaches in psychology of high ability. This tradition began with the work of Sir Francis Galton (1869/1891) on genius and heredity and his attempts to measure human intelligence. Galton's studies include an early research on both cognitive and extracognitive facets of high ability, particularly the personality of gifted individuals. Almost all researchers include certain personality traits in their theories, conceptions, and models of giftedness and creativity. Findings and achievements of the personality trait approach are very important; understanding the personality of gifted, creative, and talented individuals has great scientific significance. In general, two directions of research on personality traits of highly able individuals can be distinguished: studies of gifted children, and studies of genius and eminent persons.[2]

Studies of Gifted Children

Terman's (1925, 1954) pioneering studies of more than 1,000 gifted children continued the Galtonian tradition of research and significantly strengthened scientists' interest in personality traits of highly able individuals. Terman's investigations are the most widely recognized and frequently quoted research on the personality traits (characteristics, peculiarities, qualities, etc.) of gifted people. In his early studies, Terman found that, in tests of "character," gifted children scored higher than the control group; in trait ratings by parents and teachers, gifted children excelled in intellectual, emotional, moral, physical, and social traits. The conclusion he reached as a

---

[1]The personality trait approach can be defined as concentrating on the identification, measurement, and description of such extracognitive personality characteristics as the motivation, emotion, and character of gifted, creative, and talented individuals.

[2]Of course, it is not possible to consider all research arising from the personality trait approach in one chapter—only the most important points outlined in psychological literature are mentioned here.

result of 30 years of follow-up studies on his initial group was that notable achievement calls for more than high intelligence. In particular, he emphasized personality, especially "persistence in the accomplishment of ends, integration toward goals, self-confidence, freedom from inferiority feelings, all-round emotional and social adjustment, and drive to achieve" (Terman & Oden, 1959, p. 148).

Likewise, Hollingworth (1926, 1942) showed that gifted children manifest early interest in reading and are above average in emotional stability, as well as walking and talking earlier than other children. They were also less neurotic, more self-sufficient, and more self-confident than the population with which they were compared.

Leites' (1960, 1971, 1996) studies of extremely gifted, creative, and talented children showed that very high mental activity (i.e., the ability to carry out mental tasks, cognitive curiosity, the desire to ask questions, the capacity to engage in high intellectual learning and mental efforts, strong need for mental work, etc.) and self-regulation (i.e., independent formulation of purposes, planning one's own activities, etc.) are the most general basic factors of giftedness and are the distinguishing characteristics of these children.

Feldman (1979) also found that prodigiousness is a reflection of the strong interests and motivation of extremely gifted children.

> Perhaps the most striking quality in the children in our study as well as other cases is the passion with which excellence is pursued. Commitment and tenacity and joy in achievement are perhaps the best signs that a coincidence has occurred among child, field and moment in evolutionary time. (Feldman, 1979, p. 351)

Exceptional Adults

Cox's (1926) monumental study of great geniuses definitely deserves mention here. One of her three well-known conclusions was that "youths who achieve eminence are characterized not only by high intellectual traits, but also by the greatest degree of persistence of motive and effort, confidence in their abilities and great strength or force of character [...]. The superior youths [...] pursued high ideas, developed significant interests [...]" (Cox, 1926, p. 50).

Similarly, in her pioneering study of the characteristics of gifted adult scientists, Roe (1952, 1958, 1983) found that early in their lives, exceptional individuals all showed considerable independence and developed intense private interests that, except for the social scientists, were shared with few others. They read a lot and enjoyed school and studying; they were curious and this played a major role in their lives. Their early interests differentiated between groups. Biologists were interested in natural history, social scientists contemplated literary careers. Biologists relied heavily on rational control. Physicists were not interested in people, avoided interpersonal relationships, and were often anxious. Social scientists were concerned with human relationships. They were capable of hard work and deep concentration, and obtained a great deal of satisfaction from their work. All of Roe's subjects had a high level of commitment to their work.

More recently, MacKinnon (1960, 1978) showed the following traits to be characteristics of creative, highly effective individuals, and important in creative accomplishments: openness to experience, freedom from crippling restraints and impoverishing inhibitions, aesthetic sensitivity, independence in thoughts and actions, individuality, unquestioning commitment to creative endeavor, emotional stability or personal soundness, enthusiasm, determination, and industry.

Considering research on both exceptional children and exceptional adults, a general picture of personality characteristics of gifted, creative, and talented individuals emerges:

Motivation: drive to achieve excellence, intrinsic achievement motivation: high level of self-motivation or task motivation; the passion with which excellence is pursued; a powerful desire for self-advancement. Most researchers distinguish motivation as a central characteristic among many other traits of gifted individuals.

For example, task motivation is one of the major personality characteristics implicated in Amabile's (1983) conception of creativity. According to Amabile, task motivation includes the individual's motivation for undertaking the task and his or her perception of this motivation. Tannenbaum (1986) also asserted that "without the support of nonintellective traits, such as the capacity and willingness to work hard in achieving excellence, it is impossible to rise above mediocrity" (p. 31). Renzulli (1986) and Rahn (1986) expressed similar views. Thus, Renzulli (1986) included "task commitment" in his conception of giftedness and stressed that the "argument for including this nonintellective cluster of traits in a definition of giftedness is nothing short of overwhelming. From popular claims and autobiographical accounts to empirical research findings, one of the key ingredients that has characterized the work of gifted persons is their ability to involve themselves totally in a specific problem or area for an extended period of time" (p. 70). Rahn (1986) studied the German winners of the annual competition *Jugend forscht* (youth conducts research), and concluded that factors such as interests, individual goals, and action competencies are more important than intelligence.

Heller (1993), having analyzed high ability within the psychometric paradigm, emphasized the following personality traits of gifted individuals which are frequently mentioned in the literature—specifically, intrinsic

1. DEVELOPING HIGH ABILITY

achievement motivation, goal orientation and persistence at tasks, tolerance of ambiguity, uncertainty and complexity, clear interests, and nonconformity. He identified motivation as one of the most powerful long-range predictors of professional success in science and technology. Howe (1990, 1993) and Perleth, Lehwald, and Browder (1993) regarded curiosity and interest as important for the development of high ability.

> These motivational characteristics manifest themselves in a child's behavior [...]. During childhood, curiosity manifests itself in exploratory behavior. Therefore, the latter may be used as an early indicator of intellectual functioning [...]. (Perleth et al., 1993, p. 297)

Feldhusen and Jarwan (1993) considered various definitions of giftedness and concluded that

> trait definitions are derived from psychological characteristics that are assumed to differentiate gifted children from others [...]. Unusual curiosity, variety of interests, persistence in attacking difficult mental tasks, etc., are among the traits included in these definitions [...]. (Feldhusen & Jarwan, 1993, p. 234)

Character/temperament: perseverance, endurance, hard work; self-confidence; persistence in the accomplishment of ends, integration towards a goal; independence, preference for working alone, individualism; determination, industry; belief in one's ability to carry out important work; nonconformity; the ability to involve oneself completely in a specific problem or area for an extended period of time; self-sufficiency; positive self-concept, high self-esteem; internal locus of control; ambition, striving toward success; high self-criticism; highly developed feeling for justice; well developed self-regulation.

Emotion: freedom from feelings of inferiority; enthusiasm; special fascination for the subject matter of one's chosen field; emotional stability; joy in achievements; boundless energy; high emotional perceptiveness; and a great satisfaction with work.

The most fundamental finding of the personality trait approach is therefore the unquestioned fact of the unique personality of highly able people. Certainly, this picture does not account for all possible personality characteristics of gifted, creative, and talented individuals. However, it provides a useful demonstration of the unique personalities of those who are considered gifted. While these studies revealed key personality traits associated with high ability, another important body of work has pointed to sociocultural factors that are critical to fostering the sort of personality that produces exceptional achievements.

Sociocultural Factors

The second research tradition studying extracognitive facets of high ability explores social factors facilitating the development of human talent. Sociocultural forces include both micro- and macro-social influences on personal development. *Micro-social factors* include family, school, "significant others" (e.g., professors or mentors, peers, friends, and other people nearest the gifted at the beginning of their careers; Feldman, 1986; Gardner, 1993; Howe, 1990, 1993; McCurdy, 1992). *Macro-social forces* include cultural, political, and historical conditions under which a person lives and develops his or her talents that affect their exceptional achievements (e.g., society as a whole, culture, and the particular historical period; Csikszentmihalyi, 1996; Simonton, 1988; Sternberg & Lubart, 1995). More details on this approach are given in the chapters that follow.

Although there may be other influences on the development of exceptional ability, this dichotomy provides a broad overview of forces outside of the individual that facilitate the expression of a person's abilities.

EXTRACOGNITIVE FACTORS IN THE EXPRESSION OF HIGH ABILITY: OVERVIEW OF THE VOLUME

Besides the personality traits and social factors associated with high ability, a third direction in the research on extracognitive facets of high ability includes internally developed standards and subjective norms of intellectual creativity; specific intellectual intentions and beliefs that influence exceptional achievements; specific feelings that scientific geniuses like Albert Einstein and other highly creative individuals say contributes to their advanced development (e.g., feelings of direction, harmony, beauty, and style); specific preferences and intellectual values (e.g., the "inevitable" choice of the field of endeavor by certain geniuses); intuitive processes; and luck, chance, and other similar phenomena in extraordinary development and performance.

This is a relatively new and unexplored direction in the study of high ability. And this is why we have prepared a book on this topic; a volume that reflects cutting-edge thinking and research on the extracognitive facets in high ability. Thus, this book presents an innovative way to address the topic of high ability, within which many insights in the psychology of giftedness, creativity, genius, and wisdom may be hidden. There are many books about the cognitive bases of high ability, but, we believe none discuss the foundations of such achievements in ways that go beyond knowledge. This book is about just such facets that have tremendous impact on the development of an individual's high ability.

Extracognitive Aspects of Exceptional Creative Achievements

The book begins with a chapter by Runco, entitled "Creativity as an Extracognitive Phenomenon." He proposes that personal creativity depends on extracognitive processes, not only involving personality, but also metacognition and discretion. In particular, he emphasizes ego-strength and fostering tactics for originality such as change of perspective, analogy, and adapting or borrowing ideas from other areas of expertise. Importantly, Runco believes that much of this can be explicitly taught and will allow more children and adults to fulfill their creative potential.

In his chapter, "The Role of Unconscious Processes in the Evolvement of Creativity," Gudmund Smith adds another dimension to the discussion of extracognitive facets of high ability by noting that extraordinary creative ability implicates unconscious affective processes. Smith's studies show that important facets of human mental activity are inaccessible to everyday waking consciousness; much of perceptual and conceptual interpretation remains beyond awareness. Smith maintains that roots of the microgeneses of ideas are usually hidden, but not necessarily completely beyond reach. Although some types of memories (e.g., procedural memories) appear to be inaccessible in principle, other memories (what Tulving calls autonoetic memories) remain outside awareness because they are temporarily inapposite, or disturbing. Smith proposes that this hidden world can be retrieved and included in ways that shape our experience within our everyday frame of reference. He argues that the degree of openness to the origins of the processes shaping our existence (experienced as self and outside reality) is important for intuition and creativity, and is associated with our ability to listen inward (to remember dreams, to reconstruct early childhood memories, etc.). According to Smith, inhibitions and mental stenosis may favor order and clarity, but not new thinking.

The chapter by Dean Keith Simonton entitled "Exceptional Creativity and Chance: Creative Thought as a Stochastic Combinatorial Process," proposes that the highest-level creativity in a particular cultural domain is less a consequence of any of the preceding influences than it is a matter of chance. The phenomenon of multiple discovery and invention within communities of individuals working in the same area shows that these inventions are not merely manifestations of the personal genius of creative individuals. The role of chance as a critical extracognitive facet in high ability is examined in the light of Simonton's predictive and explanatory stochastic model of creativity. According to this model, creativity involves generating combinations of ideas through a quasi-random process. Simonton's empirical research supports his main thesis that highly creative ideas can be viewed as a result of chance or good luck, although he acknowledges the importance of serendipity in actual scientific and cultural discovery.

In their chapter, "Extracognitive Phenomena in the Intellectual Functioning of Gifted, Creative, and Talented Individuals," Larisa Shavinina and Kavita Seeratan specify and extend the scope of these many claims by considering extracognitive phenomena implicated in the intellectual functioning of Nobel laureates. Nobel laureates provide specific examples of highly able people. It is striking to hear in their own accounts of extracognitive facets of their abilities, discussion of their feeling of direction (in their own scientific activity, in their search of mentors and of their own scientific domain), their specific scientific taste and highly developed intuition about important problems, good ideas, and elegant solutions, and their feelings about the beauty of these ideas. Shavinina and Seeratan demonstrate that these phenomena determine the mental working of the exceptional scientists and propose that they express the most refined manifestation of the intellectual and creative potentials of these individuals.

Developing Extracognitive Aspects of Exceptional Abilities

Michael Howe, in his chapter, "Some Insights of Geniuses Into the Causes of Exceptional Achievement," shows that when geniuses give their own views about the personal and sociocultural attributes that lead to exceptional creative achievements, they typically place more emphasis on qualities of temperament and personality than on cognitive abilities. Howe emphasizes that, historically, a number of geniuses have specifically denied possessing any special intellectual traits, like inherent cleverness or quickness of mind. He examines the observations made by historical geniuses on a variety of the personal qualities they regard as being vital to their exceptional accomplishments. These range from single-mindedness and sense of direction to curiosity, self-confidence, doggedness and perseverance, the capacity to focus interests effectively, and a tendency to respond positively to difficulties and failures. He also notes how they made use of their social context to achieve such amazing things.

Continuing to refine this theme, Deborah Greenspan, Rebecca Solomon, and Howard Gardner in their chapter entitled, "The Development of Talent in Different Domains," explore the influence of human and artifactual agents on children's commitment to various domains of talent in America today, including gymnastics, skating, theater, music, and community service. They conducted semistructured interviews with more than 40

1. DEVELOPING HIGH ABILITY 11

students deeply involved in an activity and learned about various influences on their decision making at critical points in their young careers. These interviews discussed their initial decision to participate in the activity, whether to persevere in the task during difficult times, to what or whom they turn for advice or support, and how they evaluated their success in the activity. A taxonomy of different kinds of influence was developed, including implicit (e.g., role models), explicit (e.g., direct advice), and media (e.g., books, television).

Rena Subotnik in her chapter, "Transforming Elite Musicians Into Professional Artists: A View of the Talent Development Process at the Juilliard School," considers the development of talent when students pursue their interests to the highest levels. She explores the specific example of the Juilliard conservatory. Juilliard is America's most prestigious conservatory for classical music, and the study of a special environment such as Juilliard allows Subotnik to explore the confluence of emerging great musical talent and elite institutions renowned for having exceptional instructional curriculums honed over generations and delivered by teachers at the pinnacle of their own expertise.

**Extracognitive Aspects of High Ability
and the Ideal Ends of Development**

In his chapter, "Wisdom and Giftedness," Robert Sternberg considers extracognitive facets in wisdom. On the basis of his research on wisdom and intelligence, he argues that wisdom is in some respects the most important, but the most neglected type of giftedness. Sternberg points out that psychologists' emphasis on analytic facets of giftedness to the exclusion of those that promote wisdom can lead to the development of leaders who are intelligent and/or creative, but unwise. His chapter presents a balance theory of wisdom and discusses how wisdom can be assessed and developed. Sternberg insists that the traditional academic emphasis on abilities such as analysis and memorization have produced leaders who have brought the world to the brink of destruction, but it is education for wisdom that holds the possibility of peace.

Jin Li, in her chapter, "High Abilities and Excellence: A Cultural Perspective," explores the role of culture that transcends specific institutions in the appearance of exceptional achievements. Her research program shows how different cultures provide different extracognitive models of learning and life orientation, including beliefs about learning, ways of thinking about and experiencing learning, and plans for action in learning. Individuals' intentions and behavior are also shaped by these deep-seated cultural models of exceptional persons that provide personal embodiments of notions such as zeitgeist, paradigm, and social systems. Li presents Chinese "heart and mind for wanting to learn" as an illustrative example of her point.

Finally, Michel Ferrari, in his chapter, integrates common themes from the various chapters and highlights important points of agreement and disagreement among the contributors to this volume.

REFERENCES

Amabile, T. M. (1983). *The social psychology of creativity*. New York: Springer-Verlag.
Csikszentmihalyi, M. (1996). *Creativity*. New York: HarperCollins.
Cox, C. (1926). *The early mental traits of 300 geniuses*. Stanford, CA: Stanford University Press.
Feldhusen, J. F., & Jarwan, F. A. (1993). Identification of gifted and talented youth for educational programs. In K. A. Heller, F. J. Mönks, & A. H. Passow (Eds.), *International handbook of research and development of giftedness and talent* (pp. 233–251). Oxford: Pergamon.
Feldman, D. H. (1979). The mysterious case of extreme giftedness. In A. H. Passow (Ed.), *The gifted and talented: Their education and development*. The Seventy Eighth Yearbook of the National Society for the Study of Education (pp. 335–351). Chicago: University of Chicago Press.
Feldman, D. H. (1986). *Nature's gambit: Child prodigies and the development of human potential*. New York: Basic.
Galton, F. (1891). *Hereditary genius: An inquiry into its laws and consequences*. New York: D. Appleton & Co. (Originally published 1869)
Gardner, H. (1993). *Creating minds*. New York: Basic.
Heller, K. A. (1993). Scientific ability. In G. R. Bock & K. Ackrill (Eds.), *The origins and development of high ability* (pp. 139–150). Chichester: John Wiley & Sons (Ciba Found. Symp. 178).
Hollingworth, L. S. (1926). *Gifted children: Their nature and nurture*. New York: Macmillan.
Hollingworth, L. (1942). *Children above 180 IQ Stanford-Binet*. New York: World Book.
Howe, M. J. A. (1990). *The origin of exceptional abilities*. Cambridge, MA: Blackwell.
Howe, M. J. A. (1993). The early lives of child prodigies. In G. R. Bock & K. Ackrill (Eds.), *The origins and development of high ability* (pp. 85–105). Chichester: John Wiley & Sons (Ciba Found. Symp. 178).
Leites, N. S. (1960). *Intellectual giftedness*. Moscow: APN.
Leites, N. S. (1971). *Intellectual abilities and age*. Moscow: Pedagogica.
Leites, N. S. (Ed.). (1996). *Psychology of giftedness of children and adolescents*. Moscow: Academia.
McCurdy, H. G. (1992). The childhood pattern of genius. In R. S. Albert (Ed.), *Genius and eminence* (pp. 155–169). Oxford: Pergamon.
MacKinnon, D. W. (1960). The highly effective individual. In R. S. Albert (Ed.), *Genius and eminence: The social psychology of creativity and exceptional achievement* (pp. 114–127). Oxford: Pergamon.
MacKinnon, D. W. (1978). *In search of human effectiveness*. Buffalo, NY: Creative Education Foundation.
Perleth, C., Lehwald, G., & Browder, C. S. (1993). Indicators of high ability in young children. In K. A. Heller, F. J. Mönks, & A. H. Passow (Eds.), *International handbook of research and development of giftedness and talent* (pp. 283–310). Oxford: Pergamon.
Rahn, H. (1986). *Jugend forscht* [Youth conducts research]. Gottingen: Hogrefe.
Renzulli, J. S. (1986). The three-ring conception of giftedness: A developmental model for creative productivity. In R. J. Sternberg & J. E. Davidson (Eds.), *Conceptions of giftedness* (pp. 53–92). New York: Cambridge University Press.
Roe, A. (1952). *The making of a scientist*. New York: Dodd Mead.

Roe, A. (1958). Early differentiation of interests. In C. W. Taylor (Ed.), *The second (1957) research conference on the identification of creative scientific talent* (pp. 58–108). Salt Lake City: University of Utah Press.

Roe, A. (1983). Early background of eminent scientists. In R. S. Albert (Ed.), *Genius and eminence: The social psychology of creativity and exceptional achievement* (pp. 170–181). Oxford: Pergamon.

Simonton, D. K. (1988). *Scientific genius: A psychology of science.* Cambridge: Cambridge University Press.

Sternberg, R. J., & Lubart, T. (1995). *Defying the crowd: Cultivating creativity in a culture of conformity.* New York: Free Press.

Tannenbaum, A. J. (1986). Giftedness: A psychosocial approach. In R. J. Sternberg & J. E. Davidson (Eds.), *Conceptions of giftedness* (pp. 21–52). New York: Cambridge University Press.

Terman, L. M. (1925). *Genetic studies of genius: Vol. 1. Mental and physical traits of a thousand gifted children.* Stanford, CA: Stanford University Press.

Terman, L. M. (1954). The discovery and encouragement of exceptional talent. *American Psychologist, 9,* 221–230.

Terman, L. M., & Oden, M. H. (1959). *The gifted group at mid-life.* Stanford, CA: Stanford University Press.

EXTRACOGNITIVE ASPECTS OF EXCEPTIONAL CREATIVE ACHIEVEMENTS

II

Chapter 2

Creativity as an Extracognitive Phenomenon

Mark A. Runco
California State University, Fullerton

"High ability" is a useful but general label. There are different kinds of high ability. Picasso may have accomplished what he did by relying on skills and capacities that differed dramatically from those used by the Wright Brothers, and their talents may have, in turn, differed dramatically from the skills and capacities of the scientists who recently found the tau neutrino. Evidence to support domain differences such as these and others was provided by Wallach and Wing (1969), with a sample of young adults, and by Runco (1986), with children.

Admittedly, there is some overlap among certain domains. Several involve symbolic skills and capacities, for example, and others may share a dependence on logic or sensory and perceptual sensitivity. Such overlap can create problems for those studying the phenomena and for those trying to put research findings into practice, but they must be recognized or we will have only a simplified and unrealistic view of high ability.

Some domains require creativity. Others involve creativity only some of the time, or only at particular levels of performance. Therefore the relationship of creativity with high-level abilities varies from domain to domain. And just as creative skills often contribute to high-level performances, accomplishment can result from processes and capacities other than creativity (Runco, 1995). Creativity depends on originality; that is the only facet of creativity on which everyone agrees. Accomplishment and achievement, on the other hand, may reflect other problem-solving skills besides creative problem solving, including some that are more convergent than divergent. Accomplishment also involves persistence, *Zeitgeist,* and luck, as well as talent.

In the remainder of this chapter I focus on creativity, keeping in mind what was just proposed about creativity sometimes being involved in accomplishment, and sometimes interacting with other kinds of abilities, but also recognizing that sometimes creativity is merely potential and unrelated to accomplishment and achievement. This view is consistent with several definitions of giftedness (e.g., Albert & Runco, 1986; Renzulli, 1978) wherein creativity is one aspect of giftedness, and contributes to gifted-level performances, but at the same time can be separated from it. In this chapter I focus even further and explore the extracognitive bases of creativity. In a sense, this is an extension of my earlier work on "personal creativity" (Runco, 1995, 1996).

Cognition, Metacognition, and Extracognition

Personal creativity depends on extracognitive processes. Basic cognitive processes are also involved; these were recently reviewed by Runco (in press). We must be careful with our terms and distinguish as precisely as possible between the cognitive and extracognitive bases of creativity, and for that matter between the metacognitive and extracognitive components of creative potential. I use the term *extracognitive* to refer to all things not strictly cognitive. This is indeed a general category, then, given that creativity is best viewed as a complex (Runco & Albert, in press) with personality, attitude, emotions, and cognitive processes each contributing to it. Extracognitive contributions include everything but basic cognitive influences.[1] Metacognitive processes are also very important for creative thinking. They are related to cognition, rather than outside the cognitive realm, but they are more specific than the extracognitive aspects of the complex. Metacognitive processes are not extracognitive because they often take advantage of particular cognitive processes. (Memory is one example of a basic cognitive process that is sometimes involved in creative thinking; Runco, in press.) The critical distinguishing characteristic of metacognitive processes may be their controllability. Individuals can monitor and manipulate metacognitive processes. This distinguishes them from basic cognitive processes, and it means (a) that there are developmental differences in the metacognitive facets of creativity, and (b) that they may constitute the most

---

[1]Sometimes even this distinction can be questioned, as is apparent in the debate about the relationship between emotion and cognition (Lazarus, 1991; Zajonc, 1991). One view is that emotions are independent of cognition. Another is that we do not care (emotionally) about things we do not understand (cognitively), in which case emotions and cognition are interdependent.

2. PERSONAL CREATIVITY

important target for enhancement and educational efforts. If individuals have control over these processes, they (and those working with them) can do something about them. This is not true about certain aspects of personality nor more basic cognitive processes.[2]

I elaborate on this idea of control and enhancement later in this chapter, but first I wish to relate the definitions I have just given to the theory of personal creativity that has already been outlined (Runco, 1996). This will clarify exactly what is involved in and unique about creativity and suggest something about the relationships among the pertinent cognitive, metacognitive, and extracognitive skills and capacities.

Personal Creativity

Creative thinking involves at least three things: the cognitive *capacity to transform* experience into original interpretations, an *interest* in producing original interpretations, and *discretion*.

By discretion I mean that the individual recognizes and chooses when to invest in and retain an original interpretation, and when to look to a rote interpretation instead. Note that it is largely a matter of choice. Think how often we have an idea but then decide that it is not worth sharing or would be embarrassing to share. We edit and direct our thinking. For creative thinking, the individual may need to stick with the idea regardless of what others think. After all, if others think differently, the individual who alone has the idea is original! What may be most important is that, in this light, originality is intentional; we choose to think in an original fashion and choose when to do so. The role played by choice makes this the most metacognitive of the processes involved.

In contrast, the processes involved in constructing interpretations are less intentional. They are much like the Piagetian processes involved in adaptation, namely *assimilation* and a*ccommodation*. In the former, information is transformed so it can be brought into the individual's cognitive system. In the latter, the cognitive system changes in accordance with new information. In assimilation, the information (the data provided by experience) is altered; in accommodation, the cognitive structures change to take that new information into account.

There are two points to emphasize. First, the model of personal creativity emphasizes assimilation and not accommodation. Accommodation is often tied to insight, and in particular to the "ah-ha" feeling that we have with a sudden recognition of a solution. But in that case, the solution is out there, somewhere, waiting to be understood. The process is therefore almost

---

[2] The only possible aspect of the creativity complex that may be as reasonable (and controllable) a target for education and enhancement efforts is attitude. Attitudes play a significant role in creative thinking and are easily manipulated.

convergent. The individual merely discovers what already exists. It is accommodation in that the thinking must change to grasp this existent idea or notion or solution. It is much more creative to assimilate, transform information, and construct one's own interpretation of experience. If it is one's own interpretation, it is original. If it is one's own, it is not convergent. Recall here that originality is the key feature of creative ideas.

The second point to emphasize is that assimilation is something we all do. It is universal. It is natural. It is not in and of itself a matter of choice. In that light, the assimilatory component of creativity is not something we can do much about! We don't need to do anything; everyone assimilates with ease. We can do something about the other parts of personal creativity, and we can do things (e.g., seek challenges) to make assimilation more probable or frequent. I think it quite reassuring that everyone has the potential to think in a creative fashion. The assimilative portion, at least, is not something reserved for geniuses or highly gifted persons.

Assimilation and interpretation may seem too mundane to tie to creativity, but keep in mind that information is transformed when it is assimilated. How is it altered? It is altered such that the individual's existing cognitive system can handle it, so it can be grasped and brought into the existing cognitive system. It is, then, idiosyncratic. It is not an act of conformity. At least as important, there is a transformation involved. The interpretations that result from assimilation are often—and perhaps always—different from what is presented in objective experience. The information is transformed in response to idiosyncratic cognitive structures. Piaget (1976) said it best in the title of his monograph, *To Understand Is to Invent*. My interpretation (no pun intended) of that title is that individuals do not have a true authentic understanding of their experience unless they construct that understanding for themselves. It is one thing to memorize some datum, but quite another to discover it for one's self. Only then do we really understand. My position is that what Piaget called "invention" is a kind of creation—a creation of personal meaning. I don't think this is far from Piaget's own view; he tied assimilation to imaginative play; and surely imaginative play manifests original and creative interpretations. Empirical research has also uncovered correlations between imaginative play and creative potential (Singer & Singer, in press).

Discretion is manifested in judgments that are largely independent of traditional cognitive processes, including divergent and convergent thinking. Surely personality is relevant here; a person with ego-strength is more likely to be original than to conform. I say more about ego-strength later in the chapter when I discuss ways to enhance creativity. First I need to bring home an important point about creativity: There are times when we should be original (and transform our experiences accordingly) and times when we should not. Sometimes the unoriginal interpretation is best. For example, when my children approach a busy intersection, and the stoplight facing their direction is red, I want them to stop every time! I want them to conform. There are other times when originality is necessary, and yet other times when we could conform or be original. One part of creativity is deciding when to invest in an original interpretation and when to rely on memory, conform, and act in a conventional fashion. This is discretion: Deciding when to be original and when not to be original.

Fortunately there is a science that helps us to understand judgment, discretion, and choice. Runco, Johnson, and Gaynor (1997) reviewed this area of research and explored its implications specifically for creativity. They proposed that "the maximization of creative potential is partly a matter of making the right choices and having the right choices made by one's parents and teachers. In this light, the study of choice, judgment, and the like should increase our understanding of the fulfillment of creative potential" (p. 16). They also suggested that predictions of high-level performances will be the most accurate if judgmental processes are taken into account. This is because many other predictors, including traits and abilities, generally define a range of possible expressions. They describe capacity and what the individual is capable of. Yet, if that individual's judgments are taken into account, we know what they will in fact do. The individual may decide to devote all of their resources and capacities to a problem or task, or they may only allocate a portion of each; but if one knows what they have decided to allocate, one can also know what is being used and applied rather than what *could be* used or applied. It is for this reason that we should take judgmental tendencies into account. Decisions lead very directly to actual performance.

Developmental Trends

We must take developmental processes into account. This is because there is a metacognitive component to personal creativity, and metacognitive processes typically do not show themselves until adolescence. This is true of various kinds of metacognition, including some that are directly relevant to creativity. A useful way to view this developmentally is to compare preconventional, conventional, and postconventional thought. Runco and Charles (1995) found these to characterize moral reasoning, language, game playing, divergent thinking, and art. In the preconventional stage, young children are unaware of rules and other conventions. They are often quite creative precisely for this reason! They do not conform and follow convention and are, as a direct result, uninhibited and original. Later they enter a conventional stage where they recognize conventions of language, behavior, and rules governing games and social activities of all sorts. Moreover, they become quite respective of conventions, and as a direct result, they conform to conventions and peer pressure. They become quite literal in their interpretations, and many of them enter a fourth-grade slump in original and divergent thinking (Torrance, 1968). Their artwork becomes representational and realistic rather than uninhibited and self-expressive. Many do move into a postconventional stage, which is characterized by a recognition of conventions and rules, but a personal decision about following the rules and conforming to convention. At this point the individual is very aware of norms and rules, but thinks for him- or herself. He or she makes a decision, hopefully to conform to that which is safest, but also to express personal creativity when it is appropriate. Postconventional reasoning is another way of describing what I called judgment and discretion earlier in this chapter. It is important for the metacognitive aspect of creativity, but not something we see in young children.

This is not to say that we do not see originality in children. It simply has a different source. It reflects their lack of inhibitions rather than their intentional and metacognitive efforts. Nor does this imply that we need not worry about children's creativity. On the contrary. It is probably during childhood that we can instill an interest in creativity and provide children with the support they need to develop ego-strength. That ego-strength will allow them to stand up to peer pressure and to express themselves as individuals even if it means being different. Without ego-strength, individuals are likely to conform to others' interpretations and fear or mistrust their own insights.

One attractive aspect of this theory of personal creativity is that it applies to everyday expressions of creative potential, and not just to eminent persons and high-level achievements. This is not to say that personal creativity is unrelated to unambiguous creative achievements and eminence. As a matter of fact, I have argued that unambiguous creative achievements (eminent and otherwise) rely on personal creativity. Transformation, discretion, and interpretation are probably involved in achievement and accomplishment, just as when they are used in the more mundane but original interpretations of day-to-day life. Original interpretations, discretion, and interest are involved in significant insights and paradigm shifts, but those also involve *Zeitgeist*, knowledge, luck, and persistence. If we view the interplay of transformation, discretion, and interpretation as an intellectual mechanism, this position can be simply stated: The same mechanism is involved in both everyday insight and world-shaking discoveries.

DISCUSSION

Given the nature of the various components of personal creativity, it appears that efforts to support and enhance originality would focus on ego-strength, and tactics for originality. There are other important processes, including those emphasized early in this chapter (i.e., transformation, discretion, interest). Some of these are not, however, controllable. Assimilation, for example, is far from intentional. Enhancement efforts would be more likely to succeed if they target those aspects of personal creativity that we know can be manipulated. Logic and common observation suggest that ego-strength can be strengthened. Empirical evidence confirms that tactics, such as other expressions of metacognition, can be dramatically altered (e.g., Basadur, Runco, & Vega, 2000; Plucker & Runco, 1999).

Just as there is a science of judgment and choice, previously mentioned as useful for work on discretion, so too is there plenty to consult for tactical originality and the relevant aspects of metacognition. One useful tactic involves some sort of *change of perspective*. There are, for example, benefits to taking time away from a task, incubating, traveling, or working backwards. Each of these leads to a shift in perspective. Another general tactic involves *analogies*. Runco (1999) described the insights of Samuel Morse, Eli Whitney, Louis Pasteur, George Bissell, James Watt, and Sir Marc Brunel. Whitney, for example, conceived the cotton gin after seeing a cat trying to catch a chicken through a fence; Morse conceived the stations in the telegraph line after observing stagecoaches periodically changing their horses; Pasteur saw an analogy between grapes and human skin; Bissell drew an analogy of a brine pump being used as an oil pump; Watt designed the steam engine after observing a tea kettle; and Brunel found new ideas about underwater tunnels after thinking about worms. The benzene ring, Velcro, and numerous other inventions and creative ideas seem to have been inspired by apt analogies. A third useful tactic involves a kind of *adaptation or borrowing*. This is suggested by Piaget drawing from biology in his work on cognition and development, by Freud's applying the medical model to the human psyche, by Darwin's using geology for his theory of evolution. Musicians also adapt and borrow, as Elvis Presley did, using gospel and country music for his brand of rock'n'roll.

There are many other kinds of tactics, and these can be provided to adolescents and adults as recipes or procedures that can be used for creative work. Yet children will probably benefit the most if we reinforce their ego-strength. Although ego-strength was not part of the model of personal creativity, it is important because it should lead directly to the decision to be original and the wherewithal necessary to maintain and defend it. As mentioned earlier, it is sometimes difficult to be original because that always means the individual is doing something that others are not. It is always a kind of nonconformity, and even deviance. With ego-strength, the individual can accept deviance, at least if that is how his or her own behavior is labeled.

Both ego-strength and tactical creativity will benefit if we do several specific things:

1. Provide opportunities for practice.
2. Model specific tactics and optimal ego-strength.
3. Reinforce the use of tactics and ego-strength.
4. Insure that educational experiences increase the likelihood that the tactics will be maintained and generalize to the natural environment (Plucker & Runco, 1999). And finally, we should
5. Be certain that the individual recognizes the value of originality and creativity. They will only look to a tactic and make appropriate choices if they see the value of those choices! This is one reason that modeling is vital.

Not everyone is fulfilling his or her creative potential, but there is much that can be done in this regard, for both children and adults. In fact, the situation is almost ideal. I say this because, on the one hand, the potential for creativity is universal. We all have the ability to transform information and to construct our own interpretations. At the same time there is much we can do to direct those transformations so that we are original at appropriate times. We can learn to make the right (original) choices and learn to use the tactics that lead to creative ideas, insights, solutions, and actions. We might not make ourselves into Einsteins, but we can take advantage of the extra- and metacognitive processes involved in creative thinking to insure that we can think for ourselves and solve problems in an original fashion.

REFERENCES

Albert, R. S., & Runco, M. A. (1986). The achievement of eminence: A model of exceptionally gifted boys and their families. In R. J. Sternberg & J. E. Davidson (Eds.), *Conceptions of giftedness* (pp. 332–357). New York: Cambridge University Press.

Basadur, M., Runco, M. A., & Vega, L. (2000). Understanding how creative thinking skills, attitudes, and behaviors work together: A causal process model. *Journal of Creative Behavior.*

Lazarus, R. S. (1991). Cognition and motivation in emotion. *American Psychologist, 46,* 352–367.

Piaget, J. (1976). *To understand is to invent.* New York: Penguin.

Plucker, J., & Runco, M. A. (1999). Enhancement of creativity. In M. A. Runco & S. Pritzker (Eds.), *Encyclopedia of creativity* (pp. 669–675). San Diego, CA: Academic Press.

Renzulli, J. (1978). What makes giftedness? Re-examining a definition. *Phi Delta Kappan, 60,* 180–184.

Runco, M. A. (1986). Divergent thinking and creative performance in gifted and nongifted children. *Educational and Psychological Measurement, 46,* 375–384.

Runco, M. A. (1995). Insight for creativity, expression for impact. *Creativity Research Journal, 8,* 377–390.

Runco, M. A. (1996, Summer). Personal creativity: Definition and developmental issues. *New Directions for Child Development,* No. 72, pp. 3–30.

Runco, M. A. (1999). Tactics and strategies for creativity. In M. A. Runco & S. Pritzker (Eds.), *Encyclopedia of creativity* (pp. 611–615). San Diego, CA: Academic Press.

Runco, M. A. (in press). Creativity, cognition, and their educational implications. In J. C. Houtz (Ed.), *The educational psychology of creativity*. Cresskill, NJ: Hampton.

Runco, M. A., & Albert, R. S. (in press). *Theories of creativity* (rev. ed.). Cresskill, NJ: Hampton Press.

Runco, M. A., & Charles, R. (1995). Developmental trends in creativity. In M. A. Runco (Ed.), *Creativity research handbook: Vol. 1* (pp. 113–150). Cresskill, NJ: Hampton.

Runco, M. A., Johnson, D., & Gaynor, J. R. (1997). The judgmental bases of creativity and implications for the study of gifted youth. In A. Fishkin, B. Cramond, & P. Olszewski-Kubilius (Eds.), *Creativity in youth: Research and methods* (pp. 113–141). Cresskill, NJ: Hampton.

Singer, J., & Singer, D. G. (in press). Imagining possible worlds to confront and to create new realities. In M. A. Runco (Ed.), *Creativity research handbook* (Vol. 3). Cresskill, NJ: Hampton Press.

Torrance, E. P. (1968). A longitudinal examination of the fourth-grade slump in creativity. *Gifted Child Quarterly, 12*, 195–199.

Wallach, M. A., & Wing, C. (1969). *The talented student.* New York: Holt, Rinehart & Winston.

Zajonc, R. (1980). Feeling and thinking: Preferences need no inferences. *American Psychologist, 35*, 151–175.

Chapter 3

The Role of Unconscious Processes in the Evolvement of Creativity

Gudmund J. W. Smith
Lund University

INTRODUCTION

The notion of unconscious mental processes has stirred up many feelings during the past century. The very mention, around the 1950s, of possible effects of subliminal stimulation was deemed outrageous, primarily because it seemed to actualize subversive psychoanalytic thinking, thus eroding the (shaky) scientific status of psychology (cf. Cramer, 1998). Although subliminal activity was eventually accepted as an empirical fact—special homage should be paid to Norman Dixon's (1971, 1981) incisive reviews of the field and to such researchers as the Seattle group (e.g., Greenwald, 1992)—a fundamentalistic cognitivism surfaced again in the 1980s, relying heavily on a rationalistic approach to basic facets of human action. Emotions were either neglected or reduced to secondary side effects of no great importance.

All this seems to have been turned topsy-turvy in the nineties. Not only have such discarded psychoanalytic concepts as defense mechanisms surfaced in the papers of a new generation of psychologists, too young and innocent to have been unduly influenced during the heydays of psychodynamic thinking. Even serious experimentalists (e.g., Bargh & Chartrand, 1999) declare, in so many words, that most of our daily adaptation is regulated via unconscious channels. Many threatening situations, in particular, are mastered without conscious interference. To be true, adaptive behavior is often more efficient if allowed to run along unconscious grooves. We are easily tempted to regard conscious thought as the cause of action. As illustrated in many experiments (Libet, 1985; Wegner & Wheatly, 1999), however, the notion of rational choice, even if personally satisfying, proves to be a common illusion. Correlations between conscious intentions and actions are mostly modest.

A critical question in this context, too often neglected, is how these unconscious processes really function. When discussing subliminal stimulation many researchers asked themselves if it was less efficient than supraliminal stimulation, obviously regarding the unconscious sphere as a pale copy of consciousness. An alternative, borrowed from psychoanalytic thinking, would be that unconscious processes are qualitatively different, at least in cases where they actualize at a considerable distance from the conscious surface. It would not be too farfetched to assume that they are more governed by emotions and paralogical thinking than by rational, even if not fully illuminated deliberations. Although using their own homemade terminology to stress their dissociation from "psychodynamic" theorizing, many cognitive psychologists would nowadays agree in a general way.

This chapter is based on the assumption that processes outside awareness play a prominent role in the evolution of creative ideas. The assumption is elucidated within the frame of micro- or percept-genetic theory implying that our perceptual world is constructed by processes from "within" ourselves. During the course of such a process it is gradually more and more constrained by the stimulus context. Creativity presupposes openness to the early subjective stages, such as relative freedom from these constraints. A creative functioning test based on that assumption is introduced.

The chapter continues to discuss obstacles to creative or adaptive functioning. The other side of the coin, the benefits of a creative attitude, is illustrated by a study of breast cancer patients. As a complement to this individualizing perspective, the chapter finally brings up the question of situational factors and cites studies of creativity at the place of work and in the education system, from primary school to college and university. Asking to what extent situational factors may favor the "vertical" communication necessary to creative functioning, the opening problem of the chapter is revived.

A PAST-TO-PRESENT PERSPECTIVE

Even if the approach to creative functioning is indebted to psychoanalysis in some respects, I do not want to rouse psychoanalytic thinking from its fading past but rather, exploit a microgenetic (perceptgenetic) frame of reference. Perceptgenetic theory assumes that the real world around us is constructed from within ourselves through ultraswift processes rooted in our memory but unfolding in an independent outside reality. The assumption is not entirely new but inspired by a subjectivistic continental tradition of which H. Bergson (1912) was a prominent exponent. Already Külpe (1910) argued that reality is not immediately given but is only understood in a process of construction. Similarly, the analogous theory formulated by the neurologist Jason Brown (1991) owes a debt of gratitude to Whitehead (e.g., 1929), who regarded the world as a process and was a kindred spirit of James (1890).

Confronted with a new situation the viewer is apt to react with a general stage of readiness or arousal. In other words, his or her accumulated experiences are mobilized on a broad front. When, after renewed fixations, he or she has received more information, the mobilization is relaxed and more specialized functions are delegated to take care of the adaptive task. This implies that early stages (*P-phases*) of the perceptgenesis are characterized by a very varied experiential specter, rooted far back in life of the viewer, a specter only to a small degree constricted by the actual situation and often structured without regard for spatial and logical categories. During the ultra-short perceptgenesis, however, irrelevant and person-proximal contents are peeled off, leaving a gradually more dominant nucleus of stimulus-proximal contents. But remnants of early contents may remain until the last phase (as feelings, associations, imagery, etc.). The correct final stage is called the *C-phase*.

If we express this in terms of neurology, stimulation from the outside primarily activates the old brain, including the limbic system, and only secondarily, via the parietal cortex, the occipital area of cortex where a definite percept is produced (Brown, 1988). This subjectivist perspective, says Brown (2000, p. 56), implies "that objects are understood as exteriorized mental images." "The experiential content of a perceptual object is, in the ordinary sense, preperceptual. That is, the feeling, meaning, and recognition of an object are not attached to things out there in the world after they are perceived, but are phases ingredient in the process through which the perception occurs" (Brown, 2001, p. v). Perceptgeneses are mostly unconscious. Empirical evidence (Smith, 2001) supports the assumption that, on repetition, they quickly become abbreviated (mechanized, automatized). But the more open to the rich menu of potentialities characterizing its origins, the less likely the process is to become stereotyped.

It should be obvious by now why it seems reasonable to assume that creativity depends on a broad inward communication. To be true, the tachistoscopic program constructed to assess creativity (Smith & Carlsson, 1990, 2001) probes the willingness and ease with which a viewer abandons a correct assessment of a test stimulus and entertains more idiosyncratic interpretations of it when the tachistoscopic presentations are being gradually abbreviated. As described later, perceptgeneses can be protracted by means of a fractioning technique. If instead of a systematic prolongation of exposure times to reconstruct a perceptgenesis the procedure is reversed, the viewer is induced to travel from the stage of objective perception to more and more subjective stages, stamped by the person him- or herself, by his or her emotions and private experiences. The technique is employed in a Creative Functioning Test (CFT, Smith & Carlsson, 2001) where openness to these subjective stages is deemed synonymous with creativity.

BETWEEN FREEDOM AND CONTROL

It is not unproblematic to open your inner sluices to promote unorthodox associations. If untamed forces are let loose they must be adequately mastered. Once the bottle is uncorked, the genie may become unmanageable. In actual fact, a balance is needed between freedom and control, the state of equilibrium determined by, among other things, the individual's degree of anxiety tolerance. In our own empirical studies, such anxiety dampening control strategies as compulsive isolation and depressive retardation have proved to have a particularly negative effect on creativity. In the compulsive period of prepuberty both anxiety and creativity were lower than before and after (Smith & Carlsson, 1990). If presence of anxiety implies tolerance and absence of it, intolerance, presence can thus be regarded as an indirect sign of readiness for creative functioning. However, the word *anxiety* should not be overdramatized. What we deal with here might better be termed *medium anxiety* or a feeling of unease or discomfort. Severe anxiety or panic, signifying total lack of control, is counterproductive.

These assertions are based on a particular experimental technique constructed to make microprocesses available for observation and applied in a long series of studies (cf. Kragh & Smith, 1970; Smith, 2001). The technique was tried out already in the 1920s in Germany and Italy (Sander, 1928; Gemelli, 1928) and introduced in the United States by Heinz Werner (1956). The frame of reference of these oldtimers, however, was general psychology while workers in the perceptgenetic tradition found individual psychology more congenial. The basic assumption behind this technique is that perceptgeneses (microgeneses in the U.S.) can be prolonged if the stimulus presentation is fractionated. A first presentation of it thus gives the viewer enough time (or, illumination) to detect that something is happening. The next presentation is a little longer (or, brighter). The exposure series should be arranged in such a way that a correct report of the stimulus meaning is attained after 20 to 25 presentations. The test person is asked to report after each exposure, in some tests even to sketch his or her impressions by making drawings. Attempts are now being made to exploit the field of hearing in a similar way. This can be done by using an auditory mask and let a message gradually percolate while the mask is toned down.

A VERTICAL PERSPECTIVE

Whatever stimulation is used in these experiments, one of the first observations is that reports of impressions at different stages of the process of detection do not only—or primarily—differ with respect to degree of clarity—or quantitatively—but also qualitatively. The content of the interpretations may shift over the series, often drastically. Early interpretations also seem less strictly structured, more dreamlike, than subsequent ones. This is often reflected in the drawings or in the way the descriptions are phrased. A superficial reading of the reports may miss important qualitative modulations over the perceptgenetic series. Some of this may be retrieved if the test person is asked to associate to his or her own report after the experiment is terminated. All in all, a careful analysis of the viewer's reports is a *sine qua non* for a perceptgenetic experiment to be fully utilized.

In order to provoke control strategies into action, threatening stimulation has been inserted in the picture material. In one version of the perceptgenetic techniques, a threatening figure is placed peripherally in relation to a central identification figure, the "hero" (the Defence Mechanism Test, DMT; Kragh, 1985). In another version, a threatening picture is exposed immediately before a "hero" picture, at first masked by that picture but eventually penetrating it when exposure times are prolonged (the Meta-Contrast Technique, MCT; Smith, Johnson, Almgren, & Johanson, 2002). Whatever the technique used, on the whole, the ensuing results are analogous. The aggressive provocation can be met directly by a veridical report of its presence on the projection screen. Avoidance strategies are, however, more common. The varieties of these strategies often resemble the well-known psychoanalytic defense mechanisms. Justification for naming viewers' visual maneuvers on the screen after these mechanisms has been obtained through extensive clinical studies of different diagnostic groups.

TO CORK UP CREATIVE SOURCES

One such strategy, isolation, was previously mentioned. Basically, it implies that all emotional coloring is erased from our personal world. In one of the perceptgenetic tests (DMT) the viewer may report that the peripheral threat and the central hero are clearly separated by a barrier. In both the DMT and the MCT white painting of the threat is common. If, however, the viewer sees black color seeping through the white cover, the defense is obviously incapable of keeping anxiety (the darkness) at bay. The viewer may also avoid confrontation with the threat by retarding the perceptgenesis. That strategy is typical of states of depression. In the MCT the viewer perhaps reports that something has begun to intrude into the "hero" picture. However, that something is not unmasked but continues to be seen as a "ripple in the surface" over a long stereotyped series of exposures.

An excess of defense is obviously impeding high-level performance in many areas. One of them is advanced aviation, another accident-free car driving (Svensson & Trygg, 1994). Avoidance strategies dominating the late sections of a perceptgenesis appear to be particularly crippling. A primitive type of defense, projection, is of special interest for car driving. In the DMT it may show up as impressions that the threat figure is a friend of the hero figure, that threat and hero exchange positions, or that the identity of the hero changes at least five times. This group of signs were assumed to represent the defense of projection or projective identification and thus signify a weak identity control. What this implies for drivers involved in highway competition can easily be imagined; for example, when overtaken by another car, the driver with a weak identity is tempted to begin a dangerous highway race.

Lack of defenses is not synonymous with unbridled creativity. According to Carlsson (1992), high-creative people are characterized by flexible, variable defensive strategies. The creative person may shield him- or herself against disturbing intrusions but does not permanently block the contact with his or her unconscious self and the opportunities offered by that contact for reorganizing his or her cognitive activities. Moreover, the defenses utilized by high-creative people make demands on both hemispheres, unlike low-creative people who more often rely on only one hemisphere (the left one, in verbal tasks, etc.). Defenses were previously regarded as typically neurotic hallmarks. Nowadays, they are recognized as commonplace functions facilitating efficiency and necessary undisturbedness and relaxation (cf. Hentschel et al., 1993).

BENEFITS AND DANGERS OF CREATIVE FUNCTIONING

The problems involved can be illustrated by a study of patients suffering from breast cancer (Lilja et al., 1998), a study the results of which are now cross-validated in an ongoing study. Both studies particularly reveal the balance between openness and control. One of the previously mentioned tests, the MCT, was utilized in the study together with a test (the IT or Identification Test) where the main stimulus is a picture of an aggressor and his victim. Like in the MCT, an extra stimulus is introduced to appear before this picture. The stimulus is the word "I" which all the time is kept subliminal, such as, masked by the thematic picture. The subliminal "I" is directed toward one or the other of the figures in the picture in an attempt to manipulate the viewer to identify with either of them. An important part of the

3. UNCONSCIOUS PROCESSES   33

testing is the introductory series where the schematic stimulus is presented alone, perceptgenetic fashion starting from subthreshold values.

Many studies (see Lilja et al., 1998) have demonstrated that attempts to deny or suppress aggressive impulses are associated with a malignant cancer growth. In the group of patients referred to earlier, the aggressive theme caused considerable difficulties, a majority refusing to recognize what the picture was all about. Some of them even reported that aggressor and victim exchanged roles. However, this denial of aggression is obviously counter-checked by creativity in many cases. According to a number of biological variables such as tumor size, lymph node metastases, and DNA S-phase fraction, the patients could be split in one portion with a relatively favorable prognosis and another portion with a less favorable one. The study now showed that creativity, as defined by the test mentioned in the beginning of this chapter, was associated with a favorable prognosis. At the same time the low-creative patients blocked recognition of the aggressor–victim picture and let the two figures exchange roles.

The immediate conclusion was that creative patients had easier access to unconscious functions, including emotions with aggressive coloring. According to both previous studies and the present results, suppression of aggression was thus associated with malignant cancer growth, the question of causation left open. By redirecting the naked aggression along constructive channels, creative patients appeared to be able to keep the internal contact. Yet there were interesting exceptions. In a small group of patients with "comedo carcinoma," a different form of breast cancer, the results were turned upside down with high creativity associating with an unfavorable prognosis. The reason for this was soon traced. These patients could not easily handle the aggressive impulses let loose when functioning creatively. There were even signs of psychotic dysfunctioning in the IT, regressive reactions interfoliating more normal ones. For them it would be better to put the lid on, such as, to show a low-creative profile. Not just anyone can endure being creative, particularly not people with weak identity control.

HOW TO APPLY WHAT WE KNOW ABOUT CREATIVITY

Do these and similar results offer any guidelines for how to further creative development? It is almost a cliché nowadays that creativity is thriving in an open intellectual climate and hampered in a restrictive one. Very few creative flowers blossom under authoritarian regimes. This notion of the best hotbeds for creative development is supported in a very general way by data presented in this chapter. The central assumption is that if you throttle the communication between conscious and unconscious processes you tie your cognitive functions to ingrained trajectories and assign them to endless repetition of trivia. You even prevent the conscious processes from exploiting the work done in your unconscious backyard, among other things browsing among quickly accumulating subliminal messages and sending so-called intuitive signals to the conscious surface.

What is easy to say is much more difficult to prove. Industrial psychology seems to be the field where environmental effects on the processes of innovation have been most systematically studied. Ekvall (1999), for instance, has contrasted orthodox and unorthodox industrial departments, the former more efficient but running along fixed trajectories and unwieldy when change is required, the latter thriving because their actions are not predetermined by rigid norms of cost efficiency. Still, even in developmental sections of an industry there must be a limit to the patience with efforts aiming far beside the main goal of the enterprise at large. And perhaps such patience is needed for the really revolutionary breakthroughs to happen.

As can also be learned from the preceding presentation unlimited openness is not tolerated by everybody. It presupposes that you are able to master the impulses set free in your unconscious world, although the mastery is flexible and does not strangle the inner communication. Anger could be such a dangerous impulse as previously exemplified by studies of breast cancer patients. If one is frightened by his or her own unconscious reality, even by its apparent chaos, he or she will not function creatively unless they are given supporting tools. Some people may need therapy in order to be able to utilize their dormant creative abilities. It should also be admitted that creativity is not necessarily constructive. If not combined with a reasonable degree of intelligence the outcome of creative initiatives is often likely to be destructive. Of course, in order to be destructive on a grandiose scale, high intelligence is also needed (as shown by Nobel laureate Haber's invention of war gas during World War I).

If we want to liberate creative resources we should, of course, begin early. After what we have learned about the rapid early development of the central nervous system, it may even be too late to do something after regular school has started. On the other hand, we have also learned that a neurobiological consolidation continues far into the twenties and that, contrary to conventional textbook wisdom, new nerve cells can be formed even late in life. Dwelling on the topic of creativity, let us talk about song birds. It is known that in the breeding season, when these birds assert their territorial boundaries by means of incessant, often rather complex singing, their brains grow in size, often so much that they have to shrink quickly again in order not to be too burdensome when the season is over. This has inspired speculation about the possibility that even adults may grow new neurons and thereby enhance their creative powers even late in life.

Primary school has no doubt a decisive influence on the development of creativity. In a previous study of creativity in children aged 4 to 15 years (Smith & Carlsson, 1990) we found two creative peaks (around ages six and eleven) and valleys in between. The shift from six to seven might have been caused by the beginning of regular school in Sweden, for example, the end of freedom. However, later shifts were more difficult to combine with changes in the school curriculum. It seemed reasonable, instead, to consider part of these changes as reflections of a natural variation between periods of acquisition of new knowledge and skills and periods when these new acquisitions were utilized for personal creative efforts. We suspected, in addition, that the home atmosphere might have a more lasting influence on creativity than the school. In cases where the home background was academic, the children seemed to be less hesitant to express their creativity in full.

The next level, college and university, has been the object of much speculation but of little research. The present author and his colleagues at Lund University have had reason lately to contemplate the significance of the academic environment for young graduate researchers. We are often made to believe that big institutions have a clear advantage because of higher intellectual density and greater resources generally. But there may also be more infighting, envy and bureaucracy. At a distance small colleges and institutes may appear more free and easy, offering an optimal climate for independent thinking. But that is perhaps a distance illusion.

We have asked dissertation advisers at our home base what they believe is the most favorable approach to beginners in the fields of humanities and social sciences. The majority emphasize the importance of giving the candidates as free reins as possible, to take their suggestions seriously and not to press one's own pet ideas upon them from above. For others the need of guidance seems more important. Finally, it is not uncommon that advisers realize the dangers of provincialism in the enclosure of homogeneous departments and recommend confrontation with more diversity, with divergent theories, even heresies excommunicated by the present scientific establishment. They also advise their students to read books outside their chosen specialty. In another study of the relations between personality factors and university conditions Ryhammar and Smith (1999) found that from the perspective of creativity (measured by the CFT) the crucial variable in a university organization is openness and diversity. It also seems to be taken for granted that creativity needs a good soil of solid knowledge in order to thrive. As is well known, intuition, that indispensable tool of scientific innovation, requires long acquaintance with a field and hard work to generate fruitful ideas.

When all is said and the future for creativity painted in rosy color—provided that the advice given by pedagogical expertise is followed—one may still wonder if various external arrangements can really guarantee an augmentation of creativity, particularly the kind of creativity necessary to clear the way for radical change. Even if modifications of the atmosphere in schools and universities might favor more modest creative endeavors, why should they affect the inner tensions and contradictions out of which the more powerful creative thunderstorms arise? In the light of really pioneering creations where mighty unconscious forces are involved, artistic or scientific, our petty anxieties appear ridiculous. These people are forced to create because their working material has become part of themselves. To bridge the contradictions and defects in one's outside world thus becomes an inner necessity, overshadowing whatever minor changes the environment is ready to make for one's benefit. What is probably more urgent in these cases is not to throttle them with carping rules, moral straitjackets, or cold indifference.

SUMMARY

The pervading assumption of this chapter is that creative functioning depends on an open communication between conscious experiences and preconscious layers of the mind. What is more, in most studies cited, creativity was defined by the test subject's degree of independence of the stimulus for the benefit of personal interpretations. Creative functioning is not only important for the generation of new ideas but also, as shown by an example, for a constructive handling of affects and primitive impulses. The role of situational factors in all this is not well known. It is concluded, however, that outstanding creative accomplishments are more dependent on inner forces than on benevolent outer circumstances.

REFERENCES

Bargh, J. A., & Chartrand, T. L. (1999). The unbearable automaticity of being. *American Psychologist, 54*, 462–479.

Bergson, H. (1912). *Time and free will*. New York: Macmillan.

Brown, J. W. (1988). *Life of the mind. Selected papers*. Englewood Cliffs, NJ: Prentice Hall.

Brown, J. W. (1991). *Self and process: Brain states and the conscious present*. New York: Springer-Verlag.

Brown, J. W. (2000). *Mind and nature. Essays on time and subjectivity*. London: Whurr.

Brown, J. W. (2001). Foreword. In G. J. W. Smith, *The process approach to personality* (pp. v–x). New York: Plenum.

Carlsson, I. (1992). *The creative personality. Hemispheric variation and sex differences in defence mechanisms related to creativity*. Lund, Sweden: Department of Psychology.

Cramer, Ph. (1998). Defensiveness and defense mechanisms. *Journal of Personality, 66*, 879–894.

3. UNCONSCIOUS PROCESSES

Dixon, N. F. (1971). *Subliminal perception: The nature of a controversy.* New York: McGraw-Hill.
Dixon, N. F. (1981). *Preconscious processing.* New York: Wiley.
Ekvall, G. (1999). Creative climate. In M. A. Runco & S. R. Pritzkov (Eds.), *Encyclopedia of creativity, Vol. I* (pp. 403–412). San Diego: Academic Press.
Gemelli, A. (1928). Il comparire e il scomparire della forma. *Contributi di Laboratoria della Psicologia e Biologia, Università del Sacrio Core, 3,* 385–436.
Greenwald, A. G. (1992). New Look 3: Unconscious cognition reclaimed. *American Psychologist, 47,* 766–779.
Hentschel, U., Smith, G. J. W., Ehlers, W., & Draguns, J. G. (Eds.). (1993). *The concept of defense mechanisms in contemporary psychology.* New York: Springer-Verlag.
James, W. (1890). *The principles of psychology.* New York: Holt (1950).
Kragh, U. (1985). *Defence Mechanism Test—DMT: Manual.* Stockholm: Persona.
Kragh, U., & Smith, G. J. W. (Eds.). (1970). *Perceptgenetic analysis.* Lund: Gleerup.
Külpe, O. (1910). *Erkenntnistheorie und Naturwissenschaft.* Leipzig: Hirzel.
Libet, B. (1985). Unconscious cerebral initiative and the role of conscious will in voluntary action. *Behavior and Brain Sciences, 8,* 529–566.
Lilja, A., Smith, G. J. W., Malmström, P., & Salford, L. G. (1998). Psychological profile related to malignant tumors of different histopathology. *Psycho-oncology, 7,* 376–386.
Ryhammar, L., & Smith, G. J. W. (1999). Creative and other personality factors as defined by percept-genetic techniques and their relation to organizational conditions. *Creativity Research Journal, 12,* 277–286.
Smith, G. J. W. (2001). *The process approach to personality.* New York: Plenum.
Smith, G. J. W., & Carlsson, I. (1990). The creative process: A functional model based on empirical studies from early childhood to middle age. *Psychological Issues, Monograph 57.* New York: International Universities Press.
Sander, C. F. (1928). Experimentelle Ergebnisse der Gestaltpsychologie. *Bericht über den X. Kongress für experimentelle Psychologie, 1927.* pp. 23–28.
Smith, G. J. W., & Carlsson, I. (2001). *CFT—the Creative Functioning Test.* Lund, Sweden: Department of Psychology.
Smith, G. J. W., Johnson, G., Almgren, P.-E., & Johanson, A. (2002). *MCT—the Meta-Contrast Technique: Manual.* Lund, Sweden: Department of Psychology.
Svensson, B., & Trygg, L. (1994). *Personality, accident proneness and adaptation.* Stockholm: Almqvist & Wiksell.
Wegner, D. M., & Wheatly, Th. (1999). Apparent mental causation: Sources of experience of will. *American Psychologist, 54,* 480–492.
Werner, H. (1956). Micro-genesis in aphasia. *Journal of Abnormal and Social Psychology, 52,* 347–353.
Whitehead, A. N. (1929). *Process and reality.* New York: Macmillan.

Chapter 4

Exceptional Creativity and Chance: Creative Thought as a Stochastic Combinatorial Process

Dean Keith Simonton
University of California, Davis

In most domains of achievement, the possession of exceptional ability would seem antithetical to the operation of chance. Tiger Woods came to dominate professional golf not because of a bunch of lucky shots, but because he exhibits consistently high levels of performance. A violinist like Jascha Heifetz awed audiences not because he would try to play a difficult piece several times during a concert until he chanced on the right notes, but rather because he could maintain inspiring levels of technical virtuosity and interpretative power performance after performance. A calculation prodigy like Shakuntala Devi—who can perform phenomenal feats of mental arithmetic—amazes not only because of the speed and magnitude of the achievement but also because the calculations are absolutely free of guesswork and error.

Yet creativity seems to operate in a very different fashion from these phenomenal displays of talent or expertise. Even the most illustrious creative geniuses of history have careers riddled by both hits and misses, both successes and failures. Take the case of Albert Einstein, proclaimed as "Man of the Century" by *Time* magazine. His image has attained the status of an almost mythical icon of exceptional genius. And yet his career was plagued by terrible ideas, false starts, and surprising disasters. Having entered into a debate with Niels Bohr over the implications of quantum theory, Einstein offered a series of arguments that Bohr would counter by identifying the logical flaws. Once Bohr even demolished one of Einstein's attacks by pointing out that Einstein failed to take into consideration the theory of relativity! Even worse, Einstein wasted the final years of his career working on a unified field theory that was almost universally rejected by his colleagues. Einstein's modesty allowed him to admit his mistakes on many occasions. He himself said that his assumption of the cosmological constant was one of his biggest blunders. He even defended his missteps by noting that errors can advance science so long as the errors are not trivial. Thus, the ups and downs in Einstein's career appear diametrically opposed to what is observed in the careers of Tiger Woods, Jascha Heifetz, or Shakuntala Devi.

In this chapter I wish to explore the extent to which luck, both good and bad, participates in creative performance. Before that exploration begins, however, I must first avoid misunderstanding by defining my terms. According to the *American Heritage Electronic Dictionary* (1992), the primary definition of *luck* is a "chance happening of fortunate or adverse events." The same source then defines *chance* in a more complicated fashion. As a noun, chance can be "the unknown and unpredictable element in happenings that seems to have no assignable cause," "a force assumed to cause events that cannot be foreseen or controlled," "an accidental or unpredictable event," and "a risk or hazard; a gamble." As an adjective, chance can signify "caused by or ascribable to chance; unexpected, random, or casual." Among the idioms is the notion "to chance on," which means "to find or meet accidentally; happen upon," and "by chance," which means "without plan; accidentally." Its synonyms are *random, casual, haphazard,* and *desultory*. Its etymology, interestingly enough, comes from the Latin word for "to fall," as in the English expression "let the chips fall where they may." Coin tosses and the casting of dice both entail the deliberate quest of a chance event by letting an object freely fall. A concept closely related to chance and luck is *random*. By the same reference source, this means "having no specific pattern, purpose, or objective," "of or relating to the same or equal chances or probability of occurrence," and "without governing design, method, or purpose; unsystematically."

Given these definitions, I can show that the concepts of luck, chance, and randomness are highly descriptive of how discovery, invention, and creativity function in renowned geniuses. I begin by discussing a phenomenon that is largely confined to scientific and technological creativity—when two or more scientists or inventors independently make the same discovery or invention. I next turn to a more general phenomenon, that of creative productivity across and within careers. Models that affirm that creativity involves the ability to generate combinations of ideas through a quasi-random process will explicate both phenomena. I conclude by discussing some of the principal objections that might be raised regarding what these models imply about the creative process and person.

MULTIPLES IN SCIENCE AND TECHNOLOGY

Permit me to begin with a true story from my graduate student days. At the time I was admitted to Harvard's Department of Social Relations, it included sociologists and cultural anthropologists as well as developmental, personality, and social psychologists. Hence, not every faculty member was receptive to an individualistic perspective. This lack of sympathy emerged once when I mentioned to one professor that I was fascinated with creative genius. The response was surprising, for I was told that creativity is not an individual-level phenomenon. Instead, creativity was entirely a manifestation of sociocultural processes. At best, the individual creator is a mere spokesperson for the *Zeitgeist*, or the "Spirit of the Times." As proof of this claim, I was told to consider the phenomenon of multiples (Merton, 1961a, 1961b). A *multiple* is a discovery or invention that is contributed by two or more individuals working independently. Classic instances include the calculus by Newton in 1671 and Leibniz in 1676, the theory of evolution by natural selection by Darwin in 1844 and Wallace in 1858, and the discovery of the periodic law of the elements by DeChancourtis in 1862, Newlands in 1864, Meyer in 1869, and Mendeléev in 1869. What makes these multiples especially spectacular is that the duplicate contributions are often simultaneous as well as independent. Not only will the separate contributions occur within the same year, but also they will occasionally happen in the exact same day. This precise degree of simultaneity holds for the invention of the telephone, for Bell and Gray showed up at the U.S. Patent Office only a few hours apart.

Sociologists and anthropologists have used the multiples phenomenon to defend the theory that it is the sociocultural system, not the individual, that creates new ideas. According to their interpretation, discoveries and inventions are the direct effect of sociocultural determinism. Thus, Robert K. Merton (1961a), the distinguished sociologist, claimed that

> discoveries and inventions become virtually inevitable (1) as prerequisite kinds of knowledge accumulate in man's cultural store; (2) as the attention of a sufficient number of investigators is focused on a problem—by emerging social needs, or by developments internal to the particular science, or by both. (p. 306)

The Zeitgeist determines not just the inevitable appearance, but the precise timing besides. Alfred Kroeber (1917), the illustrious anthropologist, was impressed by the fact that DeVries, Correns, and Tschermak all rediscovered Mendelian genetics in the exact same year. So he concluded, "it was discovered in 1900 because it could have been discovered only then, and because it infallibly must have been discovered then" (p. 199). Given that the sociocultural milieu is a necessary and sufficient cause of creativity, the personal abilities of creators are irrelevant. For instance, Leslie White (1949), another distinguished anthropologist, drew this strong conclusion from the independent invention of the steamboat: "Is great intelligence required to put one and one—a boat and an engine—together? An ape can do this" (p. 212). Generalizing further, White maintained that "a consideration of many significant inventions and discoveries does not lead to the conclusion that great ability, native or acquired, is always necessary. On the contrary, many seem to need only mediocre talents at best" (p. 212). If true, creativity cannot be considered among those human behaviors that manifest exceptional ability.

Although sociocultural determinism has become the traditional explanation of this phenomenon (Lamb & Easton, 1984), many objections have been raised against the argument (Patinkin, 1983; Schmookler, 1966; Simonton, 1987). Some have criticized the nature of the data. For instance, many putative multiples were not really independent, but rather one scientist or inventor was influenced by another. To offer a specific case, many of those who worked on the invention of the steamboat were very much aware of the work of their competitors. Yet it is also possible to criticize the traditional account on theoretical grounds (Schmookler, 1966). Not only does sociocultural determinism fail to explain many crucial features of multiples, but also it is perfectly possible to account for all of the central attributes of the multiples phenomenon without assuming any kind of sociocultural determinism whatsoever (Simonton, 1987, 1999a). In place of the deterministic sociocultural system, the agent behind multiples is the individual creator, operating by means of a stochastic process. Again according to the *American Heritage Electronic Dictionary* (1992), the term *stochastic* means "involving or containing a random variable or variables," "involving chance or probability [as in] a stochastic simulation" (italics removed). This alternative, stochastic model can be outlined as follows (for more details, see Simonton, 1988b, 1999a).

1. Each scientific or technological specialty consists of a set of facts, concepts, techniques, heuristics, themes, and questions. These can be collectively referred to as the "ideas" that make up a given domain. Each scientist or inventor during the course of disciplinary education and training acquires his or her "sample" from this larger set of ideas. Naturally, a large portion of each creator's sample is shared with one or more creators working in the same domain. Even so, another portion of that sample is unique to each creator, owing to discrepancies in background and training. For instance, the scientist or inventor might have switched fields, bringing ideas that are alien to the new domain of choice (Hudson & Jacot, 1986; Simonton, 1984c).

2. The disciplinary ideas making up each creator's sample are then subjected to free recombination, with the aim of finding original and useful permutations. These ideational variations actually have a relatively low probability of arriving at a creative combination, because a large amount of time is spent sifting through useless combinations. Fortunately, however, the low likelihood of success is partially compensated by the large number of trials. Not only will each creator working within a field engage in this combinatory process for many years, but also there will usually be more than one creator subjecting roughly the same set of ideas to the same combinatory procedure.

3. Whenever a creator chances across a useful ideational combination, he or she will attempt to develop it into publishable form—as in a journal article or patent application—and thereby make others aware of the idea. The successful dissemination of these discoveries then provides new facts, concepts, techniques, heuristics, themes, or questions that enter the disciplinary pool from which creators draw their sample of ideas for the incessant rounds of combinatory activities.

4. The successful communication of a particular combination necessarily preempts others from arriving at that same combination. No one deliberately tries to reinvent the wheel. Once creators find out that they have been "anticipated," they immediately move to some other topic or issue, often incorporating the preempting discovery into the repertoire of ideas that will be subject to future combinatory processes.

5. If two or more creators have sampled roughly the same sample of ideas, and if they are subjecting their respective samples to combinatorial variation, then by chance alone, two or more individuals will arrive at the same combination. In other words, multiples essentially become creations of coincidence. Because multiples emerge naturally from random creative processes occurring in separate individuals, there is no necessity to evoke some mysterious notion of sociocultural determinism.

Once we accept the proposition that multiples are the product of a stochastic process, certain consequences directly ensue that either have no counterpart in the traditional interpretation or else directly contradict that interpretation. In particular, alternative interpretation proves superior in the explanation and prediction of multiple identity, grade, simultaneity, inevitability, and participation.

The Rarity of Truly Identical Multiples

Critics of the traditional interpretation will sometimes point out that many so-called multiples do not truly involve identical discoveries or inventions (e.g., Patinkin, 1983). Instead, the lists of putative multiples include many clear illustrations of "a failure to distinguish between the genus and the individual" (Schmookler, 1966, p. 191). Two supposed duplicates are often not actually identical, but rather a generic category has been superficially imposed on rather distinct creations. As an example, nuclear magnetic resonance was independently and simultaneously observed in 1946 by Bloch, Hansen, and Packard at Stanford and by Purcell, Torrey, and Pound at Harvard. This earned Bloch and Purcell a Nobel medal in 1957. Even so, although physicists "have come to look at the two experiments as practically identical," said Purcell, "when Hansen first showed up [at our lab] and started talking about it, it was about an hour before either of us understood how the other was trying to explain it" (cited in Zuckerman, 1977, p. 203). An even greater discrepancy occurred in the case of the steam turbine, which has been credited to four independent inventors. Detailed analysis of each invention has proven that they have quite contrasting forms and operate under rather different physical principles (Constant, 1978). None can be considered combinations containing identical elements.

The rarity of genuine multiple identity causes some embarrassment for the traditional interpretation. The sociocultural system is viewed as a "superorganic" force that imposes itself uniformly on all individuals working under the same Zeitgeist and Ortgeist (Kroeber, 1917). For the stochastic model, in contrast, the lack of multiple identity necessarily follows from the suppositions. Even when two or more creators are subjecting precisely the same collections of ideas to the combinatorial process, there is nothing to guarantee that identical combinations will result. On the contrary, each supposed multiple will have a high likelihood of containing certain elements that render each product unique. For instance, although both Newton and Leibniz are credited with the invention of the calculus, the Newtonian version was quite different from the Leibnizian version, especially in terms of notation (e.g., $\ddot{y}$ rather than d^2y/dx^2). Undermining identity even more is the fact that each scientist or inventor will include idiosyncratic ideas along with those that are shared with two or more colleagues. These components will often personalize each participant's contribution. "A mathematician will recognize Cauchy, Gauss, Jacobi, or Helmholtz, after reading a few pages, just as musicians recognize, from the first few bars, Mozart, Beethoven, or Schubert," said theoretical physicist Ludwig Boltzmann (Koestler, 1964, p. 265). Likewise, when Newton sent off an anonymous solution to a mathematical problem that had been posed as a challenge to the international community, the recipient immediately discerned "the claw of the lion."

Of course, the stochastic model of multiples does not claim that absolutely identical multiples are impossible. After all, by chance alone, two individuals might arrive at precisely the same idea. An example is the Pelton water wheel, a device that was arrived at by two independent inventors, albeit from entirely divergent initial ideas (Constant, 1978). Even so, according to the stochastic model, bona fide identity will be relatively rare. For instance, a detailed analysis of rival patent claims indicates that the separate inventions usually only overlap on a small subset of characteristics (Schmookler, 1966). It would be very valuable to conduct a systematic analysis of rival claims in order to gauge the cross-sectional distribution of the degree of identity. The stochastic model would predict a highly skewed distribution, inventions that share 90% of their definitive components being far more rare than those inventions that share only 10%. Although this prediction has never been tested, it is similar to other predictions that have been empirically confirmed, as will become apparent in the two sections that follow immediately.

The Skewed Distribution of Multiple Grades

Some multiples have more participants than others do. Only two mathematicians claimed to have devised the calculus, while four have some claim to discovering the periodic law of the elements. The calculus is a grade-2 multiple, or *doublet*, whereas the periodic law is a grade-4 multiple, or *quadruplet*. It is also apparent from the published lists of multiples that some grades may be more frequent than others are (see, e.g., Kroeber, 1917; Ogburn & Thomas, 1922). In general, the higher the grade, the lower is its frequency. The highest grade ever claimed was grade 9, or a *nonet*, but this is very rare (and the case doubtful). In contrast, grade-2 multiples are the most common, followed by grade 3, then grade 4, and so on.

From the combinatorial theory we can predict the specific shape of the probability distribution (Price, 1963; Simonton, 1978, 1979). In the first place, because the process is basically random, a large number of variants must be generated before a useful variant survives. In other words, the probability of success is relatively small. There are many trials and many errors. So, for the sake of argument, suppose that $p = .01$, meaning that the probability is only 1% of arriving at a particular discovery or invention even when all the requisite elements are in place in the creator's mind. Concomitantly, any given discipline will consist of a fairly large number of creators independently subjecting roughly the same subset of ideas to the combinatorial process. Thus, the low probability of success for any one individual is somewhat compensated by the large number of participants. Again for the sake of argument, assume that there are 100 individuals who have sampled the domain of ideas that are necessary for a given discovery or invention. That is, say $n = 100$. Because of this redundancy, the odds will be enhanced that many of the potentially useful combinations will be found by at least one member of the field. At the same time, this same redundancy will permit a certain number of multiples to emerge, even if the creators are truly working independently of each other. By the luck of the draw, there will appear multiples of grade 2, 3, 4, and so forth up to the sole grade-9 multiple.

Given these conditions, the predicted probabilities of occurrence for multiple grades must be closely described by what is called the *Poisson distribution* (Price, 1963; Simonton, 1978, 1986b). This distribution is an approximation to the binomial distribution when p is very small and n very large. That is, it handles occurrences when the number of trials is extremely large but the probability of success extremely low. In fact, research has repeatedly shown that this distribution does an excellent job of predicting the observed frequencies of events when those events are so unlikely to happen that they can only happen because there are so many attempts (e.g., the number of Prussian cavalry officers killed by horse kicks in a given period of time). The same predictive success holds for multiples as well. The Poisson-predicted frequencies have been directly compared to the actual frequencies obtained in three separate data sets (Merton, 1961b; Ogburn & Thomas, 1922; Simonton, 1979). In every case, goodness-of-fit tests prove that any departures from prediction can be ascribed to statistical error (Simonton, 1979). To illustrate, the most extensive list of multiples so far collected contained 449 doublets, 104 triplets, 18 quadruplets, 7 quintuplets, and 1 octuplet, whereas the model predicts 435, 116, 23, 4, and 0, respectively (Simonton, 1979). Moreover, the fit holds for separate domains of science and technology (Simonton, 1978). Of special interest are the resulting estimates μ, which represents both the mean and variance of the Poisson distribution. This key parameter corresponds to the parameters p and n, namely $\mu = pn$. Because the estimated μ is roughly around unity for the three data sets (Simonton, 1986c), the hypothesized values of $p = .01$ and $n = 100$ are not far off the mark.

It must be emphasized that the traditional explanation for multiples cannot accommodate these findings. Strictly speaking, sociocultural determinism maintains that discoveries and inventions are inevitable, or nearly so. As a consequence, $p \approx 1.0$. That implies that high-grade multiples should be not just extremely common, but also much more frequent than low-grade multiples (Simonton, 1979; also see Schmookler, 1966). The evidence flatly contradicts this prediction. Moreover, it will not help to argue that many multiples are missing from these data sets (Merton, 1961b). Every attempt to gather more multiples has ended up with an even higher proportion of doublets relative to the higher grade multiples. Hence, more inclusive collections of multiples only worsen the case for sociocultural determinism! Thus, the best bet is to conclude that the probability distribution of multiple grades reflects an underlying stochastic process.

The Distinctive Degree of Multiple Simultaneity

As noted earlier, sociocultural determinists make a big deal about the near simultaneity of so many multiples. This simultaneity is taken as positive proof that an invention or discovery becomes absolutely inevitable at a specified time and place in history. No room for chance here! Yet closer examination of the empirical record suggests that this argument is incredibly weak. For one thing, many multiples are not nearly so simultaneous. Merton (1961b) found that four fifths of the multiples he collected were separated by 2 or more years and about one third were 10 or more years apart! For instance, despite Kroeber's (1917) amazement that Mendel's laws were rediscovered by three independent researchers in the exact same year, the fact remains that it took 35 years for those laws to be rediscovered! It makes no sense to excuse this delay by saying that "Mendel was ahead of the times," for the "times" constitute the causal agent of sociocultural determinism.

Even more critical is the fact the stochastic model can explain this aspect of multiples with more precision. The model holds that once a new discovery or invention becomes sufficiently disseminated among those individuals working with roughly the same samples of disciplinary ideas, further multiples will be precluded. In other words, the probability of duplication decreases over time. This feature can be introduced into stochastic models by means of a "contagion" or "communication" process (Brannigan & Wanner, 1983b; Simonton, 1986a, 1986b). Models that incorporate this feature do an excellent job predicting the skewed distribution of temporal separation of the separate multiples (Brannigan & Wanner, 1983b). Although large time lags are not impossible, the odds of this happening are much smaller than simultaneous multiples.

One advantage of these contagion models is that they allow for historical trends in the efficiency of scientific communication. In the early days of the scientific revolution, there existed no scientific journals or patent offices to publish the latest discoveries and inventions. Most often novelties were disseminated by private correspondence or by large integrative books that took years to write. In time, more formal and efficient means of communication emerged, vastly speeding up the process. These historical changes alter the parameters of the stochastic model so that high-grade multiples should become even more rare, and those multiples that do manage to appear should become ever more simultaneous. A secondary analysis of Simonton's (1979) data set confirmed both predictions (Brannigan & Wanner, 1983a).

The Concept of Multiple Inevitability

Besides multiple grades of 2 or higher, one can also speak of grades 1 and 0 (Price, 1963). The first is a *singleton*, that is a discovery or invention only made once (Merton, 1961b); the second is a *nullton*, or an invention or discovery that never got made (Simonton, 1978). According to the Poisson model, the singletons invariably outnumber doublets by a pretty substantial margin, a disparity that agrees with empirical observations (Simonton, 1979). More curiously, the model also predicts a substantial number of nulltons (Price, 1963; Simonton, 1979). These are hypothetical instances where the luck ran out on a particular combination, the large n not completely compensating for the small p. Certainly this prediction of the Poisson model flatly contradicts the doctrine of inevitability promulgated by the sociocultural determinists.

The problem with this prediction is that it can never be empirically tested. Besides it might be argued that all potential combinations will eventually appear, even if it is not inevitable that they do so at a given time and place. That is, once the requisite ideas are available in the disciplinary pool from which the individual samples are drawn, sooner or later the corresponding discovery or invention will appear, even if it takes many years to do so. Thus, very often a contribution builds on a sociocultural substrate that has been around for decades, or even centuries. Take the development of paper chromatography, for which Martin and Synge shared the 1952 Nobel Prize for Chemistry. Martin minimized their accomplishment by observing "all the ideas are simple and had peoples' minds been directed that way the method would have flourished perhaps a century earlier" (cited in Daintith, Mitchell, & Tootill, 1981, p. 531). The general applicability of this remark is fully demonstrated by the many rediscoveries separated by a decade or more. If the earliest contribution is truly identical to the latest, then it must be the case that all the prerequisites had been satisfied years earlier.

It turns out that the stochastic model has no problems accommodating this complication (Simonton, 1986a). It is only necessary to introduce an "exhaustion principle" in which the trials continue until all potential combinations are generated, and thus exhausted. The only consequence of adding this mechanism is that the nulltons are eventually redistributed among the singletons and multiples. Yet the highly skewed, Poisson-like distribution of multiple grades emerges unaltered. This principle does not compromise the underlying stochastic nature of the process. Moreover, just because every viable combination will eventually appear, it does not mean that the combination that finally emerges will be indistinguishable from the one that might have appeared years earlier. If the stochastic model predicts that simultaneous multiples will seldom consist of identical ideas, the model would predict a lack of identity between what might have happened and what eventually happened even more. The longer the time delay, the greater are the changes in the set of ideas that are undergoing recombination. In addition, the ideational combinations might have appeared in a different form, perhaps even piecemeal rather than as a single discovery. The molecular biologist Gunter Stent (1972) provided a hypothetical illustration of such historical indeterminacy with respect to the discovery of DNA's structure:

If Watson and Crick had not existed, the insights they provided in one single package would have come out much more gradually over a period of many months or years. Dr. B might have seen that DNA is a double-strand helix, and Dr. C might later have recognized the hydrogen bonding between the strands. Dr. D later yet might have proposed a complementary purine-pyrimidine bonding, with Dr. E in a subsequent paper proposing the specific adenine-thymine and guanine-cytosine replication mechanism of DNA based on the complementary nature of the two strands. All the while Drs. H, I, J, K and L would have been confusing the issue by publishing incorrect structures and proposals. (p. 90)

Hence, just because the ideas are already "in the air" regarding a particular contribution, that by no means ensures that the contribution be made right away, nor that the contribution be made in exactly the same way. The sociocultural system's role in the process has been reduced to establishing the necessary conditions for a given discovery or invention—the ideas that defined the essential components.

Individual Differences in Multiple Participation

Multiple discoveries often provoke priority disputes, such as the bitter fight between Newton and Leibniz over who should get credit for the calculus. Sometimes the priority battle expands to national proportions, as when the English and the French debated over whether John Couch Adams or Urbain Leverrier should be honored for discovering Neptune. Therefore, some scientists and inventors might count themselves blessed if they manage to avoid ever getting involved in a multiple contribution anytime in their careers. According to the stochastic model of multiples, there are two factors that make one more susceptible to this happenstance (Simonton, 1999a).

First, the more ideational combinations a creator generates, the higher the probability of duplicating someone else's effort, or having one's own effort duplicated. Hence, those with the highest odds of participating in multiple discovery and invention are those who are most prolific in terms of lifetime productivity. As Merton (1961b) expressed it, those of "great scientific genius will have been repeatedly involved in multiples . . . because the genius will have made many discoveries altogether" (p. 484).

Second, the more creators who are sharing more or less the same sample of disciplinary ideas, the higher is the likelihood that two or more will come up with the same combination. In contrast, those who are working in relative isolation from others are less likely to fear this outcome. Scientists or inventors only have a high probability of multiple participation if they are subjecting very similar samples of ideas to the combinatorial process.

Both of the foregoing predictions have received empirical confirmation (Hagstrom, 1974; Simonton, 1979). The probability of participation in multiple discovery is an additive function of the total number of contributions an individual makes and the total number of colleagues independently working on the same or similar problems. Thus, the stochastic model specifies what someone needs to do to escape the threat of multiple participation: either publish very little or else publish only on unpopular topics! Nonetheless, even those who dare to make prolific contributions to hot areas have relatively little to fear. Out of one sample of nearly 2,000 scientists, only 17% had their work anticipated more than twice, even if about 60% had been anticipated at least once (Hagstrom, 1974). Hence, highly productive creators still receive sole credit for most of their contributions. The odds of multiple participation are too low for the prospect to be considered a major risk. A creative individual would have to be very unlucky indeed to have his or her entire output linked to rival claimants. The bottom line is that p remains extremely small, whatever the size of n.

CREATIVE OUTPUT ACROSS AND WITHIN CAREERS

I have just shown that a phenomenon that has been traditionally interpreted as proof of sociocultural determinism actually can be better explicated in terms of a rather contrasting model. Multiples are most likely the probabilistic consequence of an essentially stochastic process operating in the creative individuals who make up a scientific community. According to the stochastic model, the sociocultural system—the Zeitgeist or Ortgeist—has a very limited role, namely, to define the pool of facts, concepts, techniques, heuristics, themes, and questions from which each individual draws his or her sample of ideas. The recombination of those ideas to produce new discoveries and inventions, on the other hand, takes place within the creative mind. As a result, the sociocultural milieu can only be said to provide the necessary but not sufficient conditions for contributions to science and technology. If a necessary ingredient of a potential creation is missing, then none of the individuals of that time and place can be expected to generate the combination. This constraint of the sociocultural system can be easily incorporated into the stochastic model (Simonton, 1986a). In effect, the added feature sets $p = 0$ until such time as all of the requisite ideas have entered the general pool from which the creators must obtain their individual samples.

That added complication makes creativity even more a matter of luck than ever before, because many scientists and inventors may waste large segments of their careers trying to create the impossible. A classic illustration is the long list of inventors who tried to create a heavier-than-air flying machine before an efficient means of propulsion had been invented first. Airplanes and helicopters powered by steam engines rather than internal-combustion engines are simply impractical. Hence, part of the luck of exceptional creativity entails the fortune of picking solvable problems in the first place. Sometimes creators will be lucky, and sometimes not, with the consequence that their careers will be riddled with both success and failures. Even scientists as great as Galileo, Newton, Darwin, and Einstein took on tasks that were doomed to fail because the antecedent conditions had not yet been met.

Moreover, this capricious aspect of the creative process is not confined to science and technology. The same fickleness appears in artistic creativity as well. This fact will become apparent when I review what we have learned about creative output across and within careers. I first begin with a discussion of individual differences in total output, and then end with a treatment of how that output is distributed across the individual life span.

Individual Differences in Lifetime Productivity

The stochastic model of multiples predicted that an individual's involvement in such duplicates was a probabilistic function of the total number of contributions made. Hence, to comprehend more fully why scientists and inventors get entangled in these episodes, it is necessary to learn more about the basis of individual differences in the number of contributions. This latter phenomenon has two aspects: the cross-sectional distribution of lifetime output and the relation between quantity and quality of output.

Cross-Sectional Distribution. Galton (1869) was the first to define exceptional ability in terms of placement at the upper end of the normal distribution. Later Terman (1925) continued this idea by defining "genius" and "giftedness" in terms of a person's location on the IQ distribution, which was again assumed to be described by the bell-shaped curve. But soon it became apparent that when one turns to exceptional performance and achievement, the normal curve fails miserably. For instance, Burt (1943) observed that the ability to earn money appears to be best described by a highly skewed distribution, a tiny percentage of the population earning most of the income. It is for this reason that the central tendency of income tends to be reported by the median rather than the mean, because the former is less influenced by extreme scores at the upper end of the distribution. The same skewed-right curve describes high ability in a vast diversity of achievement domains (Walberg, Strykowski, Rovai, & Hung, 1984).

Individual differences in creative output are no exception (Simonton, 1999a). Typically, in any given domain of creative achievement, a relatively few producers are responsible for most of the contributions. For instance, if we divide the contributors into deciles according to the total level of output, the top 10% will usually account for about 50% of everything produced, whereas the bottom 50% can be credited with only around 15% of the contributions that define the discipline (Dennis, 1954a, 1954c, 1955). This extremely lopsided distribution has been described according to two laws. The first is the Lotka Law, which says that the number of persons making n contributions is inversely proportional to the square of n (Lotka, 1926). Stated more formally, $f(n) = k/n^2$, where k is a constant that depends on the discipline. This law is formally similar to the Pareto Law, which accurately describes the cross-sectional distribution of income (Price, 1963). The second principle is the Price Law, which states that if k represents the number of creators active in a domain, $\sqrt{k}$ gives the number of creators who are responsible for around half of the total contributions to the discipline (Price, 1963). Hence, if $k = 100$, then just 10% will be credited with 50% of the work. To appreciate better the implications of these two laws, consider what would happen if the height of human beings had the same distribution as lifetime creative productivity: the National Basketball League would have no difficulty recruiting players who were 15 feet tall!

The really interesting question is what the skewed distribution might tell us about the role of chance in exceptional creativity. Three main explanations for this distribution have been offered, each with a rather different conception of how chance participates.

1. Exceptional creativity might require the simultaneous presence of several distinct components. That is, all components must be present and all enter the determination of the ability according to some multiplicative function. This explanation was first suggested by Burt (1943), but it has been proposed by many others (e.g., Eysenck, 1995; Shockley, 1957). One specific manifestation of this explanation is the genetic concept of *emergenesis*, or nonadditive inheritance (Lykken, 1998; Simonton, 1999b). However, the collection of essential components of the ability might entail environmental factors along with innate traits (Eysenck, 1995; Simonton, 1999b; Sternberg & Lubart, 1991). This multidimensional and multiplicative conception can account for the highly skewed distribution because the cross-sectional distribution of the product of several normally distributed variables will be described by a lognormal curve (Burt, 1943; Simonton, 1999b). If this explanation is correct, then highly productive creators are those who are "lucky enough" to score high on every single requisite component. By sheer chance, they will manage to be precisely the right person at the right place at the right time.

2. Sociologists have proposed an alternative explanation in which chance plays an even more central role. It is called the principle of accumu-

4. CREATIVITY AND CHANCE

lative advantage (Allison, Long, & Krauze, 1982; Allison & Stewart, 1974). According to the model, all creators start out with the same basic abilities. However, all are obliged to seek success in a highly selective system where "many are called but few are chosen." Scientific journals, literary magazines, art galleries, and book publishers have to be selective. By chance alone, some newcomers to a field will be successful, while a larger number will fail. The successful will be encouraged to submit additional manuscripts, artwork, or other creative products, whereas the unsuccessful will be discouraged. Over time, the "rich will get richer, and the poor poorer" (Merton, 1968). This basic process has been translated into mathematical models that explicate the data pretty well, including the skewed distribution of total lifetime output (Allison & Stewart, 1974; also see Simon, 1955). If exceptional creativity is totally the function of accumulative advantage, then it may not be a psychological ability at all, but rather the upshot of accumulated chance. This has sometimes been referred to as the Ecclesiastes hypothesis (Turner & Chubin, 1976). This name comes from the biblical passage in *Ecclesiastes* 9:11 that maintained that "the race is not to the swift, nor the battle to the strong, neither bread to the wise, not yet riches to men of understanding, not yet favor to men of skill; but time and chance happeneth to them all" (quoted in Turner & Chubin, 1979, p. 437).

3. Neither of the previously mentioned explanations makes the cross-sectional distribution inherent in the creative process itself. The final explanation does, and has the additional asset of providing a theoretical link with the stochastic model of multiples. In the latter model it was assumed that each individual acquires through education and training, a sample of ideas—facts, concepts, techniques, heuristics, themes, and questions—that undergo a more or less random combinatorial procedure. These individual samples do not only differ in contents, but also in size. That is, for some creators the ideational variations will be based on relatively few given ideas, whereas for other creators these variations will be based on a very rich supply of available ideas. Let us suppose that the size of these samples is normally distributed in the population, in rough agreement with individual performance on school exams and tests (i.e., scholastic achievement). Then the distribution of potential combinations will be described by a highly skewed lognormal distribution (Simonton, 1988b, 1997). This happens because the number of potential combinations tends to grow exponentially with the total number of available ideas that feed the combinatorial process. Hence, for this third interpretation, the skewed cross-sectional distribution of lifetime output emerges from the nonlinear relation between the number of ideas and the number of ideational combinations those ideas can produce (see also Barlow & Prinz, 1997). Chance then participates at the must fundamental level, in the combinatorial process that generates the ideational variations.

It is certainly conceivable that all three explanations account for some portion of the observed distribution of creative ability. Yet the third has two virtues over the remaining two, namely that it connects directly with the stochastic interpretation of the multiples phenomenon already given, and the forthcoming explanations of several critical aspects of the creative career. One of these aspects is the relationship between productivity and creativity, or quantity and quality.

Quantity and Quality. Not all of the ideas that come out of the combinatorial process are equally good. Some combinations will be absolutely excellent, perhaps even of breakthrough quality. Other combinations will be more mediocre, and maybe downright bad. Even the greatest creators have terrible ideas.[1] If the creative individual is subjecting a given sample of ideas to free recombination, then the good and bad must come together. Those who generate more total ideas will produce more hits, and more misses. As W. H. Auden noted, because great writers produce such a large body of work, "the chances are that, in the course of his lifetime, the major poet will write more bad poems than the minor" (cited in Bennet, 1980, p. 15). The career of Thomas Edison, like that of Albert Einstein, shows that the same principle operates among great inventors. Edison still holds the record for the most patents bestowed by the U.S. Patent Office—well over a thousand—yet not all of his inventions were in the same class as the phonograph. For instance, Edison wasted much effort on a failed system for separating iron ore. The developmental costs of his useless experiments had even wiped out all that he had then earned on the electric light bulb!

But is quality simply a function of quantity? Do hits and misses, successes and failures really have to go together? On the one hand, there might exist perfectionists who produce very little, but what they do produce has been polished to perfection. The perfectionists would constitute creators who somehow manage to escape the stochastic nature of creativity by having some guaranteed method to achieve success. On the other hand, there might exist mass producers who generate a large quantity of really bad stuff, with little or anything that comes close to being notable. The mass producers somehow lack whatever it takes to arrive at a really good idea.

---

[1] I must stress that the quality of creative products forms a continuous ratio scale that ranges from those that have zero impact (e.g., never performed, never cited) to those that are highly acclaimed as masterpieces (e.g., repertoire war horses, citation classics). For specific illustrations of such assessments, see Simonton (1980, 1990, 1998) for aesthetic creations and Shadish (1989) and Redner (1998) for scientific journal articles. Hence, the demarcation of "good" and "bad" works—"hits" and "misses"—is somewhat arbitrary. Thus, for journal articles, the line might be drawn between cited and uncited papers or between papers cited 10 or more times and those cited less than 10 times. Fortunately, it does not matter very much where the cutoff is placed (see, e.g., Quételet, 1835/1968; Simonton, 1977).

Yet, if creativity at bottom involves a stochastic combinatorial process, then true perfectionists and bona fide mass producers would be very rare (Simonton, 1999a). A perfectionist would have had to acquire a sample of ideas that only generated good combinations, whereas a mass producer would have had to acquire a sample of ideas that could only generate bad combinations. The chances of that happening are probably extremely small. The biggest difference separating creators working in the same domain is most likely the size of the sample, not whether the ideational sample is good or bad. On the average, therefore, the more ideas that can be fed into the combinatorial hopper, the more hits will emerge, and the more misses. Quality will be a function of quantity, exceptions like the perfectionists and the mass producers representing no more than statistically expected scatter around the regression line linking total output to influential output (Simonton, 1999a). Those exceptions will not constitute outliers, nor will they cluster in the scatterplot to form distinctive types. They are simply the direct repercussion of the fact that the combinatorial process is presumed to be stochastic. By mere chance, some will have a higher percentage of hits than others. If a group of people toss a coin several times, some will get more heads, and others more tails, without the coin being in any way biased, or without certain participants being adept at psychokinesis.

All of the foregoing implications of the proposed model have been endorsed in the empirical literature (e.g., S. Cole & J. R. Cole, 1973; Davis, 1987; Feist, 1997; Simonton, 1997). The single best predictor of output quality is output quantity. Moreover, this relation holds across different criteria of quality (e.g., citations, eminence, influence) and various ways of assessing quantity (e.g., total counts, counts weighted according to type of work, counts confined to a particular major type, such as journal articles). In line with the view that creativity consists of stochastic recombinations, the correlation is not perfect. Typically, around 50% of the variance is shared. This magnitude of effect leaves sufficient latitude for residuals that might be classified as either perfectionists or mass producers. But these residuals cannot be considered outliers by the standard statistical tests. Furthermore, if you calculate the quality ratio—the number of hits divided by total attempts—that that ratio is distributed randomly across the productivity distribution (Platz & Blakelock, 1960; Simonton, 1985, 1999a). In other words, the most productive individuals, on the average, do not have higher or lower quality ratios than the least productive individuals. This has been called the *equal-odds rule* because the most prolific creators have the same likelihood of success as do the least productive, on a product-for-product basis (Simonton, 1994). This rule again indicates that perfectionists and mass producers define nothing more profound than occasional departures from statistical expectation. More critically, the equal-odds rule follows logically from the argument that creativity ultimately involves a stochastic process for generating combinations of ideas contained within individual ideational samples.

One consequence of the equal-odds rule is that findings that apply to total output also work when applied to select output. For instance, the cross-sectional distribution for high-impact products is the same as that for total products. The Price Law can be used to illustrate this point. Based on concert programs, it has been determined that approximately 250 composers have produced at least one work of sufficient importance to have entered the classical repertoire (Moles, 1958/1968). The square root of this number is 15.8, which, since you cannot have part of a composer, rounds off to 16. This root should give the number of composers who account for half of all compositions performed. That is exactly the case (Simonton, 1984b).

The equal-odds rule will show up again in the next section, when I discuss how creativity changes across the life span.

Longitudinal Changes in Output Rate

As best I can determine, the first scientific study of exceptional creativity was conducted by Quételet (1835/1968). This investigator was specifically interested in how creative output changes across the life span. The longitudinal relation between age and productivity has been studied by many other researchers in the intervening years, most notably by Lehman (1953, 1962) and Dennis (1966). My own first publication was on this very topic (Simonton, 1975), and I have addressed this issue many times over the past quarter century, including empirical studies (Simonton, 1991a, 1991b), literature reviews (Simonton, 1988a), and theoretical models (Simonton, 1984a, 1997). On the basis of the cumulative body of research, I believe that Quételet's (1835/1968) two most critical findings have been replicated so many times that they have assumed the status of well-established empirical facts. These two facts concern the specific age function and the relation between quantity and quality over the career course.

The Age Function. Quételet (1835/1968) reported that creative output was not evenly distributed across the course of the career, but rather productivity tended to be an inverted-backward-J function of age. That is, the output rate first increased fairly rapidly to a period of peak productivity, and thereafter declined gradually. Subsequent research has replicated this finding, with only two major qualifications. First, the longitudinal trend should be better defined in terms of career age rather than chronological age (Simonton, 1988a, 1997). By "career age" is meant the length of time the creator has been active in the particular domain. Hence, if a creator gets a late start, or launches a new career, the whole trajectory is shifted over in a proportional amount. Second, the specific shape of the age curve, and especially the location of the peak productive age, varies across different domains of creativity (Dennis, 1966; Lehman, 1953; Simonton, 1989, 1991b). Some domains, like mathematics, display rapid ascents to early peaks followed by somewhat precipitous declines. Other domains, like philosophy, reach the peak more slowly, and the peak is correspondingly displaced toward older ages, with relatively little age decrement thereafter. Furthermore, many of these interdisciplinary contrasts in the age curves appear to be transhistorically and cross-culturally invariant. For instance, the peak for writing poetry comes at a younger age than the peak for writing prose for all of the world's literary traditions, from the ancient Greeks to the 20th century and from Europe to Asia and the Americas (Simonton, 1975).

Taken together, these two qualifications suggest that the age curve has psychological rather than biological or sociocultural origins (Simonton, 1988a). If the career trajectory was rooted in the biological changes associated with maturity and aging, then it would be hard to explain why productivity is more determined by career age than age per se. It would also be difficult to understand the basis for interdisciplinary contrasts in the age curves. At the same time, it is not easy to ascribe the longitudinal changes to sociocultural factors—such as differential role expectations—to the extent that the trajectories are invariant across time and place. All of the world's literary traditions, for example, would have to agree that poetry is part of the young person's role, whereas prose is more appropriate to older persons. If the age curves are a function of neither biological changes nor sociocultural influences, then what remains is most likely human psychology. In particular, the trajectory in productivity may result from the cognitive process underlying creativity.

I have pursued this explanation by developing a two-step combinatorial model of the creative process (Simonton, 1984a, 1989, 1991a, 1997). The model begins with the concept of *initial creative potential*, a variable that determines the total number of contributions an individual is potentially capable of making in an unlimited life span. This individual-difference variable is essentially the same as the size of the ideational sample that played so prominently in both the stochastic model of multiples and the combinatorial explanation of the skewed cross-sectional distribution of lifetime output. In short, the larger the personal repertoire of domain-relevant facts, concepts, techniques, heuristics, themes, and question, the greater the number of combinations that can be generated, and hence the higher the probable creative output. At the beginning of the career, each individual exploits this initial creative potential in two steps: ideation and elaboration. Ideation is the combinatory process that generates novel ideas, whereas elaboration is the process by which these ideas are developed, tested, and articulated into publishable form, whether a journal article, painting, poem, or architectural drawing. These two processes were more precisely defined as differential equations that, when solved, led to the following equation:

$$p(t) = c(e^{-at} - e^{-bt}),$$

where $c = abm/(b - a)$. This equation specifies the productivity rate p as a function of time t, where m is the initial creative potential, a is the ideation rate, b the elaboration rate, and e is the exponential constant (≈ 2.718). In the special case where the two information-processing parameters are identical ($a = b$), the equation becomes $p(t) = a^2 m e^{-at}$, a slightly simpler form, but with essentially the same predicted career trajectory. In line with what was said earlier, t is not chronological age, but rather career age. That is, $t = 0$ at the moment the individual begins generating ideational variations in a particular domain. The location of the career peak in terms of career age is determined by the ideation and elaboration parameters, whereas its location in terms of chronological age is determined by the age at which $t = 0$ (i.e., the age at career onset). The parameter m, in contrast, has no impact on the location of the peak, but only its height. In other words, initial creative potential determines the maximum output rate that occurs at the career peak.

This equation generates an inverted-backward J curve that corresponds extremely well with several distinct data sets, including those of Dennis (1966) and Lehman (1953). The correlations between observed and predicted output levels are typically in the upper .90s (Simonton, 1984a, 1989; see also Crozier, 1999). The predicted curve even handles the specific details of the observed longitudinal distribution well, such as the concave downward initial segment, the single-peaked function, and the concave upward concluding segment. Just as important, the two-step combinatorial model provides a means to accommodate interdisciplinary contrasts in the career trajectory. The ideational samples that feed the two-step procedure vary greatly in attributes such as degree of abstraction, complexity, and richness of the ideas they contain. For instance, the ideas that make up the creative potential of a mathematician are far more abstract, well-defined, and finite in comparison to the ideas that constitute the creative potential of a geologist. The ideation and elaboration rates will respond accordingly, mathematicians generally having faster rates than geologists, with corresponding changes in the shape of the career trajectory (viz., later career peaks for the latter discipline). When the ideation and elaboration rates are estimated by applying nonlinear techniques on the observed trajectories, the estimates come out exactly as expected (Simonton, 1989). The same

4. CREATIVITY AND CHANCE 59

holds for other interdisciplinary contrasts, such as that between poetry and prose literature.

The two-step combinatorial model can explicate another critical feature about creative productivity across the career—its longitudinal stability across the career course. Empirical research shows that the level of productivity in any given career decade will correlate highly with the level of productivity in any other career decade. In other words, the prolific tend to be highly productive throughout their careers, whereas the relatively unproductive tend to maintain their low output across their career course (Cole, 1979; Dennis, 1954b). According to the combinatorial model, the output rate in any given period—controlling for discipline and age at career onset—will be a function solely of initial creative potential (m). That is, the correlations among the various periods will be adequately described by a single-factor latent-variable model, a prediction that has been empirically confirmed (Simonton, 1997). This confirmation is significant because accumulative advantage makes a very different prediction, namely that the amount of output in a particular career period is a function of the output in the preceding period. For instance, output in the 60s would be a function of output in the 50s, which in its turn would be a function of output in the 40s, and so on. This autoregressive process would necessarily yield a correlation matrix that exhibits a characteristic structure (viz. simplex or quasi-simplex). Specifically, the productivity in adjacent periods would be more highly correlated than those in nonadjacent periods, the correlations declining with the degree of temporal separation. That prediction has been soundly disconfirmed (Simonton, 1997).

At present, there exists no other theoretical model—biological, sociocultural, or psychological—that can explain and predict all of the following:

1. the generic age curve,
2. the specific form the curve assumes in particular creative endeavors, and
3. the distinctive latent-variable structure of longitudinal stability in output across the career course (Simonton, 1997).

But the explanatory power of two-step combinatorial model does not stop here.

Quantity and Quality. Besides scrutinizing the overall longitudinal trend, Quételet (1835/1968) examined whether the trend was the same for both major and minor creative products. He reported that the trends are basically the same, those periods of the career that contain the most hits also containing the most misses. Subsequent secondary analyses of his data using techniques unavailable in his day endorsed this conclusion; the correlations averaged in the upper .80s (Simonton, 1997). Even more interesting are the trends for the quality ratio, defined here as the number of notable works divided by the total output for each period of the career. That ratio neither increases nor decreases, nor exhibits a curvilinear form (Simonton, 1997). This result has been replicated on many other data sets (e.g., Simonton, 1977, 1984b, 1985, 1997; Weisberg, 1994). The implications should be obvious: The equal-odds rule that describes the quantity–quality relation for cross-sectional data applies just as well to longitudinal data. Creative individuals do not learn how to increase their hit rate as they acquire more expertise, nor do they betray any decline in their hit rate as they enter their final years.[2]

Needless to say, this is precisely what would be expected from the two-step combinatorial model if the ideation process is essentially stochastic, as proposed in the earlier model of multiples. The ideational variations must be largely blind with respect to which combinations are most likely to be successful in the long run, and so good and bad ideas will be randomly distributed throughout the career. The odds of a success during the course of a creator's career will be a probabilistic function of the total attempts, so that hits will tend to correlate with failures. This statistical association between quantity and quality across the career course leads to some important predictions about the location of the three main *career landmarks* (Raskin, 1936; Simonton, 1991a, 1997). These are the age at which a creator produces the first success, the age at which he or she produces the best single work, and the age at which the last success is produced. In the first place, because different disciplines display distinct age curves for total output according to their respective ideation and elaboration rates, they will also exhibit different longitudinal placements of the first, best, and last major contribution (Simonton, 1991a, 1997). For instance, those domains with earlier peaks for the maximum output rate will also have the best works appear at younger ages. Likewise, those creative domains with precipitous post-peak declines will show younger ages for the last successful work in contrast to those domains with far more gradual post-peak decrements. These and related predictions have been empirically confirmed (Simonton, 1991a). The longitudinal placement of the first, best, and last major contributions are contingent on the underlying distribution of total output.

---

[2]Space is insufficient to discuss the fascinating issue of why creators cannot learn to improve their hit rates over the course of their careers. May it suffice to say here that the failure results from several factors, including the complex configurational character of the creative product, the ambiguous and often contradictory nature of environmental feedback, the temporal instability of the relevant aesthetic or scientific criteria, and the intricate interplay between overtraining and crosstraining effects (Simonton, 1999a, 2000). Taken together, these factors indicate that at the cutting edge of any creative domain, each product more or less must be a "shot in the dark."

Yet the two-step combinatorial and stochastic model also accounts for differences in the longitudinal placement of the three career landmarks even when the creators are working within the same discipline or domain. These differences emerge owing to individual differences among creators with respect to the age of career onset and the initial creative potential. Because these two factors are uncorrelated on both empirical and theoretical grounds (Simonton, 1997), a fourfold typology results: high-creative early bloomers, high-creative late bloomers, low-creative early bloomers, and low-creative late bloomers (Simonton, 1991a). Even more important, cross-sectional variation on these two parameters of the two-step model lead to many predictions that can be subjected to empirical tests (Simonton, 1991a, 1997). For example, the model predicts that correlation between age at first contribution and the age at last contribution will become negative after partialing out either age at best contribution or age at maximum output rate. The model also predicts that the age at best work will have a zero correlation with either lifetime productivity or the maximal output rate at the career peak. These and several other distinctive predictions have received empirical confirmation (Simonton, 1991a, 1991b, 1992, 1997). Hence, the two-step combinatory model not only handles interdisciplinary contrasts in the placement of the career landmarks, but also individual differences in their placement for colleagues active in the same field.

I hasten to point out that the empirical confirmations of the two-step combinatorial model do not mean that it explains all or even most of the variance. Quite the contrary is true. Because the process is at bottom stochastic in nature, the relation between prediction and observation is necessarily probabilistic, not deterministic. Consequently, the predictions of the model only hold when applied to large samples of creators. When the output is averaged across many careers, the random departures will cancel out. For instance, although the two-step model can account for almost all of the longitudinal variance in output when that output is averaged across dozens if not hundreds of creators, it will account for far less when applied to the career of a single creative individual (Simonton, 1988a). Yet rather than disconfirm the general thesis of this article—that creativity is closely linked with chance—this empirical limitation actually reinforces the claim. Creative productivity is less predictable at the individual level than it is when averaged across many individuals because the stochastic nature of the process can fully materialize. This heavy influx of unpredictability is amply demonstrated by results that Huber (1998a, 1998b) has recently obtained using an entirely different analytical strategy. Huber has concentrated on "inventivity," or the production of inventions, which he assessed by looking at thousands of patents granted to hundreds of inventors by the U.S. Patent Office. Besides replicating previous findings regarding the highly skewed cross-sectional distribution, Huber has closely examined how the patents were distributed across the inventor's career. Two results are especially provocative.

First, the number of patents granted in any single time period corresponds closely to a Poisson distribution (Huber, 1998a, 1998b). This is precisely what would be expected if the likelihood of coming up with a patentable idea is so extremely small, that it only happens at all because there are so many attempts. Hence, the most common outcome is no invention at all, followed by just one invention, then two, and so forth. Because the mean is usually much less than unity (i.e., $\mu <1$), it would take the concerted effort of many inventors before there would be much chance for a technological multiple to appear.

Second, according to run tests, the patents are distributed randomly across the years of each inventor's career (Huber, 1998a, 1998b). There is certainly no tendency for them to cluster in one year or another, whether the beginning, middle, or end. This means that the creator is not acquiring any expertise that enables him or her to produce patents at an accelerated rate as the career progresses. By the same token, there is no evidence here that some aging process or knowledge obsolescence intrudes to cause the invention rate to decelerate at the career close.

Admittedly, the null results of the run tests also signify that there is no tendency for the patents to cluster in the middle of the career, which would seem to contradict the single-peak function of the two-step model. Yet, as Huber (1998b) himself observed, the amount of variance explained by the curvilinear age curve is insufficient to ensure that the clustering will appear at the level of a single inventor's career. Only when aggregated across many careers will the clustering emerge at the career peak. Hence, when the curve predicted by the combinatorial model is fit to the longitudinal productivity of 44 inventors who produced 646 inventions (from Dennis, 1966), a correlation .90 obtains across the 6 consecutive career decades from the 20s to the 70s (Simonton, 1989). Yet this correlation would only be one tenth as large were the curve fit to a single inventor who averaged only one invention every four years, even though this would constitute an average rate of output. Only in the case of an extremely prolific inventor would the clustering emerge at the expected career peak. This remark is not mere speculation, for it has been empirically proven in the case of the greatest all-time inventor, Thomas Edison. The correlation between his output and theoretical prediction according to the two-step combinatorial model is an impressive .87 (Simonton, 1989).

OBJECTIONS

I think a strong case has been made that exceptional creativity is ultimately based on some kind of stochastic combinatorial process. In particular, models based on random ideational combinations have successfully explicated the specific phenomenon of multiple discovery and invention and the general phenomenon of creative output across and within careers. Moreover, unlike any alternative explanations currently available, these models generate precise empirical predictions that have received extensive empirical confirmation. Even so, these models most likely would provoke objections from psychologists who have very different conceptions about exceptional creativity. These objections either concern the creative process or the creative person (for more extended discussion, see Simonton, 1999a).

The Creative Process

Some cognitive psychologists might be inclined to reject the conclusions drawn about the creative process. Cognitive processes were not studied directly, but rather were only inferred on the basis of models that assumed creativity operated in a certain way. Whatever the success in predicting the data regarding multiples and careers, it might be possible to devise alternative models that have the same predictive precision but hypothesize an entirely different cognitive mechanism. This latter possibility is suggested by two influential research traditions in cognitive psychology. In the first, cognitive psychologists have conducted numerous laboratory experiments that endeavor to prove that creativity is nothing but problem solving, and that problem solving entails a deliberately logical inferential process (e.g., Qin & Simon, 1990). In the second tradition, the same ideas about problem solving and creativity are translated into computer programs that purport to demonstrate creativity (Boden, 1991; Johnson-Laird, 1993). The most notable are the various discovery programs that claim to rediscover established scientific laws after processing the same data used by the original discoverers (Langley, Simon, Bradshaw, & Zythow, 1987; Shrager & Langley, 1990). Taken together, this research implies that any model based on a stochastic combinatorial process is untenable a priori.

To these arguments I can offer the following three responses:

1. The bulk of the laboratory experiments on problem solving require college student participants to solve well-defined problems with known solutions. Therefore, it is a moot question whether the findings have any direct relevance to the issue of genuine creativity. Furthermore, participants are given open-ended problems that require truly creative solutions, the results become more supportive of the cognitive process presumed to operate in the stochastic combinatorial models (Simonton, 1999a). For instance, creativity has been shown to be enhanced by the influx of quasi-random, incongruent, or otherwise unpredictable stimuli (e.g., Finke, Ward, & Smith, 1992; Proctor, 1993; Rothenberg, 1986; Sobel & Rothenberg, 1980).

2. The discovery programs and other computer simulations of human creativity fall far short of realistic simulations (Miller, 2000; Simonton, 1999a; Sternberg, 1989; Tweney, 1990). It is one thing to rediscover what has already been discovered, quite another to make a new discovery altogether. There is something inherently suspicious about a researcher writing a computer program post hoc to discover a law or principle already known to exist. Even worse, the computer programs that do successfully exhibit something comparable to human creativity invariably incorporate some kind of stochastic process, often in the guise of the standard random number generator (Boden, 1991). Perhaps the most remarkable development here is the emergence of genetic algorithms (Goldberg, 1989; Holland, 1992) and genetic programming (Koza, 1992, 1994), which offer original solutions to problems using a Darwinian blind-variation and selective-retention principle (also see Adleman, 1994). The computational process is perfectly compatible with what is hypothesized for the stochastic combinatorial models of multiple discovery and creative productivity (Simonton, 1999a).

3. The fact that the creative process was assumed to be stochastic and combinatorial rather than empirically demonstrated is not inherently wrong. Mathematical models often begin by hypothesizing an underlying process, and then work out the empirical implications of the presumed mechanism. The classic example is Newton's *Principia Mathematica*. Contrary to folklore, Newton did not *discover* gravity, but rather only *assumed* its existence in order to construct a celestial mechanics that could simultaneously explain both Galileo's mechanics and Kepler's laws of planetary motion—plus offer a host of empirical predictions. Although Cartesians of his day criticized this fundamental feature of Newtonian theory, the predictive and explanatory success of his system won in the end. It was not until Cavendish that gravity was actually measured, and not until Einstein's general theory of relativity that it was given a firm (if transformed) theoretical foundation. Yet even today, despite much speculation about gravitons and gravity waves, along with diverse attempts to integrate gravity with the other basic forces of nature, a complete comprehension of gravitation remains out of reach. Physicists know much more about how gravity behaves than what it actually is. Conceivably, the creative process is at least as complex and elusive as the process of gravitational attraction. But at least we have some idea about how creativity behaves—namely very much like a stochastic combinatorial process.

In the final analysis, those cognitive psychologists who still believe that exceptional creativity constitutes a straightforward exercise in logic should proceed by constructing their own models that account for everything the stochastic combinatorial models can explain. Once that is accomplished, they can administer the coup de grace by showing that their alternative handles aspects of the phenomenon totally inconsistent with the idea that creativity incorporates chance as an essential ingredient.

The Creative Person

The notion that exceptional creativity incorporates a considerable amount of luck or chance seems to run counter to the commonplace image of the great creative genius. Such an individual is often seen as capable of simply sitting down and conceiving grand acts of creativity by the sheer power of his or her intellectual brilliance. Is Ludwig van Beethoven far better known than Anton Reiche because the former had all the luck? Did Albert Einstein prove a more influential scientist than Friedrich Hasenöhl because the latter was dealt a bad hand by fate? It seems absurd, almost peevish, to suggest that the illustrious status of these two exalted figures can be ascribed to pure chance. This appears to take the art of genius debunking to a new low.

One way of responding to this objection is simply to observe that illustrious creators themselves frequently report the critical role of chance and chance-like processes in their creative activities (e.g., Ghiselin, 1952). For instance, the surrealist artist Max Ernst described the place of chance in his use of frottage, and Henry James described how a random fragment of a conversation inspired a story. This stochastic influx even holds in the sciences, where logic and fact should reign supreme (Cannon, 1940; Mach, 1896). The most obvious illustrations come from the very numerous cases of serendipitous discoveries (Austin, 1978; Kantorovich & Ne'eman, 1989; Roberts, 1989; Shapiro, 1986). According to the dictionary, *serendipity* is the "faculty of making fortunate discoveries by accident," where *accident* means something "unforeseen," "unexpected," or "by chance" (*American Heritage Electronic Dictionary*, 1992). Especially remarkable are those serendipitous discoveries that were not even solutions to given problems, such as the advent of X-rays and radioactivity. Such events often propel both the individual scientist and the scientific community in a direction that no one could have foreseen (Kantorovich & Ne'eman, 1989).

Even more dramatic are the many introspective reports in which creators of immense stature report engaging in some variety of combinatorial procedure with strong stochastic overtones (Campbell, 1960; Hadamard, 1945; Simonton, 1999a). For example, Henri Poincaré (1921), the great French mathematician, once recorded how "ideas rose in crowds; I felt them collide until pairs interlocked, so to speak, making a stable combination" (p. 387). He compared this process to "the hooked atoms of Epicurus" that jiggle and bump "like the molecules of gas in the kinematic theory of gases" so that "their mutual impacts may produce new combinations" (p. 393). This comparison of the creative process to the kinetic theory of gases is quite tell-ing. The original inspiration for the two-step combinatorial model of the age–productivity relation was the realization that the creative process was analogous to what occurs in certain gaseous chemical reactions (Simonton, 1984a). In any case, it is not being critical of great creators if they themselves will acknowledge the role of a process that departs very little from the purely stochastic generation of ideational combinations.

Besides, "chance favors the prepared mind," as Louis Pasteur is often quoted as saying (Beveridge, 1957, p. 46). This preparedness means two things. First, creators must exhibit an intense fascination with their field, an incessant curiosity about its phenomena and potentialities (Cox, 1926; Roe, 1953). Without this exceptional interest, it is doubtful that individuals would even notice that "Lady Luck" has sent something their way, nor would they care much if they did notice (Mach, 1896). Even more critically, preparedness usually means that the creative genius has already established considerable expertise in the domain. This expertise acquisition is often expressed in terms of the "10-year rule," which says to make world-class contributions to a creative activity one must first devote 10 years to acquiring the domain-relevant knowledge and skills (Ericsson, 1996; Hayes, 1989). Although there is reason to believe that exceptional geniuses take less time than the norm (Simonton, 1991b) and that it is possible to acquire excessive expertise (Simonton, 2000), it remains true that it is virtually impossible for anyone to make even a single contribution to a field without first obtaining a minimal level of domain mastery. It must be remembered that all of the stochastic combinatorial models presume that the individual has acquired a sufficient sample of domain-relevant facts, concepts, techniques, heuristics, themes, and questions—the ideas that make up initial creative potential.

Finally, this disciplinary fascination and expertise must be coupled with cognitive and dispositional traits that render the individual capable of generating the stochastic combinations (Simonton, 1999a). A certain minimal level of intelligence is certainly essential, especially in order to acquire a sufficient sample of disciplinary facts, concepts, techniques, heuristics, themes, and questions (Simonton, 1994). Yet this intellect must be structured in a manner that permits divergent thinking, remote association, homospatial and janusian thinking, primary process or primordial imagery, and other cognitive processes associated with creativity (Guilford, 1967; Martindale, 1995; Mednick, 1962; Rothenberg, 1979; Suler, 1980). Some of these cognitive capacities are linked with dispositional traits, such as openness to experience and risk taking (Eysenck, 1995; McCrae, 1987; Sternberg & Lubart, 1995). Especially interesting is Eysenck's (1995) claim that high scores on his psychoticism scale are linked with a cognitive tendency not to filter out supposedly "irrelevant" information, a tendency that ex-

4. CREATIVITY AND CHANCE

poses the creator to "random" thoughts and stimuli. Psychoticism is also associated with a dispositional inclination toward independence, even anticonformity, another trait conducive to free thought (Crutchfield, 1962; Eysenck, 1995). Finally, it is absolutely critical to acknowledge the role of drive, persistence, and determination (Cox, 1926; Roe, 1953). According to the stochastic combinatorial models, the creative career is a life of few hits and many misses. Solutions to problems are not guaranteed by some secure method or logic, rather errors predominate. Thus, Hermann von Helmholtz (1891/1898) admitted that

> I only succeeded in solving such problems after many devious ways, by the gradually increasing generalisation of favourable examples, and by a series of fortunate guesses. I had to compare myself with an Alpine climber, who, not knowing the way, ascends slowly and with toil, and is often compelled to retrace his steps because his progress is stopped; sometimes by reasoning, and sometimes by accident, he hits upon traces of a fresh path, which again leads him a little further; and finally, when he has reached the goal, he finds to his annoyance a royal road on which he might have ridden up if he had been clever enough to find the right starting-point at the outset. In my memoirs I have, of course, not given the reader an account of my wanderings, but I have described the beaten path on which he can now reach the summit without trouble. (p. 282)

Hence, no one is going to reach the top of the creativity distribution without being able to face the numerous obstacles and frustrations that will be thrown in their way.

To be sure, this persistence can be maladaptive if carried to an extreme. The creator might waste an entire career pursuing the impossible. Moreover, the solution to one problem might be suggested by a solution to a seemingly different problem (see e.g., Poincaré, 1921). Accordingly, exceptional creators adopt a work style that enables them to avoid unnecessary perseveration. Rather than think about just one problem at a time in a sequential manner, creators adopt the practice of contemplating several problems simultaneously, many of which are only peripherally related to each other. This "network of enterprises" (Gruber, 1989) permits a great deal of "crosstalk" (Tweney, 1990) between separate projects in various stages of completion. Furthermore, creative individuals have the flexibility to take on new projects whenever the unexpected arises. B. F. Skinner (1959), for instance, emphasized "a first principle not formally recognized by scientific methodologists: when you run into something interesting, drop everything else and study it" (p. 363).

In a nutshell, exceptional creators have the capacity and inclination to ensure that luck is on their side. They exploit chance to produce genius.

REFERENCES

Adleman, L. M. (1994). Molecular computation of solutions to combinatorial problems. *Science, 266,* 1021–1024.
Allison, P. D., Long, J. S., & Krauze, T. K. (1982). Cumulative advantage and inequality in science. *American Sociological Review, 47,* 615–625.
Allison, P. D., & Stewart, J. A. (1974). Productivity differences among scientists: Evidence for accumulative advantage. *American Sociological Review, 39,* 596–606.
American heritage electronic dictionary (3rd ed.). (1992). Boston: Houghton Mifflin.
Austin, J. H. (1978). *Chase, chance, and creativity: The lucky art of novelty.* New York: Columbia University Press.
Barlow, L. W., & Prinz, J. J. (1997). Mundane creativity in perceptual symbol systems. In T. B. Ward, S. M. Smith, & J. Vaid (Eds.), *Creative thought: An investigation of conceptual structures and processes* (pp. 267–307). Washington, DC: American Psychological Association.
Bennet, W. (1980, January–February). Providing for posterity. *Harvard Magazine,* pp. 13–16.
Beveridge, W. I. B. (1957). *The art of scientific investigation* (3rd ed.). New York: Vintage.
Boden, M. A. (1991). *The creative mind: Myths & mechanisms.* New York: Basic Books.
Brannigan, A., & Wanner, R. A. (1983a). Historical distributions of multiple discoveries and theories of scientific change. *Social Studies of Science, 13,* 417–435.
Brannigan, A., & Wanner, R. A. (1983b). Multiple discoveries in science: A test of the communication theory. *Canadian Journal of Sociology, 8,* 135–151.
Burt, C. (1943). Ability and income. *British Journal of Educational Psychology, 12,* 83–98.
Campbell, D. T. (1960). Blind variation and selective retention in creative thought as in other knowledge processes. *Psychological Review, 67,* 380–400.
Cannon, W. B. (1940). The role of chance in discovery. *Scientific Monthly, 50,* 204–209.
Cole, S. (1979). Age and scientific performance. *American Journal of Sociology, 84,* 958–977.
Cole, S., & Cole, J. R. (1973). *Social stratification in science.* Chicago: University of Chicago Press.
Constant, E. W., II (1978). On the diversity of co-evolution of technological multiples: Steam turbines and Pelton water wheels. *Social Studies of Science, 8,* 183–210.
Cox, C. (1926). *The early mental traits of three hundred geniuses.* Stanford, CA: Stanford University Press.
Crozier, W. R. (1999). Age and individual differences in artistic productivity: Trends within a sample of British novelists. *Creativity Research Journal, 12,* 197–204.
Crutchfield, R. (1962). Conformity and creative thinking. In H. E. Gruber, G. Terrell, & M. Wertheimer (Eds.), *Contemporary approaches to creative thinking* (pp. 120–140). New York: Atherton.
Daintith, J., Mitchell, S., & Tootill, E. (1981). *A biographical encyclopedia of scientists* (Vol. 1). New York: Facts on File.
Davis, R. A. (1987). Creativity in neurological publications. *Neurosurgery, 20,* 652–663.
Dennis, W. (1954a, September). Bibliographies of eminent scientists. *Scientific Monthly, 79,* 180–183.
Dennis, W. (1954b). Predicting scientific productivity in later maturity from records of earlier decades. *Journal of Gerontology, 9,* 465–467.
Dennis, W. (1954c). Productivity among American psychologists. *American Psychologist, 9,* 191–194.
Dennis, W. (1955, April). Variations in productivity among creative workers. *Scientific Monthly, 80,* 277–278.
Dennis, W. (1966). Creative productivity between the ages of 20 and 80 years. *Journal of Gerontology, 21,* 1–8.

Ericsson, K. A. (1996). The acquisition of expert performance: An introduction to some of the issues. In K. A. Ericsson (Ed.), *The road to expert performance: Empirical evidence from the arts and sciences, sports, and games* (pp. 1–50). Mahwah, NJ: Lawrence Erlbaum Associates.
Eysenck, H. J. (1995). *Genius: The natural history of creativity.* Cambridge, England: Cambridge University Press.
Feist, G. J. (1997). Quantity, quality, and depth of research as influences on scientific eminence: Is quantity most important? *Creativity Research Journal, 10,* 325–335.
Finke, R. A., Ward, T. B., & Smith, S. M. (1992). *Creative cognition: Theory, research, applications.* Cambridge, MA: MIT Press.
Galton, F. (1869). *Hereditary genius: An inquiry into its laws and consequences.* London: Macmillan.
Ghiselin, B. (Ed.). (1952). *The creative process: A symposium.* Berkeley: University of California Press.
Goldberg, D. E. (1989). *Genetic algorithms in search, optimization, and machine learning.* Reading, MA: Addison-Wesley.
Gruber, H. E. (1989). The evolving systems approach to creative work. In D. B. Wallace & H. E. Gruber (Eds.), *Creative people at work: Twelve cognitive case studies* (pp. 3–24). New York: Oxford University Press.
Guilford, J. P. (1967). *The nature of human intelligence.* New York: McGraw-Hill.
Hadamard, J. (1945). *The psychology of invention in the mathematical field.* Princeton, NJ: Princeton University Press.
Hagstrom, W. O. (1974). Competition in science. *American Sociological Review, 39,* 1–18.
Hayes, J. R. (1989). *The complete problem solver* (2nd ed.). Hillsdale, NJ: Lawrence Erlbaum Associates.
Helmholtz, H. von (1898). An autobiographical sketch. In *Popular lectures on scientific subjects, second series* (E. Atkinson, Trans., pp. 266–291). New York: Longmans, Green. (Original work published 1891)
Holland, J. H. (1992). Genetic algorithms. *Scientific American, 267*(1), 66–72.
Huber, J. C. (1998a). Invention and inventivity as a special kind of creativity, with implications for general creativity. *Journal of Creative Behavior, 32,* 58–72.
Huber, J. C. (1998b). Invention and inventivity is a random, Poisson process: A potential guide to analysis of general creativity. *Creativity Research Journal, 11,* 231–241.
Hudson, L., & Jacot, B. (1986). The outsider in science. In C. Bagley & G. K. Verma (Eds.), *Personality, cognition and values* (pp. 3–23). London: Macmillan.
Johnson-Laird, P. N. (1993). *Human and machine thinking.* Hillsdale, NJ: Lawrence Erlbaum Associates.
Kantorovich, A., & Ne'eman, Y. (1989). Serendipity as a source of evolutionary progress in science. *Studies in History and Philosophy of Science, 20,* 505–529.
Koestler, A. (1964). *The act of creation.* New York: Macmillan.
Koza, J. R. (1992). *Genetic programming: On the programming of computers by means of natural selection.* Cambridge, MA: MIT Press.
Koza, J. R. (1994). *Genetic programming II: Automatic discovery of reusable programs.* Cambridge, MA: MIT Press.
Kroeber, A. L. (1917). The superorganic. *American Anthropologist, 19,* 163–214.
Lamb, D., & Easton, S. M. (1984). *Multiple discovery.* England: Avebury.
Langley, P., Simon, H. A., Bradshaw, G. L., & Zythow, J. M. (1987). *Scientific discovery.* Cambridge, MA: MIT Press.
Lehman, H. C. (1953). *Age and achievement.* Princeton, NJ: Princeton University Press.
Lehman, H. C. (1962). More about age and achievement. *Gerontologist, 2,* 141–148.
Lotka, A. J. (1926). The frequency distribution of scientific productivity. *Journal of the Washington Academy of Sciences, 16,* 317–323.

Lykken, D. T. (1998). The genetics of genius. In A. Steptoe (Ed.), *Genius and the mind: Studies of creativity and temperament in the historical record* (pp. 15–37). New York: Oxford University Press.

Mach, E. (1896, January). On the part played by accident in invention and discovery. *Monist, 6*, 161–175.

Martindale, C. (1995). Creativity and connectionism. In S. M. Smith, T. B. Ward, & R. A. Finke (Eds.), *The creative cognition approach* (pp. 249–268). Cambridge, MA: MIT Press.

McCrae, R. R. (1987). Creativity, divergent thinking, and openness to experience. *Journal of Personality and Social Psychology, 52*, 1258–1265.

Mednick, S. A. (1962). The associative basis of the creative process. *Psychological Review, 69*, 220–232.

Merton, R. K. (1968, January 5). The Matthew effect in science. *Science, 159*, 56–63.

Merton, R. K. (1961a). The role of genius in scientific advance. *New Scientist, 12*, 306–308.

Merton, R. K. (1961b). Singletons and multiples in scientific discovery: A chapter in the sociology of science. *Proceedings of the American Philosophical Society, 105*, 470–486.

Miller, A. L. (2000). *Insights of genius: Imagery and creativity in science and art*. Cambridge, MA: MIT Press.

Moles, A. (1968). *Information theory and esthetic perception* (J. E. Cohen, Trans.). Urbana: University of Illinois Press. (Original work published 1958)

Ogburn, W. K., & Thomas, D. (1922). Are inventions inevitable? A note on social evolution. *Political Science Quarterly, 37*, 83–93.

Patinkin, D. (1983). Multiple discoveries and the central message. *American Journal of Sociology, 89*, 306–323.

Platz, A., & Blakelock, E. (1960). Productivity of American psychologists: Quantity versus quality. *American Psychologist, 15*, 310–312.

Poincaré, H. (1921). *The foundations of science: Science and hypothesis, the value of science, science and method* (G. B. Halstead, Trans.). New York: Science Press.

Price, D. (1963). *Little science, big science*. New York: Columbia University Press.

Proctor, R. A. (1993). Computer stimulated associations. *Creativity Research Journal, 6*, 391–400.

Qin, Y., & Simon, H. A. (1990). Laboratory replication of scientific discovery processes. *Cognitive Science, 14*, 281–312.

Quételet, A. (1968). *A treatise on man and the development of his faculties*. New York: Franklin. (Reprint of 1842 Edinburgh translation of 1835 French original)

Raskin, E. A. (1936). Comparison of scientific and literary ability: A biographical study of eminent scientists and men of letters of the nineteenth century. *Journal of Abnormal and Social Psychology, 31*, 20–35.

Redner, S. (1998). How popular is your paper? An empirical study of the citation distribution. *European Physical Journal B, 4*, 131–134.

Roberts, R. M. (1989). *Serendipity: Accidental discoveries in science*. New York: Wiley.

Roe, A. (1953). *The making of a scientist*. New York: Dodd, Mead.

Rothenberg, A. (1979). *The emerging goddess: The creative process in art, science, and other fields*. Chicago: University of Chicago Press.

Rothenberg, A. (1986). Artistic creation as stimulated by superimposed versus combined-composite visual images. *Journal of Personality and Social Psychology, 50*, 370–381.

Schmookler, J. (1966). *Invention and economic growth*. Cambridge, MA: Harvard University Press.

Shadish, W. R., Jr. (1989). The perception and evaluation of quality in science. In B. Gholson, W. R. Shadish, Jr., R. A. Neimeyer, & A. C. Houts (Eds.), *The psychology of science: Contributions to metascience* (pp. 383–426). Cambridge, England: Cambridge University Press.

Shapiro, G. (1986). *A skeleton in the darkroom: Stories of serendipity in science*. San Francisco: Harper & Row.

Shockley, W. (1957). On the statistics of individual variations of productivity in research laboratories. *Proceedings of the Institute of Radio Engineers, 45*, 279–290.
Shrager, J., & Langley, P. (Eds.). (1990). *Computational models of scientific discovery and theory formation.* San Mateo, CA: Kaufmann.
Simon, H. A. (1955). On a class of skew distribution functions. *Biometrika, 42*, 425–440.
Simonton, D. K. (1975). Age and literary creativity: A cross-cultural and transhistorical survey. *Journal of Cross-Cultural Psychology, 6*, 259–277.
Simonton, D. K. (1977). Creative productivity, age, and stress: A biographical time-series analysis of 10 classical composers. *Journal of Personality and Social Psychology, 35*, 791–804.
Simonton, D. K. (1978). Independent discovery in science and technology: A closer look at the Poisson distribution. *Social Studies of Science, 8*, 521–532.
Simonton, D. K. (1979). Multiple discovery and invention: Zeitgeist, genius, or chance? *Journal of Personality and Social Psychology, 37*, 1603–1616.
Simonton, D. K. (1980). Thematic fame, melodic originality, and musical zeitgeist: A biographical and transhistorical content analysis. *Journal of Personality and Social Psychology, 38*, 972–983.
Simonton, D. K. (1984a). Creative productivity and age: A mathematical model based on a two-step cognitive process. *Developmental Review, 4*, 77–111.
Simonton, D. K. (1984b). *Genius, creativity, and leadership: Historiometric inquiries.* Cambridge, MA: Harvard University Press.
Simonton, D. K. (1984c). Is the marginality effect all that marginal? *Social Studies of Science, 14*, 621–622.
Simonton, D. K. (1985). Quality, quantity, and age: The careers of 10 distinguished psychologists. *International Journal of Aging and Human Development, 21*, 241–254.
Simonton, D. K. (1986a). Multiple discovery: Some Monte Carlo simulations and Gedanken experiments. *Scientometrics, 9*, 269–280.
Simonton, D. K. (1986b). Multiples, Poisson distributions, and chance: An analysis of the Brannigan-Wanner model. *Scientometrics, 9*, 127–137.
Simonton, D. K. (1986c). Stochastic models of multiple discovery. *Czechoslovak Journal of Physics, B 36*, 138–141.
Simonton, D. K. (1987). Multiples, chance, genius, creativity, and zeitgeist. In D. N. Jackson & J. P. Rushton (Eds.), *Scientific excellence: Origins and assessment* (pp. 98–128). Beverly Hills, CA: Sage Publications.
Simonton, D. K. (1988a). Age and outstanding achievement: What do we know after a century of research? *Psychological Bulletin, 104*, 251–267.
Simonton, D. K. (1988b). *Scientific genius: A psychology of science.* Cambridge, England: Cambridge University Press.
Simonton, D. K. (1989). Age and creative productivity: Nonlinear estimation of an information-processing model. *International Journal of Aging and Human Development, 29*, 23–37.
Simonton, D. K. (1990). Lexical choices and aesthetic success: A computer content analysis of 154 Shakespeare sonnets. *Computers and the Humanities, 24*, 251–264.
Simonton, D. K. (1991a). Career landmarks in science: Individual differences and interdisciplinary contrasts. *Developmental Psychology, 27*, 119–130.
Simonton, D. K. (1991b). Emergence and realization of genius: The lives and works of 120 classical composers. *Journal of Personality and Social Psychology, 61*, 829–840.
Simonton, D. K. (1992). Leaders of American psychology, 1879–1967: Career development, creative output, and professional achievement. *Journal of Personality and Social Psychology, 62*, 5–17.
Simonton, D. K. (1994). *Greatness: Who makes history and why.* New York: Guilford Press.
Simonton, D. K. (1997). Creative productivity: A predictive and explanatory model of career trajectories and landmarks. *Psychological Review, 104*, 66–89.

Simonton, D. K. (1998). Fickle fashion versus immortal fame: Transhistorical assessments of creative products in the opera house. *Journal of Personality and Social Psychology, 75*, 198–210.

Simonton, D. K. (1999a). *Origins of genius: Darwinian perspectives on creativity.* New York: Oxford University Press.

Simonton, D. K. (1999b). Talent and its development: An emergenic and epigenetic model. *Psychological Review, 106*, 435–457.

Simonton, D. K. (2000). Creative development as acquired expertise: Theoretical issues and an empirical test. *Developmental Review, 20*, 283–318.

Skinner, B. F. (1959). A case study in scientific method. In S. Koch (Ed.), *Psychology: A study of a science* (Vol. 2, pp. 359–379). New York: McGraw-Hill.

Sobel, R. S., & Rothenberg, A. (1980). Artistic creation as stimulated by superimposed versus separated visual images. *Journal of Personality and Social Psychology, 39*, 953–961.

Stent, G. S. (1972). Prematurity and uniqueness in scientific discovery. *Scientific American, 227*, 84–93.

Sternberg, R. J. (1989). Computational models of scientific discovery: Do they compute? [Review of Scientific discovery: Computational explorations of the creative process]. *Contemporary Psychology, 34*, 895–897.

Sternberg, R. J., & Lubart, T. I. (1991). An investment theory of creativity and its development. *Human Development, 34*, 1–31.

Sternberg, R. J., & Lubart, T. I. (1995). *Defying the crowd: Cultivating creativity in a culture of conformity.* New York: Free Press.

Suler, J. R. (1980). Primary process thinking and creativity. *Psychological Bulletin, 88*, 144–165.

Terman, L. M. (1925). *Mental and physical traits of a thousand gifted children.* Stanford, CA: Stanford University Press.

Turner, S. P., & Chubin, D. E. (1976). Another appraisal of Ortega, the Coles, and science policy: The Ecclesiastes hypothesis. *Social Science Information, 15*, 657–662.

Turner, S. P., & Chubin, D. E. (1979). Chance and eminence in science: Ecclesiastes II. *Social Science Information, 18*, 437–449.

Tweney, R. D. (1990). Five questions for computationalists. In J. Shrager & P. Langley (Eds.), *Computational models of scientific discovery and theory information* (pp. 471–484). San Mateo, CA: Kaufmann.

Walberg, H. J., Strykowski, B. F., Rovai, E., & Hung, S. S. (1984). Exceptional performance. *Review of Educational Research, 54*, 87–112.

Weisberg, R. W. (1994). Genius and madness? A quasi-experimental test of the hypothesis that manic-depression increases creativity. *Psychological Science, 5*, 361–367.

White, L. (1949). *The science of culture.* New York: Farrar, Straus.

Zuckerman, H. (1977). *Scientific elite.* New York: Free Press.

Chapter 5

Extracognitive Phenomena in the Intellectual Functioning of Gifted, Creative, and Talented Individuals

Larisa V. Shavinina
Département des Sciences Administratives,
Université du Québec en Outaouais, Canada

Kavita L. Seeratan
University of Toronto, Canada

INTRODUCTION

Autobiographical and biographical findings on distinguished scientific geniuses demonstrate that their mental functioning is determined in part by *specific feelings, preferences, beliefs,* and other similar phenomena. However, psychologists, working in the field of high ability, rarely study these phenomena, which can be referred to as "extracognitive phenomena." One of the greatest minds of the 20th century, Albert Einstein, in discussions with Max Wertheimer (1959) about the development of the theory of relativity and the way of thinking which led to it, emphasized that:

> during all those years there was the *feeling of direction,* of going straight toward something concrete. It is, of course, very hard to express that feeling in words; but it was decidedly the case, and clearly to be distinguished from later considerations about the rational form of the solution. (p. 228; italics added)

Similarly, Jacques Hadamard (1954) in his study on the psychology of invention in the mathematical field cited Henri Poincaré, a famous French scientist, who asserted that:

> it may be surprising to see emotional sensibility invoked a propos of mathematical demonstrations which, it would seem, can interest only the intellect. This would be to forget the *feeling of mathematical beauty,* of the *harmony of numbers and forms,* of *geometric elegance.* This is a true esthetic feeling that all real mathe-

mathematicians know, and surely it belongs to emotional sensibility. (p. 31; italics added)

Poincaré (1913) also insisted that "pure logic would never lead us to anything but tautologies. It is by logic that we prove. It is by *intuition* that we discover" (p. 208; italics added). In a similar way, Rosenblueth and Wiener (1945) emphasized that:

> An *intuitive flair* for what will turn out to be the most important general question gives a basis for selecting some of the significant among the indefinite number of trivial experiments which could be carried out at that stage. Quite vague and tacit generalizations thus influence the selection of data at the start. (p. 317)

Even such a brief account shows the extremely significant role that "feeling of direction," "sense of beauty," those processes usually referred to as "intuition," and other similar phenomena played, and still play, in the appearance of some of the most celebrated creative scientific discoveries.

In the context of this chapter, the phenomenon of the extracognitive refers to four interrelated, and at the same time, obviously different components. These are:

1. specific intellectual feelings (e.g., feelings of direction, harmony, beauty, and style),
2. specific intellectual beliefs (e.g., belief in elevated standards of performance),
3. specific preferences and intellectual values (e.g., the "inevitable" choice of the field of endeavor by certain geniuses and internally developed standards of intellectual working), and
4. intuitive processes.

The frequently used word *specific* embodies the uniqueness of these components in the intellectual functioning of gifted, creative, and talented individuals. It is interesting to note that other psychologists also use the word *specific* in their accounts of the intellectually creative processes at the highest level. For example, Marton, Fensham, and Chaiklin (1994) wrote about a "specific form" of the feeling of being right and made reference to other "specifics" in their study of scientific intuition in Nobel Prize winners.

The following findings are a result of three different directions that our research has taken. The first one was the study of the extracognitive phenomenon in the case of Vladimir I. Vernadsky, a famous Russian scientist/genius of Nobel caliber. The second was the study of this phenomenon in three intellectually gifted adolescents. The third was an investigation of the extracognitive phenomena in Nobel laureates. The goal of this chapter is to concurrently examine these research findings and to consequently present the concept of the extracognitive phenomenon. The chapter consists of six parts. The first part deals with methodological issues related to the use of biographical and autobiographical literature as well as case-study approaches as a means of investigating the psychological underpinnings of gifted, creative, and talented individuals. The second, third, and fourth parts of this chapter present findings regarding the extracognitive phenomena of Vernadsky, gifted adolescents, and Nobel laureates, respectively. The fifth part, a discussion, considers the relationship between the components of the extracognitive, its link to metacognition, and its functions. Finally, the sixth part concludes that the extracognitive should be viewed as the highest level of the manifestation of the intellectual and creative potentials of an individual, and consequently, as an important criterion of intellectually creative giftedness.

METHODOLOGICAL ISSUES

Three main data sources were used in our studies:

1. biographical and autobiographical accounts on Vernadsky and Nobel laureates,
2. a modified version of the case-study method for investigating the learning patterns and characteristics of three gifted adolescents, and
3. the analysis and amalgamation of research literature presenting the psychological investigations as well as other related studies pertaining to Nobel laureates.

The use of the biographical and autobiographical accounts and the case-study method can be, and has been to a certain extent, a controversial matter. However, any attempt at a comprehensive review of the research, for example, on Nobel laureates and other distinguishing individuals, is unfeasible without some reliance on such accounts. These accounts and the case-study method are perfectly suited for capturing the special characteristics of highly creative and intellectual individuals and their discoveries or inventions. Autobiographical and biographical literature is essential for the research and description of persons or events distinguished by their rarity as is the case with Nobel laureates. Using this literature, psychologists can describe the idiosyncratic features of gifted, creative, and talented individuals including a focus on the characteristics of their extracognitive phenomena. Often biographical and autobiographical accounts provide a holistic view of the subject (Frey, 1978) allowing psychologists to develop and validate theories grounded in a more direct "observation" of the individuals (Gross, 1994). The analysis of subjective phenomena such as the individual's feelings, preferences, beliefs, and views enables a more comprehensive "picture" of the individual than that which is possible with only objective methods.

However, the use of autobiographical and biographical literature for the study of outstanding individuals such as Nobel scientists presents certain limitations, such as:

1. The possible subjectivity of biographers resulting from their individual interpretations of events, thoughts, and states. These interpretations may be influenced by their personal attitudes toward the person about whom they write, an attitude potentially swayed in part by whether the latter is living or not. Autobiographers can also be very subjective and contradictory in their accounts of their own thinking processes, psychological states, and the surrounding events that lead up to and follow their particular innovative breakthroughs in science.

2. The time of writing the biography or autobiography, normally after an individual has already become a brilliant personality, often relies on vague memories of one's thinking processes that may have likely been weakened or altered over time. Hence, the conclusions and reports of autobiographers and especially of biographers are not always reliable. It certainly raises the issue surrounding the validity and reliability of subjective reports when they are used as data. This problem has been addressed extensively in literature (Brown, 1978, 1987; Ericsson & Simon, 1980). However, despite such critiques, scholars in the field of creativity view the use of self-reports as an "effective means of learning about scientific thinking" (John-Steiner, 1985, p. 181).

It should be noted that Nobel laureates and other distinguishing personalities, who are themselves the subjects of biographies and autobiographies, grasped the above-mentioned problems very well. For example, Einstein himself realized this clearly when he wrote at the beginning of his *Autobiographical Notes*:

> The exposition of that which is worthy of communication does nonetheless not come easy; today's person of 67 is by no means the same as was the one of 50, of 30, or of 20. Every reminiscence is colored by today's being what it is, and therefore by a deceptive point of view.... (Einstein, 1949, p. 47)

Holton (1973) further pointed out that it is not only growth or change that colors one's interpretations, but it is also the difference between experience lived and experience reported.

5. EXTRACOGNITIVE PHENOMENA

In this case it is well possible that such an individual in retrospect sees a uniformly systematic development, whereas the actual experience takes place in kaleidoscopic particular situations. (Einstein, 1949, p. 47)

However, even with these limitations in mind, the use of biographical and autobiographical literature is probably the single best source available for the investigation of the extracognitive phenomenon in gifted, creative, and talented persons because such accounts are enriched with information pertaining to an individual's specific feelings, preferences, beliefs, and intuitive processes.

THE EXTRACOGNITIVE PHENOMENA IN THE CASES OF FULFILLED AND DEVELOPING GIFTEDNESS

Our initial research on the extracognitive included the case study of this phenomenon in one prominent Russian scientist, V. I. Vernadsky, and the case studies of this phenomenon in three gifted, creative, and talented students in physics and mathematics. The findings regarding their extracognitive phenomena are presented next.

The Extracognitive Phenomena in an Outstanding Scientist

Vladimir I. Vernadsky was a famous geologist, biochemist, geochemist, geobiochemist, philosopher, and historian of science. He was a founder of such sciences as geochemistry, biochemistry, geobiochemistry, and of many scientific theories like the theory of the biosphere, and the theory of the noosphere. We have investigated Vernadsky's extracognitive intelligence by studying relevant biographical materials (i.e., letters, diaries, etc.). The following components of his extracognitive were found in our study.

First, we should point out Vernadsky's *aspiration to harmony and beauty* in everything (in cognition, science, and life as a whole). His feeling of harmony and beauty is seen in various spheres of his life and work. Let us mention just a few examples to illustrate.

1. In the field of cognition, he asserted: "Looking for clarity where there is scarcely *harmony*...." "There is a strong mathematical dependence in the shape of crystals; having measured 4–5 angles you can find out all the *harmony*." "The idea is becoming clearer and clearer and I begin to recognize *the beauty—the harmony*... and I have a *feeling* that I will sort out everything soon" (Vernadsky, 1988, p. 105; italics added).

2. As to his versatile interests in the arts, Vernadsky (1988) noticed: "According to my present mood... I prefer theatre, rather than novels and

tales. There is something in the former which is not worth looking for in the latter.... This is the *beauty of construction, the beauty of architecture.* You feel the real *whole beauty* in the shape of this creation as in good architecture or sculpture" (p. 91; italics added).

3. With regards to his private life, he wrote, for example, to his wife: "I greatly appreciate that you possess a *beautiful harmony of thoughts* and that you live *in harmony with thoughts"* (Vernadsky, 1988, p. 115; italics added).

4. In life as a whole, Vernadsky, admitting the fact that beauty and harmony exist, tried to understand what they are all about and tried to find in them something more general. Therefore, he asked himself, "Is it not the case that *beauty is in thought, in the belief in truth?"*

According to Vernadsky, the creation of harmony in the universe is only possible through the work of the human mind. He claimed: "Thought is the background of personality.... It is deathless.... It is the *creator of harmony* in universal chaos" (Vernadsky, 1988, p. 78; italics added). He also wrote:

> How important is the purity of thought! It seems to me that it is more important than anything else in life, because through it we experience the *desire to seek harmony*. The *feeling of harmony* is brought about this way. One must not think about the negative, or distract oneself with everyday problems and anxieties when all around there is so much space to think *more harmonic, more beautiful,* more important thoughts. (Vernadsky, 1988, p. 113; italics added)

Vernadsky's well-developed *"feeling of style"* is related to his *"harmonious vision of reality."* He noticed, for example, in his diary: "I am reading the books of *Marcus Aurelius* with great pleasure. They are so *wonderful,* there is so much humanity, strength" (Vernadsky, 1988, p. 63; italics added). He wrote in one of his letters: "What a *wonderful* book—*Don Quixote!* There is so much humanity!" (Vernadsky, 1988, p. 112; italics added). We think it is possible to conclude that Vernadsky had a harmonious vision of the world around him and an aesthetic vision of life as a whole. His aspiration to harmony and beauty—and this should be especially emphasized—had a generalized character as it was directed to "life as a whole."

The second component of the extracognitive in Vernadsky's mental functioning is his *understanding of the value of mind work,* the consideration of Thought (Vernadsky wrote this word with a capital letter) as the most important thing in the life of human beings. He was convinced that:

> *Thought is the most important thing* in the whole life of human beings. It means everything. Goodness, dedication and feelings have a meaning for the life of individual persons.... Of course, it is impossible to live without that.... But

5. EXTRACOGNITIVE PHEOMENA

for the whole society and for all the people *Thought replaces everything.* I clearly and *very strongly feel* that it is very important and I am distressed and irritated by everything which could possibly restrict Thought. (Vernadsky, 1988, pp. 75-76; italics added)

Vernadsky could not endure the fact, that "*Thought is not yet accessible for everyone.*" He wrote: "There is no mental search, there are no doubts for the majority of people. They have a quiet family life . . . far from eternal, profound and excruciating, but at the same time *beautiful* problems, which are proposed by human history" (Vernadsky, 1988, p. 116; italics added). His strongly expressed *faith in the power of ideas* is the special manifestation of this component of his extracognitive. He asserted:

There is one power and one strength—an idea. (Vernadsky, 1988, p. 115). I think, there is nothing more important than *the power of the idea*: it drives everything. (Vernadsky, 1988, p. 107; italics added)

The third component of the extracognitive in Vernadsky's intellectual activity is his *feeling of "the eternal."* He wrote: "It seems to me that *I feel the pulse of eternity* in each place and everywhere" (Vernadsky, 1988, p. 260; italics added). As was mentioned previously, Vernadsky also saw the beauty of life in its "eternal change." A special manifestation of the feeling of eternity is Vernadsky's *feeling of "historical process."* He pointed out: "I now have a very strong *feeling . . . of historical process*" (p. 249; italics added). Vernadsky was interested in history as a whole and in the history of various scientific disciplines for a very long time. He tried to consider every single scientific event or problem from a historical perspective and in all aspects of its historical connections.

The fourth component of the extracognitive in Vernadsky's mental functioning is connected with his *aspiration to the "endlessness"* in scientific cognition: he tried to understand the essence of scientific cosmogony, biochemistry, and so on as the most synthetic events of the objective world. For example, he wrote: "It seems to me, I have a subconscious understanding of scientific cosmogony problems. Once again, *my mind longs for the endlessness*" (Vernadsky, 1988, p. 230; italics added).

The fifth component of the extracognitive in Vernadsky's intellectual activity is his *aspiration to seek clarity* in everything. In this connection he pointed out: "I often seek the clarity in there, where there is no harmony" (Vernadsky, 1988, p. 81). One of the distinctive characteristics of Vernadsky's cognitive experience was his wish to understand the absolutely unknown puzzles of the world, of human origins, accompanied by his reflections about the obvious. For example, he wrote:

It seems to me so clear, that it is not worth writing about. However, usually everything which is most clear is the source of delusions of all kinds, because the human mind thinks very little about these problems, because they seem lucid. (Vernadsky, 1988, p. 142)

Therefore, the extracognitive phenomenon in Vernadsky's intellectual functioning was characterized by a unique combination of his feelings, preferences, beliefs, and intuitive processes. They guided his mental activity on the way to his outstanding scientific discoveries.

The Extracognitive Phenomena in Gifted Adolescents

The extracognitive phenomena in the case of developing intellectual giftedness were studied in three gifted students in physics and mathematics. These boys have made real-life achievements such as participation and winning first prize in local, national, and international Olympiads in physics and mathematics. They were studying in a physics-mathematics school, the only one in the Ukraine, and were evaluated by teachers as "the most gifted." They were in the ninth or tenth grade and ranged in age from 15 to 16 years old.

Psychological methods for studying the extracognitive phenomenon do not exist at present. It is well known that the initial research on any new scientific phenomenon lacks adequate methods. For this reason, the method used by Max Wertheimer in his research on Einstein's way of thinking that led to the eventual discovery of the theory of relativity, was adopted; conversations with gifted students were used in the same way Wertheimer used discussions with Einstein. During long conversations we questioned students about the characteristics of their thinking and cognitive experience. None of our questions were directly related to the extracognitive. The findings arose indirectly during the conversations. The results of the research showed that the following components of the extracognitive were typical of these gifted students.

In the first of the boys, there was a very significant manifestation of the extracognitive in his *aspiration to harmony*, which has a multidirectional character in its application to different aspects of his life. For example, in the field of his scientific interests, he asserted: "Each physicist is . . . a lyric poet in the depths of the soul. . . . The physicist feels *the harmony in shape, in form* and *in a nice theory*." Of his daily life he pointed out: "It is essential to try *to reach harmony*. . . . Daily life should not be very modest, but it should encourage activity and stimulate only the positive. . . . It should be *in harmony* with a person."

Two components of the extracognitive were found in the second student. One of them can be classified as including *beliefs*. For example, when questioned if it is easy to get interested in new ideas, he answered: "I get interested if *it seems to me that the idea is correct*. And I reject it if *I believe* that the

5. EXTRACOGNITIVE PHENOMENA

idea is wrong.... Perhaps, it is not generally correct, but personally for me it seems correct.... A new idea is great if *I feel it in my heart*."

The next component of the extracognitive in the mental functioning of this student is his understanding of the high value of the mind per se, that is one of his specific intellectual values. In particular, he believes that: "*Thought alone makes a human being.* If Thought dies, then the person will also die." His answer to a question about his life slogan also shows the extremely important status of Thought in his intellectual activity. He said: *"Think!* It is very simple, because if you think—you exist. If you do not think—you do not exist."

The third student's extracognitive profile consisted of the feeling of direction: for example, to the question: Who is your ideal in science? he answered: "I do not know.... But *I feel* at the same time, that *I aspire to something.*"

Special beliefs: for example, his answer to the question What kind of feeling do you have, when new ideas come to your mind? was the following: "When ideas come, I think about their practical realization. Sometimes such ideas come into my mind, although I do not know how to put them into practice.... At the same time I very strongly want to do this. I *believe* that *it will happen in the future.*"

The feeling of truth, which is objectively correct and true: When asked whether it was easy for him to become interested in new ideas, he replied, "I get interested easily, if the idea looks promising. *I get a feeling of whether it is correct or wrong.*"

These findings demonstrate a fascinating similarity of the components of the extracognitive in both gifted adolescents as well as the distinguished scientist, Vernadsky. Mental functioning of gifted adolescents is also influenced by the extracognitive. It would be wrong to assert that the extracognitive phenomenon plays an extremely important role only in the intellectual activity of outstanding creators in science and art. In his investigation of intuitive processes in famous scientists, Miller (1996) noted that it is impossible to reveal such processes in individuals other than adults. The earlier findings provide some support that such processes also exist within adolescents. Specifically, we found that both intellectually gifted adults and adolescents are distinguished by:

1. a specific feeling of direction in their creativity and in their life as a whole. In this respect the study of the extracognitive of such individuals is closely related to current research on the subconscious and unconscious processes of creativity. Hence, the study of the extracognitive can be viewed as instrumental in advancing the study of creativity.
2. specific beliefs. The world of these beliefs is very diverse and includes the feeling of truth, faith in the power of ideas, and so on.

3. specific preferences, including the aspiration to harmony and beauty, the understanding of mind work as very valuable and the consideration of Thought as an important aspect of human life. The feeling of the "eternal," the aspiration to "endlessness" and clarity in everything are among these preferences.

The results of these case studies allowed us to conclude that the phenomenon of the extracognitive plays an exceptionally important role in intellectual functioning of gifted adults and adolescents. The third direction of our research on the extracognitive deals with this phenomenon as applied to Nobel laureates.

THE EXTRACOGNITIVE PHENOMENA IN NOBEL LAUREATES

As it is well known from the history of science, any new field or topic—being at the initial stages of its development—starts with a descriptive stage. Since the research on Nobel laureates is not a well-developed topic and the study of the extracognitive is a relatively new one, the findings presented below are descriptive in nature. That is, they describe the different components of the extracognitive phenomenon in Nobel laureates and, as such, act to provide an introduction to this new concept.

The purpose of this section is to draw at least an approximate picture of the extracognitive in Nobel laureates. In order to do so, we primarily examine autobiographical and biographical accounts of Nobel laureates and existing psychological studies on these outstanding scientists. However, taking into account the fact that psychological publications on this topic are not numerous, we also refer to appropriate sociological investigations—for example, a famous study of Nobel laureates in the United States carried out by Harriet Zuckerman (1977). Here, we present the findings regarding each of the four previously mentioned components of the extracognitive phenomenon.

Specific Intellectual Feelings

Specific Scientific Taste, Including Sense of "Important Problems," "Good" Ideas, "Correct" Theories, and Elegant Solutions, and Feeling of Being Right

Zuckerman (1977, 1983) showed that a *specific scientific taste* is an extremely important virtue of Nobel Prize winners. Its primary criteria include a *sense* for distinguishing the important problem and an appreciation of stylish solutions. For them, "deep problems and *elegant solutions* distinguish excellent science from the merely competent or commonplace" (Zuckerman, 1983, p. 249; italics added). For example, discussing his own feelings in the process of scientific creativity, Stanley Cohen, Nobel laureate in medicine, 1986, noted:

> to me it is *a feeling of* Well, I really don't believe this result, or This is a trivial result, and This is an important result, and Let us follow this path. I am not always right, but *I do have feelings about what is an important observation and what is probably trivial.* (quoted in Marton et al., 1994, p. 463; italics added)

Analyzing Nobel laureates' replies to the question "In the absence of rational, logical support for scientific intuitions, what makes the scientist follow them?" Marton et al. (1994) found that 9 out of 72 laureates said that it was a "feeling" that made them persevere. Marton et al. (1994) pointed out that the feeling could be "a *feeling of being right, being wrong,* or *having come across something important.* . . . The feeling is often an immediate, intense feeling of certitude, of being right, especially when an answer to a problem one has been struggling with appears suddenly, without any preceding steps whatsoever" (p. 463). It is interesting to note that Marton et al. (1994) perceived a "*feeling of great certitude*" in Nobel laureates.

Marton et al. (1994) also found that the "feeling of being right often seems to originate from artistic and/or, in the metaphoric sense, sensory or quasi-sensory qualities. One senses, sees, recognizes, feels in one's fingers or produces certain qualities" (p. 463). As Paul Berg, Nobel laureate in chemistry, 1980, highlighted:

> There is another aspect that I would add to it, and that is, I think, *taste. Taste in almost the artistic sense.* Certain individuals see art in some undefinable way, can put together something which has a *certain style,* or a certain class to it. A certain rightness to it. (quoted in Marton et al., 1994, p. 463; italics added)

Csikszentmihalyi's (1996) study of ten Nobel Prize winners in science, among another 91 exceptionally creative persons, provided additional evidence for the existence of a *sense* for an "important problem." He pointed out that Nobel laureates seem to have an ability to distinguish between "good" and "bad" ideas. For example, Manfred Eigen, Nobel laureate in chemistry, 1967, was one of several scientists in Csikszentmihalyi's study who asserted that the only difference between them and their less creative colleagues was that they could tell whether a problem was soluble or not, and this saved enormous amounts of time in addition to many false starts. Similarly, at Linus Pauling's (Nobel laureate in chemistry, 1954) sixtieth birthday celebration, a student asked him, "Dr. Pauling, how does one go about having good ideas?" He replied, "You have a lot of ideas and throw away the bad ones" (Csikszentmihalyi, 1996, p. 67). Likewise, George Stigler, Nobel laureate in economics, 1982, claimed:

> I consider that I have *good intuition and good judgment on what problems are worth pursuing and what lines of work are worth doing*. I used to say (and I think this was bragging) that whereas most scholars have ideas which do not pan out more than, say, 4 percent of the time, mine come through maybe 80 percent of the time. (quoted in Csikszentmihalyi, 1996, p. 61; italics added)

Arthur L. Schwalow, Nobel laureate in physics, 1981, says the following about a similar feeling accompanying his scientific creativity:

> you store in your mind a *feeling for a magnitude of things*, how big things really are, so you'll get a *feeling whether something will go, or not*, if you try to put two ideas together. (quoted in Marton et al., 1994, p. 466; italics added)

Similarly, Niels Bohr's *feeling for correct and incorrect theories* was a legendary one. For example, after hearing Wolfgang Pauli present to a professional audience a new theory of elementary particles, Bohr summarized the subsequent discussion by saying that "we are all agreed that your theory is crazy. The question which divides us is whether it is crazy enough to have a chance of being correct. *My own feeling is that it is not crazy enough*" (quoted in Cropper, 1970, p. 57).

In an overview of Robert Burns Woodward's accomplishments, who was one of the great organic chemists of all time and Nobel laureate in chemistry, 1965, his friend and colleague at Harvard University, Frank Westheimer stated:

> Even scientists who mastered his methods could not match his *style*. For there is an *elegance* about Woodward's work—his chemistry, his lectures, his publications—that was natural to him, and as unique as the product itself. (quoted in C. E. Woodward, 1989, p. 229; italics added)

Therefore, the personal accounts of Nobel laureates demonstrate that specific scientific taste is a very critical facet in scientific creativity of an exceptionally high level. As was documented by various examples, this taste expresses itself in a variety of feelings, senses, and styles.

Feeling of Beauty

Describing his discovery of the positron, Paul Adrienne Maurice Dirac (1977) emphasized that:

> It was sort . . . of faith . . . that any equations which describe fundamental laws of Nature must have *great mathematical beauty* in them [e.g.,] . . . the *beauty of*

5. EXTRACOGNITIVE PHENOMENA

relativity. . . . [I was working on] the physical interpretation and transformation theory of quantum mechanics. (p. 136; italics added)

Also, on receiving the Nobel Prize for physics, Dirac (1963) remarked:

> It seems that if one is working from the point of view of *getting beauty* in one's equations and if one has really sound insight, one is on a sure line of progress. (p. 47; italics added)

Likewise, Dirac (1963), discussing why Ervin Schrodinger failed to publish a relativistic wave equation, asserted that "it is more important to *have beauty in one's equations* than to have them fit experiment" (p. 47; italics added). Similarly, physicist Allan Cormack, Nobel laureate in medicine, 1979, said in an interview with Rothenberg (1996):

> The abstractions [I do in mathematics] are just as *beautiful* [as in art] and I find them more satisfactory. . . . I think there's a great deal of satisfaction in seeing ideas put together or related. And there is a structural thing there just as much as in sculpture or painting or anything of that sort—form and economy of means. . . . Very often in biology you say, "If such-and-such went that way, will this go that way?" Very often the reason you ask why is because you found the previous thing to be *attractive* somehow. (p. 212; italics added)

Werner Heisenberg (1971) wrote the following about his own feeling of beauty and its role in scientific creativity:

> You may object that *by speaking of simplicity and beauty I am introducing aesthetic criteria of truth*, and I frankly admit that *I am strongly attracted by the simplicity and beauty of the mathematical schemes* which nature presents us. You must have felt this too: the almost frightening simplicity and wholeness of the relationship, which nature suddenly spreads out before us. (p. 68)

Similarly, describing his investigations in the area of x-ray crystallography, Robert Huber, Nobel laureate in chemistry, 1988, asserted in an interview with Rothenberg (1996):

> It's not just joy. This first stage [in x-ray crystallography] of seeing a crystal is not only a *beauty*, there's also so much promise behind it, so many hopes. And, then, very much later, when analysis has succeeded, ah, to see the molecule for the first time, that's similar. (p. 212; italics added)

In the same way, recalling his research on the discovery of the instructed mixture paradigm, Jean-Marie Lehn, Nobel laureate in chemistry, 1987, pointed out in an interview with Rothenberg (1996): "Once you have recognized this *harmony* which exists in self-recognition, then you should say, 'But what is the self/non-self?' " (p. 229; italics added). Ochse (1990) pointed out that "Max Born hailed the advent of relativity as making the universe of science not only grander but also more *beautiful*" (p. 123).

Likewise, R. B. Woodward's daughter wrote about her famous father's "*feeling for art*" in the synthesis of organic compounds (C. E. Woodward, 1989, p. 235; italics added). In the Cope talk of 1973, in which he reviewed the background of his orbital symmetry work in chemistry, Robert Burns Woodward asserted:

> For almost 50 years now, I have been involved in an affair with chemistry. It has been throughout a richly rewarding involvement, with numerous episodes of high drama and intense engagement, with the joys of enlightenment and achievement, with the special pleasures which come from the *perception of order and beauty in Nature*—and with much humor. (quoted in C. E. Woodward, 1989, p. 230; italics added)

In general, R. B. Woodward perceived an amazing sense of beauty in chemistry. This sense of beauty manifested itself in every facet of his work. For example, he claimed "I love crystals, the *beauty of their forms*—and their formation" (quoted in C. E. Woodward, 1989, p. 237; italics added). His daughter wrote,

> the *aspects of art and beauty in Woodward's work* are contained not only in the forms found in or built into the fixed structures of molecules. They have perhaps more to do with the way in which he manipulated the molecules, in his design of the synthetic steps, in a process that was not tortuous but *harmonious*, that *felt right* and was *elegant*. (C. E. Woodward, 1989, p. 234; italics added)

Ethologist, artist, writer, and Nobel laureate in medicine Konrad Lorenz (1952) expressed a general attitude of a man to the beauty of nature when he wrote that:

> He who has once seen the intimate *beauty of nature* cannot tear himself away from it again. He must become either a poet or a naturalist and, if his eyes are good and his powers of observation sharp enough, he may well become both. (p. 12)

It should be acknowledged that other researchers have also discussed and highlighted the importance of the feeling of beauty so strongly expressed by creative scientists. Ochse (1990) considered the feeling of beauty in the context of the analysis of aesthetic sensitivity; Rothenberg (1996) in the context of aesthetic motivation; Kuhn (1970) in the context of aesthetic considerations; and McMorris (1970), Miller (1981, 1992), and Wechsler (1978) in the context of aesthetics in science as a whole. Furthermore,

Kuhn (1970) argued that application of aesthetic sensitivity—that scientists mainly express as a feeling or sense of beauty—was indeed essential to the progress of science:

> Something must make at least a few scientists *feel they are on the right track*, and sometimes it is only *personal and inarticulate aesthetic considerations* that can do that. Men have been converted by them at times when most of the articulate technical arguments pointed the other way ... even today Einstein's general theory attracts men principally on *aesthetic grounds,* an appeal that few people outside of mathematics have been *able to feel.* (Kuhn, 1970, p. 158; italics added)

Ochse (1990) suggests that behind every famous scientist's expressions about their sense of beauty is "the suggestion that underlying scientific creativity is an intellectual motivation that is fuelled by a positive evaluation of learning and achievement, and guided by aesthetic sensitivity—which may relate to a need for emotional satisfaction" (p. 124).

Feeling of Direction and Similar Feelings (in One's Own Scientific Activity, in Search of Mentors and of One's Own Unique Domain in Science, and so on)

As it follows from Albert Einstein's (Nobel laureate in physics, 1921) citation at the beginning of this article, the feeling of direction played an important role in his work on the development of the Theory of Relativity. Michael S. Brown, Nobel laureate in medicine, 1985, described a similar feeling in a roundtable discussion—called "Science and Man"—with the Nobel laureates in physics, chemistry, and medicine:

> And so ... as we did our work, I think, *we almost felt at times that there was almost a hand guiding us.* Because we would go from one step to the next, and somehow we would *know which was the right way to go.* And I really can't tell how we knew that, how we knew that it was necessary to move ahead. (quoted in Marton et al., 1994, pp. 461–462)

It can be said that intellectually creative individuals have very specific manifestations of cognitive direction in the studying of scientific problems and of the world as a whole.

Zuckerman (1977, 1983) found that the Nobel laureates, "in their comparative youth, sometimes went to great lengths to *make sure* that they would be working with those they considered the best in their field" (Zuckerman, 1983, pp. 241–242; italics added). This belief (i.e., self-confidence, which is very often explained as good fortune, luck, fate, or chance, etc.) led them to the masters of their craft—to the scientists of Nobel caliber. It is thus possible to confirm the existence of a feeling of direction in the scientific elite. For instance, the biochemist Hans Krebs, Nobel laureate in chemistry, (1967) noted:

> If I ask myself how it came about that one day I found myself in Stockholm, I have not the slightest doubt that I owe this *good fortune* to the circumstance that I had an outstanding teacher at the critical stage in my scientific career. (p. 1444; italics added)

The "good fortune" that Hans Krebs so humbly refers to is nothing else but the deep intellectual *feeling of direction* in the fulfillment of his own scientific career.

Likewise, recalling his work on the creation of monoclonal antibodies, Georges Kohler, Nobel laureate in medicine, 1984, said in an interview with Rothenberg (1996):

> I was one of the first Ph.D. students in an institution [Basel Institute] which turned out, later on, to be a very important one. I studied genetic diversity of antibodies and I thought that [the somatic mutation hypothesis] was a very clever idea: to have one gene, and from that somatically you can have many variants. I knew there were variants because I started on that in my Ph.D. And variants were made by Cesar Milstein in the lab, so I said, "*Okay, I'm going to study how these variants are going to be made. I am going to Cesar Milstein. . . .*" I knew that the Cesar Milstein group had done experiments with cell fusion—another field in which I was reading a book and was interested. And I remember that when I was about to go to Cambridge, I was talking to somebody in the library and saying, "*I'm going to Cesar Milstein and make a lot of fusions.*" (p. 227; italics added)

These accounts bring to light the exceptional role of one's "feeling of direction" and similar feelings that are in fact one's more latent manifestations of the feeling of direction to the intellectual activity of Nobel laureates. Their scientific creativity is determined by such feelings, which guide Nobel laureates in their work.

Specific Intellectual Beliefs

Belief in Specific Standards of Performance

Kholodnaya (1991) pointed out that a belief in the existence of some principles and specific standards, by which the nature of scientific research is determined, and a priori confidence in the truth of a certain vision of things are among important beliefs of outstanding scientists. Thus, C. E. Woodward (1989) highlighted R. B. Woodward's "*feeling for experimentation*" that was based on his conviction that theory without experimental proof was worthless. "Ideas and theory could have an aesthetic aspect but their beauty and elegance were always tied to a concrete relationship with a physical reality" (C. E. Woodward, 1989, p. 237, italics added). Similarly, Zuckerman (1977) found that *elevated standards of performance* (the methods and quality of first rate research) are essential for Nobel laureates. The previously considered studies of the phenomenon of the extracognitive in Vernadsky and gifted adolescents allow us to conclude that their specific beliefs determine their exceptional self-confidence and the extraordinary stability of their intellectually creative activity.

Specific Intellectual Preferences (e.g., Choice of "Difficult" Scientific Problems or Problems at the Leading Edge of Science)

Specific intellectual preferences of Nobel laureates manifest themselves in a variety of ways. Some have a preference for "difficult" scientific problems, which were and had remained unsolved for many decades. Richard Feynman is a fine example of this pursuit to solve the unsolved. Feynman, in his early twenties at Los Alamos, was an "*enfant terrible,* bubbling with quick brilliance on the theoretical problems of bomb building that came his way" (Wilson, 1972, p. 10). Feynman's account is as follows:

> It was a succession of successes—but easy successes. After the war, I moved over to the kind of problems (like the self-energy of the electron) that men spend years thinking about. On that level there are no easy successes; and the satisfaction you get when you're proved right is so great that even if it occurs only twice in a lifetime, everything else is worth it! (quoted in Wilson, 1972, pp. 10–11)

Nobel laureates' preference for problems at the very frontiers of science is another way their specific intellectual preferences manifest. This desire to decipher, understand, and explore the relatively unknown areas of a particular field is demonstrated as we follow the life trajectory of Nobel Prize winner, Enrico Fermi. In the 1920s, he was:

> one of the leaders among the young European physicists who were developing the quantum mechanical wave theories of atomic structure. Then in 1929 Fermi made a sharp decision. Fermi felt that . . . the only remaining area of physics to attack where all was still unknown at that time was the heart of the atomic structure—nuclear physics. So in 1929 Fermi moved away from research in atomic theory, where he had made a great reputation, and went into the unknown of neutron physics, where he worked with such ingenuity on the interaction between neutrons and atomic nuclei that within seven years he won a Nobel prize. Fifteen years later, at the end of World War II in 1945,

Fermi changed again. By that time, he probably had learned more about the neutron than anyone else in the world, but now it was nuclear physics that seemed to have been all cleaned up for him. So once again he moved on—this time into the uncharted domain of high-energy particles. To Fermi, it was always necessary to be at work where the big mystery was. (Wilson, 1972, p. 16)

Such examples allowed Wilson (1972) to conclude that "when there is no longer enough mystery in a subject to attract" scientists, "they move on to new fields" (p. 16). In other words, they always follow their inner, specific intellectual preferences.

Highly Developed Intuitive Processes

As emphasized in the psychological literature, certain individuals have an intuitive feeling, as they begin their intellectual activity, about what their final product will be like (Hadamard, 1954; Gardner & Nemirovsky, 1991; Gruber, 1974; Ochse, 1990; Policastro, 1995; Simonton, 1980). This is especially true in the case of Nobel laureates. It is widely recognized by these great scientists that intuition is an essential component of creative thinking that leads to innovative discoveries. For example, Max Planck asserted that the pioneer scientist working at the frontier of science "must have a vivid *intuitive* imagination, for new ideas are not generated by deduction, but by an artistically creative imagination" (Planck, 1950, p. 109). At the same time, he recognized that intuition alone is not sufficient. For instance, in his autobiographical account on the discovery of the constant and the quantum of action, Max Planck wrote:

> So long as it [the radiation formula] had merely the standing of a law disclosed by lucky *intuition*, it could not be expected to possess more than a formal significance. For this reason, on the very day that I formulated this law, I began to devote myself to the task of investing it with true physical meaning. (Planck, 1950, p. 41; italics added)

Similarly, Einstein highly appreciated intuition in creative processes. Thus, he wrote about "Bohr's *unique instinct*, which enabled him to discover the major laws of spectral lines and the electron shells of the atoms" (Einstein, 1949, cited in John-Steiner, 1985, p. 194). Clearly, "Bohr's *unique instinct*," as referred to by Einstein, is nothing else but his "unique intuition." Wilson (1972) exemplified the value placed on intuition in this personal observation about the famous Enrico Fermi:

> Years ago, as a graduate student, I was present at a three-way argument between Rabi, Szilard, and Fermi. Szilard took a position and mathematically stated it on the blackboard. Rabi disagreed and rearranged the equations to

5. EXTRACOGNITIVE PHENOMENA

the form he would accept. All the while Fermi was shaking his head. "You're both wrong," he said. They demanded proof. Smiling a little he shrugged his shoulders as if proof weren't needed. "*My intuition tells me so,*" he said. I had never heard a scientist refer to his intuition, and I expected Rabi and Szilard to laugh. They didn't. The man of science, I soon found, works with the procedures of logic so much more than anyone else that he, more than anyone else, is aware of logic's limitations. *Beyond logic there is intuition.* (pp. 13–14; italics added)

Another example where the importance of intuition becomes evident came from the work on the discovery of DNA's structure, for which James Watson and Francis Crick were awarded the Nobel Prize. Thus, following her conversation with Sir Francis Crick, John-Steiner (1985) pointed out that one of Crick's contributions to the team's efforts—that led to the discovery of DNA's structure—was his "*intuition* and his ability to work with a minimum number of assumptions while approaching a problem" (p. 187).

Marton et al. (1994) studied intuition of Nobel Prize winners analyzing interviews conducted between 1970 and 1986 with laureates in physics, chemistry, and medicine by a Swedish Broadcasting Corporation. Practically all the laureates regard scientific intuition as a "phenomenon distinctively different from drawing logical conclusions, step by step" (Marton et al., 1994, p. 468). Eighteen out of 72 subjects in this study emphasized that intuition *feels* different from logical reasoning and cannot be explained in logical terms. Marton et al. (1994) concluded that Nobel laureates consider scientific intuition as "an alternative to normal step-by-step logical reasoning" (p. 468). Nobel laureates in their scientific activity:

> do something or something happens to them without their being aware of the reasons or the antecedents. The acts or the events are, however, guided or accompanied by feelings which sometimes spring from a quasi-sensory experience. Intuition is closely associated with a sense of direction, it is more often about finding a path than arriving at an answer or reaching a goal. The ascent of intuition is rooted in extended, varied experience of the object of research: although it may *feel* as if it comes out of the blue, it does *not* come out of the blue. (Marton et al., 1994, p. 468)

To date, Marton et al.'s (1994) study is the only one that conducts a systematic investigation of intuition in Nobel laureates.

So far, we emphasized the important positive role of intuitive processes in scientific creativity of an extremely high level by quoting exceptionally accomplished scientists. However, it is also pertinent to mention the case when the absence of scientific intuition resulted in quite mediocre work. For example,

Robert Oppenheimer was a brilliant interpreter of other men's work, and a judge who could make piercing evaluations of other men's work. But when it came time—figuratively speaking—to write his own poetry in science, his work was sparse, angular, and limited, particularly when judged by the standards he himself set for everyone else. He knew the major problems of his time; he attacked them with style; but *he* apparently *lacked that intuition*—that faculty beyond logic—*which logic needs in order to make great advances.* If one were speaking not of science but of religion, one could say that Oppenheimer's religiosity was the kind that could make him a bishop but never a saint. (Wilson, 1972, p. 13; italics added)

Although the personal accounts of Nobel laureates mentioned earlier demonstrate that "intuition" plays a significant role in highly creative and intellectual processes, we do not know for sure its psychological nature and origin. The common wisdom is to use the term *intuition* in association with the term *insight*, which does not follow logically from available information, and is interpreted as inexplicable (so-called "instinctive" insights) (Ochse, 1990). This kind of insight is often considered to be an innate quality explained by superior functioning of the right hemisphere of the brain. Hadamard (1954) described intuition as something "felt," in contrast to something "known," emphasizing that it involves emotional empathy.

Ochse (1990) attributed intuitive thinking to the operation of automatic mental routines, "unconsciously triggered by configurations of exogenous and/or endogenous stimuli. More specifically, intuition may be viewed as unconsciously triggered *automatic integration of relevant elements of information,* and an 'intuitive feeling' may be seen as part of the experiential outcome of such processes—somewhat equivalent to a feeling of recognition" (p. 243). His standpoint fits perfectly to Bruner's (1960) idea that "intuitive thinking does not characteristically advance in careful well-planned steps. It tends to involve manoeuvres based on an implicit perception of the total problem. The thinker arrives at an answer, which may be right or wrong, with little if any awareness of the process by which he reached it" (pp. 57–58).

Ochse (1990) also suggested that creators develop "well-established bases for intuition because they are constantly involved with their subject of interest, and this practice would lead to the establishment of routines that enable them to integrate relevant actions and items of information. Moreover, creators work independently rather than following prescribed curricula and instructions, which favors the acquisition of a relatively wide repertoire of *generalizable routines*" (p. 244).

Policastro (1995) distinguishes between phenomenological and technical definitions of creative intuition. According to the first, intuition is defined as "a vague anticipatory perception that orients creative work in a promising direction" (p. 99). This definition is phenomenological in that it points to the subject's experience: How does it feel to have a creative intuition? What is that like? The study by Marton et al. (1994) mentioned earlier analyzed mainly this kind of intuition in Nobel laureates.

According to the technical definition, intuition is "a tacit form of knowledge that broadly constrains the creative search by setting its preliminary scope" (Policastro, 1995, p. 100). This implies that intuition is based on cognitive foundations in the sense that it arises from knowledge and experience. Similarly, Simonton (1980) stressed that intuition involves a form of information processing that might be more implicit than explicit, but which is not at all irrational. Policastro (1995) emphasized that both definitions (phenomenological and technical) are important because they complement each other in fundamental ways.

Bowers, Regher, Balthazard, and Parker (1990) defined *intuition* as "a preliminary perception of coherence (pattern, meaning, structure) that is at first not consciously represented, but which nevertheless guides thought and inquiry toward a hunch or hypothesis about the nature of the coherence in question" (p. 74). Bowers et al. conducted experimental studies of intuition, two of which revealed that "people could respond discriminatively to coherences that they could not identify" (p. 72). A third experiment showed that this tacit perception of coherence "guided people gradually to an explicit representation of it in the form of a hunch or hypothesis" (p. 72).

In spite of the differences in the psychological interpretation of the nature of intuition in general and scientific intuition in particular, it is however clear that intuitive processes are extremely important for the productive functioning of human mind. The truth is that any successful scientist—and first of all Nobel laureates—relies on his or her intuition. It is important to note that other psychologists also include intuitive processes in their conceptualizations of higher psychological functions. For example, Sternberg et al. (2000) consider intuition as one of the prototypical forms of developed practical intelligence.

Findings from autobiographical and biographical accounts of Nobel laureates as well as related data from the research literature regarding their extracognitive phenomena were presented in this section. The main conclusion of the study is that the previously described specific scientific taste, intellectual feeling of beauty, feeling of direction, specific beliefs, intellectual preferences, scientific intuition, and their variants are exceptionally important characteristics in extraordinary creative achievements of the world's best scientists, Nobel laureates. The integration of the autobiographical and biographical findings on Nobel laureates with the findings of the psychological studies on these distinguishing scientists demonstrates that their mental functioning is determined—at least in part—by their extracognitive abilities.

DISCUSSION

A range of intellectual phenomena, which describe and comprise the four components of the extracognitive, was presented earlier. Now we would like to address the issue of the relationship between these components taking as an example the relationship between a feeling of direction and intuitive processes. To start the discussion, it seems appropriate to raise the following question: What is behind the feeling of direction? Marton et al. (1994) suggested that this is one's own intuition. They found that although famous examples of intuition associated with names such as Archimedes, Kekule, and Poincaré emphasize arriving at answers or the solutions to problems, other Nobel laureates in their sample stressed the outcome of intuition as their starting rather than end points. In other words, if intuition is considered by Nobel laureates as outcome or result (i.e., intuition denotes an idea, a thought, an answer, or a feeling), then there are the two main alternative ways of experiencing what intuition yields. The first has to do "with *direction* when moving *from* a certain point *toward* something as yet unknown" (Marton et al., 1994, p. 462; underline added). It concerns "finding, choosing, *following a direction, a path*" (Marton et al., 1994, p. 461; italics added). For instance, 37 out of 72 Nobel laureates see the result of scientific intuition as "finding or following a path" (Marton et al., 1994, p. 462). It seems safe to assert that such an understanding of intuitive processes is behind the "feeling of direction." The other main way of experiencing the outcome of intuition by Nobel Prize winners deals with *coming* to a certain point, *arriving at* an answer, "which one was moving toward that is illuminated and seen clearly" (i.e., end points; Marton et al., 1994, p. 462). Marton et al. (1994) concluded that "the most fundamental aspect of scientific intuition is that the scientists choose directions or find solutions for which they do not have sufficient data in the computational sense" (p. 468). In describing the close relationship between intuition and sense of direction, Marton et al. (1994) came close to the introduction of the concept of the extracognitive in intellectual functioning of gifted individuals, identifying some of its main components.

It seems that there are reciprocal relationships between intuition and various feelings of Nobel laureates as just described. We submit that not only does intuitive processes form a basis for the actualization and subsequent development of these feelings, but the latter may also influence the growth of intuition. As a result of their study of the experience of intuition in Nobel laureates, Marton et al. (1994) described a "cumulative structure" of intuition consisting of its higher and lower levels. On the lower level subjects simply indicated that "the experience of scientific intuition differs from the experience of making explicit, logical conclusions based on available information" (p. 463). On the higher level a crucial component is "a feeling, a feeling of something being right (or, occasionally, something being wrong)" (Marton et al., 1994, p. 464). On the next level again a specific form of this feeling is emerged: "the sudden appearance of an idea or of an answer accompanied by a feeling of great certitude" (Marton et al., 1994, p. 464). Consequently, as one can see on the example of the feeling of direction and intuitive processes, the components of the extracognitive are closely related to each other.

THE EXTRACOGNITIVE PHENOMENA AND METACOGNITION

It appears that there is a reciprocal relationship between the extracognitive phenomena and the metacognitive processes of an individual. In other words, if an individual possesses any component of the extracognitive—say, feeling of direction or feeling of beauty (but the findings show that any Nobel laureate has all previously described components of the extracognitive)—then he or she is also expected to possess highly developed metacognitive abilities.

Metacognition is broadly defined as "any knowledge or cognitive activity that takes as its object, or regulates, any aspect of any cognitive enterprise" (Flavell, 1992, p. 114). The essence of metacognition already implies some psychological phenomena, which exist at the intersection of metacognition and the extracognitive. For example, psychologists studying metacognition use and investigate such concepts as awareness and self-awareness (Ferrari & Sternberg, 1996) and feeling of knowing (Brown, 1978), just to mention a few. The most basic form of self-awareness is the "realization that there is a problem of knowing what you know and what you do not know" (Brown, 1978, p. 82). Very often an individual unconsciously comes to such a realization. Probably, intuition is behind any unconscious understanding of any object of cognition including his or her own cognitive apparatus.

Moreover, the well-known title of Brown's (1978) famous article, "Knowing *When*, *Where*, and *How* to Remember: A Problem of Metacognition," which can be considered synonymously with the definition of metacognition, indicates that feeling of direction, specific scientific taste, and feeling of beauty also play a role in metacognitive functioning. Thus, the feeling of direction corresponds to *where* (i.e., *guiding function* of the extracognitive). Specific scientific taste and the feeling of beauty relate to *how* (i.e., *function of evaluation and judgment* of the extracognitive). Altogether—including intuition—they correspond to *when*. Therefore, the phenomenon of the extracognitive contributes to the development of a person's meacognitive abilities. We would even add that the extracognitive lies somewhere in the heart of metacognition and, consequently, allows psychologists to better understand its anatomy and, hence, its nature. In its turn, metacognition leads to the further development of the extracognitive, strengthening and crystallizing its components in an individual's intellectual functioning. For example, the individual with developed metacognitive abilities will be more open to his or her own feeling of direction, feeling of beauty, and intuitive processes.

Empirical findings support our view about the existence of a direct link between the extracognitive and metacognition. Thus, Marton et al. (1994) concluded that scientific intuition of Nobel laureates can be interpreted in terms of awareness, namely as an "initially global grasp of the solution, a kind of metaphorical 'seeing' of the phenomenon being searched for, an *anticipatory perception* of its 'shape' or its gross structure" (p. 468). For example, the choice of a direction in scientific work might possibly be understood as "reflecting a marginal (not fully conscious) awareness of the nature of a phenomenon, a metaphorical 'seeing' of the phenomenon as a whole without knowing its parts, a seeing 'through a glass, darkly' " (Marton et al., 1994, pp. 468–469).

THE FUNCTIONS OF THE EXTRACOGNITIVE IN SCIENTIFIC CREATIVITY

The goal of this section is to discuss the roles the extracognitive phenomenon plays in intellectual creative activity at exceptionally high levels, as that of Nobel laureates and other gifted individuals. It appears reasonable to distinguish the following functions of the extracognitive: cognitive function, guiding function, function of evaluation and judgment, criterion function, aesthetic/emotional function, motivational function, quality/ethical function, and advancing function.

Cognitive function implies that intuitive processes, specific intellectual feelings, beliefs, and preferences provide a mode of acquiring new scientific knowledge—in the form of novel ideas, solutions, models, theories, and approaches. As it was mentioned earlier, intuition can be, for example, interpreted as "intuitive understanding" (Marton et al., 1994) or "intuitive thinking" (Bruner, 1960). The extracognitive is, therefore, a particular cognitive mode of human thinking that appears in advance of any logical, conscious accounts of an individual's intelligence.

Guiding function of the extracognitive implies that specific feelings, beliefs, preferences, and intuition lead scientists in the process of their creative endeavors toward right theories, approaches, and models. The extracognitive phenomenon guides scientists' "sense of 'this is how it has to be,' their sense of rightness" (Wechsler, 1978, p. 1) or scientific truth. The quotations of Albert Einstein, Michael S. Brown, Pierre-Gilles de Gennes, Hans Krebs, Georges Kohler, Vladimir Vernadsky, and gifted adolescents highlighted in this chapter clearly demonstrate the guiding function of the extracognitive in their work. Analyzing the Nobel laureates' views of scientific intuition, Marton et al. (1994) concluded that there appears to be an "experience of the phenomena the scientists are dealing with which is of a quasi-sensory nature and which may encompass all relevant previous experiences of the phenomena. When this experience yields an *intensely felt verdict on the direction to go, the step to take or on the nature of the solution to the problem* the scientist is engaged in what we speak of 'scientific intuition' " (p. 471; italics added).

The *function of evaluation and judgment* means that the phenomenon of the extracognitive plays a key role in the appreciation and, consequently, acceptance or disapproval and, hence, rejection of any new idea, theory, model, or approach. The considered earlier accounts of Vladimir Vernadsky, gifted adolescents, Niels Bohr, Stanley Cohen, Paul Berg, George Stigler, Paul Dirac, Werner Heisenberg, and other Nobel laureates underline this function of specific feelings, developed intellectual beliefs, preferences, and intuitive processes. These are just "*feelings* which enable scientists to follow their intuitions in the absence of rational, logical support" (Marton et al., 1994, p. 467).

Probably, the scientists' very first evaluation of everything new in science is unconscious in its nature. At the same time, as one can see from the Nobel laureates' accounts, it is not, however, entirely unconscious. The phenomenon of the extracognitive—for example, feelings of direction and of beauty, specific preferences, beliefs, and intuition—provide certain criteria for creative work of scientific minds. This is what the *criterion function* is all about. It should be noted that other functions of the extracognitive also execute to some extent the criterion function (e.g., the aesthetic/emotional function).

The *aesthetic/emotional function* highlights the important role of feeling of beauty and specific scientific taste in scientific creativity. First, passionately pursuing their intellectual quest, scientists feel intense *aesthetic pleasure* (Wilson, 1972) in discovering new laws of nature. Second, the phenomenon of the extracognitive helps to generate "*aesthetic criteria of truth*" (Heisenberg, 1971), which aesthetic experience presents to scientists. This is well illustrated by Heisenberg's (1971) quotation mentioned earlier which definitely attests to the importance of the feeling of beauty in his work. In this respect the aesthetic/emotional function of the extracognitive is closely related to its function of evaluation and judgment: the feeling of beauty and specific scientific taste delineate the very initial basis for such evaluation and judgment.

Feeling pride, enjoyment, and delight in discovering new ideas and theories, in funding new problems and fresh perspectives, in penetrating new puzzles of nature, and in solving very old and previously unsolved problems, scientists experience great pleasure and personal happiness, feelings which motivate them go further and further in their intellectual search. This is what the *motivational function* of the extracognitive is all about. As Wilson (1972) pointed out, scientists' "*success stimulates* themselves and their colleagues to still more exacting studies of the phenomena of nature" (p. 16; italics added).

Quality/ethical function of the phenomenon of the extracognitive is closely related to scientists' belief in high and far-reaching standards of scientific activity. Having elevated inner standards of performance, outstanding scientists assure an exceptionally high quality of first-rate research choosing or inventing the methods, approaches, and techniques necessary to do so. Because of that they very often cannot accept a work of poor quality. Due to their own superior standards of work and certain principles, by which the nature of scientific research is determined, Nobel laureates set new or transcend old ethical rules in science. It can concern the behavior of scientists, their important role in the public arena, their social and moral responsibility, and so on (Gruber, 1986, 1989). Very often such scientists act as role models for future generations of scientists.

Advancing function refers to the important role of the phenomenon of the extracognitive in advancing science in general and the intellectually creative activity of individual researchers in particular. It is commonly accepted that in order to advance any field of science, scientists must build on it. Not only must they have a great deal of comprehensive and complex knowledge in the particular discipline but at the same time, they should be able to step outside of it consequently expanding it (Csikszentmihalyi, 1996; Marton et al., 1994). Considering this position of scientists as a paradoxical one, Marton et al. (1994) assert that intuition resolves this paradox providing a sudden shift in the structure of a scientist's awareness. "Scientific intuition is just a special case of intuitive understanding. It is a sudden shift from a simultaneous awareness of all that it takes for that understanding to come about, to a highly singular, focused awareness of that which the understanding is an understanding of" (Marton et al., 1994, p. 469).

Therefore, the phenomenon of the extracognitive plays a critical role in exceptional scientific creativity performing the cognitive, guiding, aesthetic/emotional, motivational, and advancing functions, as well as the function of evaluation and judgment, criterion function, and quality/ethical function.

SUMMARY

The findings presented in this chapter demonstrate that the mental functioning of Nobel laureates and other gifted individuals is determined in part by subjective, internally developed feelings, beliefs, preferences, standards, and orientations, as well as intuitive processes, which constitute the different components of the extracognitive phenomenon. In this light, their negative reaction to any attempts to impose external standards on intellectually creative behavior is not surprising.

The extracognitive phenomenon guides these outstanding scientists and gifted adolescents in their understanding of the nature providing intuitive aesthetic/emotional criteria for the appropriate evaluations and judgments leading to quality work and high ethical standards. This phenomenon also motivates Nobel laureates to go beyond the limits of their intellectual pursuits and advance scientific knowledge about the world.

There are at least a few reasons to assert that the phenomenon of the extracognitive should be considered as the highest level of the manifestation of the intellectual and creative potentials of an individual. First, the fact that so many Nobel laureates—whose extraordinary intelligence and creativity are unquestionable

1. expressed almost all components of the extracognitive,
2. were very attentive to its manifestations in their own work, and
3. stressed its important role in scientific search,

testifies to the exceptionally high status of the extracognitive in the structure of an individual's giftedness (Shavinina & Kholodnaya, 1996). Second, taking into account the direct link between metacognition and the extracognitive phenomenon, it becomes apparent that developed metacognition is strongly associated with highly developed intelligence (Sternberg, 1985, 1988). From this, one can suggest that a person displaying feelings of direction and of beauty, specific scientific taste, preferences, and intuition is also distinguished by exceptional intellectual abilities. Third, the phenomenon of the extracognitive carries out such versatile and multidimensional functions in the functioning of human mind during the process of scientific creativity, which probably no other psychological processes could do. One can, consequently, suggest that if an individual exhibits his or her extracognitive in his or her own activity, then it means that this individual has already reached an integrated, well-balanced, and advanced level in his or her intellectually creative development. Altogether, these reasons allow us to conclude that the phenomenon of the extracognitive is probably the highest level of the manifestation of the intellectual and creative resources of a personality and, therefore, an important criterion of intellectually creative giftedness.

This conclusion has essential educational implications. For example, this criterion should be taken into consideration in the process of the identification of gifted and talented children and adolescents for special educational options. Also, gifted education programs—both enrichment and acceleration classes—must include elements that would direct the development of pupils' extracognitive abilities. At the same time, intelligence and creativity tests should be developed or modified in ways that would allow us to examine an individual's extracognitive abilities.

To conclude, this chapter presented rich findings regarding the phenomenon of the extracognitive that covers a whole field of unexplored or weakly explored scientific phenomena (i.e., specific feelings, beliefs, preferences, and intuition). The above-considered findings indicate that the phenomenon of the extracognitive predicts scientific productivity of the highest level resulting in significant discoveries and, as such, showing an outstanding talent of Nobel caliber.

Research on the extracognitive phenomenon in exceptional individuals is a new enterprise. This chapter does not attempt to account for all possible facets of the extracognitive in gifted, creative, and talented individuals, and it is sometimes both vague and speculative in its formulations. However, it nevertheless provides a useful attempt to understand and conceptualize the valuable psychological phenomena in the successful functioning of highly able minds. Future investigations will help to unravel many more unknown components and manifestations of this phenomenon.

REFERENCES

Bowers, K. S., Regher, G., Balthazard, C., & Parker, K. (1990). Intuition in the context of discovery. *Cognitive Psychology, 22,* 72–110.
Brown, A. L. (1978). Knowing when, where, and how to remember: A problem of metacognition. In R. Glaser (Ed.), *Advances in instructional psychology: Vol. 1* (pp. 77–165). Hillsdale, NJ: Lawrence Erlbaum Associates.
Brown, A. L. (1987). Metacognition, executive control, self-regulation, and other even more mysterious mechanisms. In F. E. Weinert & R. H. Kluwe (Eds.), *Metacognition, motivation, and understanding* (pp. 64–116). Hillsdale, NJ: Lawrence Erlbaum Associates.
Bruner, J. S. (1960). *The process of education.* Boston: Harvard University Press.
Cropper, W. H. (1970). *The quantum physicists.* New York: Oxford University Press.
Csikszentmihalyi, M. (1996). *Creativity.* New York: HarperPerennial.
Dirac, P. A. M. (1963, May). The evolution of the physicist's picture of nature. *Scientific American.*
Dirac, P. A. M. (1977). Recollections of an exciting era. *Varenna Physics School, 57,* 109–146.
Einstein, A. (1949). *Autobiographical notes.* In P. A. Schlipp (Ed.), *Albert Einstein: Philosopher and scientist* (pp. 3–49). New York: The Library of Living Philosophers.
Ericsson, K. A., & Simon, H. A. (1980). Verbal reports as data. *Psychological Review, 87,* 215–251.
Ferrari, M. J., & Sternberg, R. J. (1996). *Self-awareness.* New York: Guilford Press.
Flavell, J. H. (1992). Perspectives on perspective taking. In H. Beilin & P. Pufall (Eds.), *Piaget's theory: Prospects and possibilities* (pp. 107–139). Hillsdale, NJ: Lawrence Erlbaum Associates.
Frey, D. (1978). Science and the single case in counselling research. *The Personnel and Guidance Journal, 56,* 263–268.
Hadamard, J. (1954). *The psychology of invention in the mathematical field.* New York: Dovers Publications.

Heisenberg, W. (1971). *Physics and beyond*. New York: Harper & Row.
Holton, G. (1973). *Thematic origins of scientific thought: Kepler to Einstein*. Cambridge, MA: Harvard University Press.
Gardner, H., & Nemirovsky, R. (1991). From private intuitions to public symbol systems. *Creativity Research Journal*, 4(1), 3–21.
Gross, M. U. M. (1994). The early development of three profoundly gifted children of IQ 200. In A. Tannenbaum (Ed.), *Early signs of giftedness* (pp. 94–138). Norwood, NJ: Ablex.
Gruber, H. E. (1974). *Darwin on man*. Chicago: University of Chicago Press.
Gruber, H. E. (1986). The self-construction of the extraordinary. In R. J. Sternberg & J. E. Davidson (Eds.), *Conceptions of giftedness* (pp. 247–263). Cambridge: Cambridge University Press.
Gruber, H. E. (1989). The evolving systems approach to creative work. In D. B. Wallace & H. E. Gruber (Eds.), *Creative people at work* (pp. 3–23). New York: Oxford University Press.
John-Steiner, V. (1985). *Notebooks of the mind: Explorations of Thinking*. Albuquerque, NM: University of New Mexico.
Kholodnaya, M. A. (1991). Psychological mechanisms of intellectual giftedness. *Voprosu psichologii*, 1, 32–39.
Krebs, H. (1967). The making of a scientist, *Nature*, 215, 1441–1445.
Kuhn, T. (1970). *The structure of scientific revolutions*. Chicago: University of Chicago Press.
Lorenz, K. (1952). *King Solomon's ring*. New York: Crowell.
Marton, F., Fensham, P., & Chaiklin, S. (1994). A Nobel's eye view of scientific intuition: Discussions with the Nobel prize-winners in physics, chemistry and medicine (1970–86). *International Journal of Science Education*, 16(4), 457–473.
McMorris, M. N. (1970). Aesthetic elements in scientific theories. *Main Currents*, 26, 82–91.
Miller, A. I. (1981). *Albert Einstein's special theory of relativity: Emergence (1905) and early interpretation (1905–1911)*. Reading, MA: Addison-Wesley.
Miller, A. I. (1992). Scientific creativity: A comparative study of Henri Poincaré and Albert Einstein. *Creativity Research Journal*, 5, 385–418.
Miller, A. I. (1996). *Insights of genius: Visual imagery and creativity in science and art*. New York: Springer Verlag.
Ochse, R. (1990). *Before the gates of excellence: The determinants of creative genius*. Cambridge: Cambridge University Press.
Planck, M. (1950). *Scientific autobiography and other papers*. London: Williams & Norgate.
Poincaré, H. (1913). *Mathematics and science*. New York: Dover, 1963. (Originally published by Flammarion in 1913)
Policastro, E. (1995). Creative Intuition: An Integrative Review. *Creativity Research Journal*, 8(2), 99–113.
Rothenberg, A. (1996). The Janusian process in scientific creativity. *Creativity Research Journal*, 9(2&3), 207–231.
Rosenblueth, A., & Wiener, N. (1945). Roles of models in science. *Philosophy of Science*, XX, 317.
Shavinina, L. V., & Kholodnaya, M. A. (1996). The cognitive experience as a psychological basis of intellectual giftedness. *Journal for the Education of the Gifted*, 20(1), 3–35.
Simonton, D. K. (1980). Intuition and analysis: A predictive and explanatory model. *Genetic Psychology Monographs*, 102, 3–60.
Sternberg, R. J. (1985). *Beyond IQ: A triarchic theory of human intelligence*. New York: Cambridge University Press.
Sternberg, R. J. (1988). *The triarchic mind: A new theory of human intelligence*. New York: Viking.
Sternberg, R. J., Forsythe, G. B., Hedlund, J., Horvath, J. A., Wagner, R. K., Williams, W. M., Snook, S. A., & Grigorenko, E. L. (2000). *Practical intelligence in everyday life*. New York: Cambridge University Press.
Vernadsky, V. I. (1988). *Diaries and letters*. Moscow: Molodaja Gwardia.

Wallace, D. B., & Gruber, H. E. (1989). *Creative people at work*. New York: Oxford University Press.
Wechsler, J. (1978). *On aesthetics in science*. Cambridge, MA: MIT Press.
Wertheimer, M. (1959). *Productive thinking*. Westport, CT: Greenwood Press.
Wilson, M. (1972). *Passion to know*. Garden City, NY: Doubleday.
Woodward, C. E. (1989). Art and elegance in the synthesis of organic compounds: Robert Burns Woodward. In D. B. Wallace & H. E. Gruber (Eds.), *Creative people at work* (pp. 227–253). New York: Oxford University Press.
Zuckerman, H. (1977). *Scientific elite*. New York: Free Press.
Zuckerman, H. (1983). The scientific elite: Nobel Laureates' mutual influences. In R. S. Albert (Ed.), *Genius and eminence*. Oxford: Pergamon Press.

DEVELOPING EXTRACOGNITIVE ASPECTS OF EXCEPTIONAL ABILITIES

Chapter 6

Some Insights of Geniuses Into the Causes of Exceptional Achievements

Michael J. A. Howe
University of Exeter

The adjectives that first come to mind when we think about geniuses as a category of people are largely cognitive ones—clever, insightful, knowledgeable, sharp, creative, and intelligent. For me, it came as a surprise to discover, on starting to make efforts to explain how and why some individuals have become capable of the achievements that justify calling someone a genius, that many of the most powerful mental influences are ones that are largely extracognitive rather than specifically intellectual.

On reflection, that is not totally surprising. When geniuses themselves are asked to account for their exceptional abilities, most of the words they use to describe the qualities they regard as having been crucial are extracognitive ones. Geniuses perceive themselves as being curious, often intensely or passionately so, and they also tend to describe themselves as being determined or dogged, and capable of maintaining their interest in a particular issue. Geniuses sometimes admit to being unusually optimistic. Samuel Smiles, who is best known as the author of *Self-Help* (which first appeared in 1859) but who was also the biographer of a number of prominent inventors including the great railway engineer George Stephenson (Smiles, 1884), wrote of "perseverance" as being especially crucial among the determinants of success: it is hard to think of any genius who would seriously question that judgement.

So geniuses provide us with reasons for switching attention away from cognitive factors and toward extracognitive ones when looking for the key influences on human abilities. Another reason is that qualities belonging in the extracognitive rather than the cognitive category are the ones that come to mind when we try to list attributes that most geniuses have in common. Geniuses are, to say the least, an extremely diverse group. Some think predominantly in words, others contemplate images; some geniuses are highly intuitive, others are sharply analytical in their reasoning. But where character and temperament are concerned, shared attributes are more prominent. As I have already suggested, terms such as *curious, determined,* and *diligent* apply to almost all the highly creative achievers whose early lives I have explored (Howe, 1982; 1989; 1999). In this chapter I examine some of the ways in which the extracognitive attributes of geniuses have contributed to their extraordinary capabilities.

Initially, it is important to clarify what is meant by the term *genius*. To the surprise of some investigators, arriving at a clear and simple definition has proved impossible. There is a simple explanation for that. Although it is true that when people introduce the term *genius* as a label for a particular individual, they seem to be describing that individual, when what they are actually doing is very different. Essentially, they are acknowledging that person's achievements, and not describing the person at all.

When we call someone a genius it is usually because that person has created something, or made some kind of discovery, that we greatly admire or appreciate. Mozart is deemed to be a genius because of the music he composed, Shakespeare is regarded as a genius because of his plays, and Galileo is seen in that light because of his scientific contributions. Hence, what we are actually doing when we call someone a genius is not describing them but placing a kind of accolade on them. The process has more in common with that of awarding a prize to a person than that of providing a description of someone. To say that someone is a genius is to acknowledge them as a creator of major accomplishments.

One consequence of this is that there is a great deal of disagreement about who is entitled to be called a genius and who is not. Subjectivity is inevitable, because there are no firm defining characteristics against which individuals can be assessed. For better or worse, there is nothing equivalent to a Nobel Prize Committee for deciding who should receive the genius accolade. My genius is your nongenius, and *vice-versa*, and there is no way to say which of us is right.

Because it is an accolade rather than a description, and because it resists being satisfactorily defined, the term *genius* is not an especially helpful one for promoting scientific understanding. However, the word is a common one and a necessary one in everyday life, and ignoring it is not a realistic option. In my work I have opted to introduce the term somewhat unrestrictedly and inclusively: I use the word *genius* to refer to any person who is widely regarded to have produced major creative achievements.

In other words, a genius, for the purposes of pursuing the questions I am addressing here, is any person who substantial numbers of men and women have regarded as being a genius. Loose and uncritical as that choice of criterion may appear, it has the big advantage of coinciding with the usual everyday procedures that result in the genius appendage being applied to one or another individual. It could of course be argued that because my real interest is in "individuals who have produced major creative achievements," it might be wiser to replace the word *genius* with that alternative phrase. But doing that would not make a substantial improvement, because the same subjectivity and imprecision that permeates *genius* still remains when that term is replaced by a phrase including the words *major* and *creative*.

Further difficulties are encountered as soon as one tries to distinguish between cognitive and extracognitive. By no means can all human qualities invariably be assigned to either an exclusively cognitive category or an exclusively extracognitive one. For convenience I consider a trait or attribute to be extracognitive when it is one in which qualities relating to temperament, character, or personality have prominent roles. Hence, perseverance and diligence are seen as instances of extracognitive traits, but intelligence and insight are not. Curiosity seems to lie squarely on the borderline.

ELEMENTS OF AN APPROACH

In this chapter I list some of those extracognitive factors and attributes that are commonly encountered in geniuses, and explore the ways in which these qualities can contribute to high abilities and impressive attainments. But prior to doing that, it may be helpful to sketch out the main characteristics of the broad approach I have followed in my own efforts to understand geniuses and learn from their experiences and insights.

My starting point was a feeling of dissatisfaction with the widespread view of genius as some kind of miracle or mystery explicable only, if at all, by making the assumption that certain people are born possessing special innate powers or "gifts." That view is implied by Kant's assertion that geniuses have an incommunicable gift that nature mysteriously imparts to certain artists. It is echoed in the insistence of certain present-day writers on genius, who insist that genius simply resists understanding. According to that view, when we say that someone was only able to produce a creative masterpiece because he or she was a genius, we are essentially admitting that we do not know how it was done (Murray, 1989).

I was aware, of course, that it was conceivable that genius really is a complete mystery. However, it struck me that it is definitely worth making an effort to demystify genius. An approach that seemed promising involved trying to trace the early lives and progress of a sample of geniuses, and attempting to lay bare the routes that took them from being young children with no exceptional powers toward becoming adults possessing the special capabilities that make creative achievements possible (Howe, 1982; 1997). Of course, doing that is not always possible. It would be fascinating to be able to trace the early progress of William Shakespeare, but the dearth of factual information about his early life makes that quite impossible in practice. When it is possible to trace somebody's early progress, my experience is that much of what initially appears to be mysterious or miraculous about geniuses becomes appreciably less mysterious.

For example, brief accounts of Charles Darwin's life and achievements give the impression that although Darwin as a child was not at all exceptional, in his late twenties he mysteriously and rather dramatically transformed himself, becoming a great scientist. In fact, however, when the actual course of his early life is examined as closely as the available evidence permits, it becomes clear that his daily pursuits and interests gave him a superb preparation for his career as a scientist. It is true that he did not excel in any of the areas of accomplishment valued by the teachers at his school, and in Darwin's own autobiographical account, written in old age, he implies that as a young man he was somewhat aimless (Darwin, 1958). All the same, it is evident from his correspondence (Burkhardt & Smith, 1985) that the activities Darwin engaged in as he pursued his compelling interest in natural history equipped him with knowledge and skills that were certainly impressive, albeit unnoticed by adults (Browne, 1995; Howe, 1999). Some of the letters suggest that even at the age of seventeen he was already a fiercely determined and diligent young natural historian, and not at all aimless when he was pursuing his scientific interests (Howe, 1999, p. 28).

Similarly, a summary of the career of the great scientist Michael Faraday may lead readers to infer that as a young man he was totally unprepared for his adult career, having left school at age thirteen to spend his adolescent years in a position as an apprentice bookbinder that provided none of the education and training required of a scientist. In fact, however, the circumstances of his apprenticeship were stimulating and highly supportive for a young person who was keen to learn (Jones, 1870; Williams, 1965; Cantor, 1991). In particular, the ready availability of books (then an expensive luxury) in his working environment gave the young Faraday some real advantages. Of course, Faraday suffered from not attending school, but not in relation to his education as a scientist. Schools at that time (the first decade of the 19th century) taught no science at all. Even 20 years later, when the young Charles Darwin was attending one of the best schools in Britain, there was no science on the curriculum. Darwin's own interest in chemistry was derided by the headmaster, who told Darwin that engaging in scientific experiments was a complete waste of his time (Browne, 1994; Desmond & Moore, 1991; Howe, 1999).

My own efforts to trace the early lives of a number of geniuses (Howe, 1999) have led me to conclude that when we follow the route that a genius's

6. INSIGHTS ON GENIUSES

early life actually takes, although we certainly encounter much that is remarkable or admirable, and often extraordinary, we do not find that the person's progress has been totally inexplicable. On the contrary, there are strong grounds for believing that the events and experiences that were responsible for one child's development into an adult genius are not fundamentally distinct from those that have led to other children becoming unexceptional adults. Geniuses go further, of course, and sometimes their progress is faster, but there are no sudden or inexplicable leaps ahead. There are no points at which the individual has moved forward in ways that would be totally impossible for any other man or woman. Similarly, there are no reasons for supposing that their progress cannot be accounted for except by identifying causes or mechanisms that are entirely different from the causes of progress in other people.

One consequence of having a degree of success at demystifying genius is that one becomes increasingly aware that geniuses and ordinary people have much in common with one another. By tracing the early lives of individual geniuses it becomes possible to establish, somewhat convincingly, that these people are by no means the godlike figures, forming a kind of separate breed, that the view of geniuses as a mystery encourages us to believe in. By and large, geniuses live their lives, and create their triumphs and their failures, by the same rules that govern everyone else. Of course, geniuses, with their dazzling achievements and often amazing feats, are undoubtedly superior to other people in what they can achieve. Even so, the underlying capabilities that make their achievements possible are not necessarily completely distinct from, or qualitatively different to, the lesser and more mundane capabilities of other men and women. And there is clearly no sharp dividing line between geniuses and non-geniuses.

When we direct our attention to the ways in which geniuses are not totally unlike other people—rather than simply allow ourselves to be dazzled by their achievements—we also become aware that there is much that ordinary people can learn from geniuses. For a start, we can learn from knowing about the events and experiences that encouraged geniuses to make progress, because this information can provide information about the kinds of experiences that may also give ordinary people opportunities to extend their abilities. Once we discard the idea of geniuses as a breed apart, we can see that knowledge about formative events in the early lives of geniuses has considerable relevance to the rest of us.

Also, seeing geniuses as members of the human species whose early progress depends on essentially the same kinds of influences that affect development in other men and women, makes us aware that geniuses' own writings and statements about influences that help determine a person's abilities are highly relevant to other people. As we shall see, the sayings and writings of geniuses form a rich source of insights into the causes of high attainments and capabilities. Once we free ourselves from the delusion that what applies to geniuses does not apply to other people (a view that can no longer be maintained once the assumption that genius is a mystery has been abandoned), it becomes possible to open our minds to, and learn from, all the insights into human learning and the causes of expertise that geniuses have made available.

What *can* we learn from geniuses concerning the extracognitive factors that contribute to high abilities? In the remainder of this chapter I attempt to answer that question by examining three of the extracognitive qualities that many geniuses share, namely diligence, the capacity to respond positively to difficulties, and social capabilities. I also look at some of the remarks that geniuses themselves made about those qualities and the various roles they play.

THE NECESSITY FOR DILIGENCE

The first extracognitive attribute that geniuses share is the broad propensity to be diligent and to persevere at arduous and time-consuming tasks. It is hard to think of any geniuses who have not relished hard work, or who have not been dogged in pursuit of their aims.

Diligence makes many things possible. The necessity for it is colourfully emphasized in a remark of J. M. W. Turner, the early 19th-century English painter, to the effect that, "the only secret I have got is dammed hard work." (Cited in Hamilton, 1997, p. 128.) Diligence enables individuals to keep working on problems over a lengthy period of time. A number of geniuses have reflected on their capacity to do that. Charles Darwin, who insisted that he lacked the quickness of understanding that clever people possess and claimed that he had only a limited ability to follow abstract trains of thought (Darwin, 1958, p. 140), remarked that his own capacity to keep on reflecting for years on an unexplained problem was a key ingredient of his own success. Many geniuses, ranging from Newton and Mozart to Darwin and Einstein had the capacity to remain absorbed in their work for long periods of time.

Diligence is especially crucial when a person is engaged in the study and training upon which expertise at difficult skills almost always depends. To gain high levels of expertise it often takes many years of hard work. As Sir Joshua Reynolds, the 18th-century British artist, observed about skill at drawing, it, "like that of playing upon a musical instrument, cannot be acquired but by an infinite number of acts" (cited in Hamilton, 1997, p. 23). In music, for instance, it takes around 3000 hours of practice and training to achieve the standard of a good amateur performer (Sloboda, Davidson, Howe & Moore, 1996). To achieve the standard necessary in a professional musician requires regular practising over a period of years, totaling in the region of 10,000 hours (Ericsson, Krampe, & Tesch-Römer, 1993). That is a very considerable period of time, the equivalent of around 3 hours per day for 10 years. Comparable periods of time need to be devoted to study and training in order to reach very high levels of competence in other fields of skill, ranging from chess and mathematics to athletics and various sports.

Of course, there are variations in the precise amounts of time different individuals spend practising. However, contrary to what is widely believed, there are no short cuts that a few especially gifted people make in the amount of time that must be devoted to training. In one investigation (Sloboda et al., 1996) it was found that in order to make a given degree of progress there was no difference between unusually competent and considerably less able young musicians in the amount of time they needed to devote to practice. The more competent players did move ahead faster, but it appears that one of the main reasons why they did so was that they spent more time practising.

Even geniuses have to devote very substantial amounts of time to training and practicing activities. One investigator measured the period of years, so far as could be calculated from the available biographical evidence, that each of 70-odd major composers devoted to training and preparation prior to the time at which their first major and original composition was composed (Hayes, 1981). It might have been expected that the majority of composers would need to spend a substantial period of time training, but a few geniuses would reach a very high level of creative achievement in considerably less time than the others. Reports of individuals composing during childhood, as Mozart did, appear to confirm this. However, the findings firmly contradicted the view that a few geniuses can thrive in the absence of the lengthy training that other people require. It was discovered that with very few exceptions (none of whom are among the greatest composers), no composers produce major works of music until they have devoted at least 10 years to rigorous and intense training. Even Mozart had to spend that amount of time in careful preparation. He did indeed compose as a young child, but the more impressive of his childhood compositions were often closely modelled on those of this teachers and mentors, who included J. S. Bach's son, Johann Christian Bach.

For certain geniuses, gaining access to the preparation and training that was necessary for them to become exceptionally skilled or accomplished required immense and sustained determination in addition to all the hard work that went into the training activities. Consider, for instance, the early life of Michael Faraday (1791–1867), the great early nineteenth-century scientist whose discoveries paved the way for the practical applications of electricity. Faraday left school at age 13 and became apprenticed to a London bookbinder (Williams, 1965). His family was very poor, and there was nothing in his background that encouraged him to even consider the possibility of becoming a scientist. But he was an alert and curious youngster and with the encouragement of a sympathetic employer he began to delve into some of the books that he encountered in the course of his work. By late adolescence he seems to have become a voracious reader, and increasingly attracted to science.

There is the world of difference, however, between an enthusiastic young person who despite a lack of formal education happens to be interested in science, and somebody who makes a prolonged and disciplined study of science. That demands intense efforts and a systematic approach. Lacking teachers and a formal course structure, it would have been extremely difficult for a young man to gain the necessary training. Faraday succeeded, all the same, supported only by his own intense interest and his desire to learn. He did so because he was immensely determined, extremely diligent, and highly organized. On his own initiative, he managed to gain access to a range of appropriate learning experiences and opportunities, reading avidly, conscientiously attending lectures, from which he made notes, improved them, extended them, and revised them.

Faraday was aided by encountering an excellent eighteenth-century "self-help" book that had been written by Isaac Watts (who is better known as a writer of a number of hymns that are still widely sung), entitled *On the Improvement of the Mind* (Watts, 1801). That book is an excellent guide to studying, and Faraday followed its good advice with extreme—almost obsessive—diligence. For instance, Watts' book recommends a number of actions that will help a learner gain the maximum benefit from attending lectures. First, Watts says, the learner should listen carefully and write down on a sheet of paper the most prominent words, and also important short sentences, titles of experiments, names of substances being described, and so on. Afterwards, on arriving home after the lecture, the student should begin on a second set of notes. These should be based on the earlier ones, but should be more detailed, and also more legible and more coherent. Then, having (presumably) already devoted a fair amount of time to this task, the student should proceed to yet another stage, at which an attempt is made to re-create and write down the whole lecture, with the notes already available serving as a guide.

This advice is certainly well-founded, and it can be confidently predicted that anyone who conscientiously follows it will be likely to gain a good mastery of the material in the lecture. The only problem is that the challenge of engaging in all of the activities Watts recommended is likely to be extremely time-consuming and onerous. Few mere mortals would ever succeed in doing all the things Watts advised. But Faraday did. He did not merely read Watts' suggestions, as many other young people did; he also carefully and conscientiously followed them.

One suspects that remarkably few of Watts' other readers ever did. Had they done so, in as determined and sustained a manner as Faraday did, they might well have made comparable progress to his. Although Faraday's early accomplishments of learning were remarkable, there is no suggestion in the biographical accounts of his progress (Jones, 1870; Williams, 1965) of him possessing an unusual ability to learn. So far as one can tell, the young Michael Faraday learned more than others not because he was an inherently better learner, but largely because of his quite remarkable diligence and determination.

Michael Faraday was not the only genius to benefit from being diligent and determined to an extent that is rarely encountered. Another was George Stephenson (1781–1848), the great English engineer and inventor, whose advances made it possible for passengers to travel on railways by the power of steam. Whereas Faraday left school at an early age, Stephenson never went to school at all, and he was not even given any opportunity to learn to read until he was over 18 years old. But despite his total lack of formal education, Stephenson made himself into a superb engineer.

Stephenson, a truly heroic figure, achieved that through immense and sustained determination, in the face of numerous setbacks, and with remarkably little encouragement. He was—as his biographer Samuel Smiles recognised in an account of Stephenson's life that appeared in 1857 soon after Stephenson's death—the epitome of perseverance. It is this that marks him apart from others. When his early progress is traced, with the aid of the information of his early life that is provided in Smiles' biography (Smiles, 1881), no compelling evidence is encountered to suggest that Stephenson acquired knowledge or gained new skills faster or more easily than another person would have done. However, there is plenty of evidence that he worked at educating himself with exceptional intensity and perseverance. As in the case of Faraday, it seems to have been these qualities, rather than any inherently special cognitive powers, that largely accounted for his remarkable accomplishments.

The belief that although most people have to devote large amounts of time and effort to practice and training, there are a few special individuals who do not need to, is one that dies very hard. Perhaps there are some areas of skill in which inspiration is more crucial than effort. But if they do exist, they are certainly hard to locate. In the visual arts, Reynolds' previously mentioned insistence on the necessity for lengthy repetitive training appears to be almost universally valid. Even great artists like Picasso have had to spend long periods of time working at improving their skills. When those young men and women who eventually become major artists are learning their craft they have to go through the same stages of mastery and overcome just the same problems that less exceptional artists have to master in order to achieve a high degree of expertise (Weisberg, 1999).

Great writers, too, have needed to invest considerable time and effort to the task of gaining the skills which a writer draws on. Even those authors who achieved enormous success at an early age have taken their training very seriously. Charles Dickens, for instance, who was already famous before he was 25, began his writing career by working at a series of reporting jobs and positions in journalism: in his spare time he studied assiduously in the reading room of the British Museum. Dickens recalled many years later that his hours of study there had been among the most valuable of his life (Hibbert, 1983, p. 127).

All three of the Brontë sisters were constantly engaged in writing projects throughout their childhoods. Their early stories were highly dramatic episodic accounts, written in numerous installments, concerning people and events in imaginary nations (Barker, 1994). For the contents of their stories, the sisters drew on whatever they happened to be reading at the time: they each wrote their episodes purely for enjoyment, to be read only by one another. At first, as is evident from the numerous surviving examples of their juvenilia, the writing was thoroughly childish, poorly spelled and grammatically incorrect. But very gradually, over the years the Brontës' fiction became increasingly accomplished and mature.

PERSEVERING IN THE FACE OF DIFFICULTIES

Another trait that appears to be more common in genius than in other people, and one that is distinct from diligence but not unrelated to it, can best be described as a capacity to keep persisting in the face of obstacles that threaten to bar a person's progress. One kind of persistence against what appear to be insuperable difficulties is epitomised in accounts of the efforts of Marie and Pierre Curie, whose struggles involved enduring fatiguing physical labor as well as overcoming various other daunting barriers to progress (Howe, 1999). The intensity of a genius' concentration may go beyond anything that is dictated by mere diligence. One of Newton's contemporaries described him as having worked so hard that he would have killed himself were it not for the fact that the practical necessities of conducting experiments gave him some respite from the stress induced by continuous thinking (Westfall, 1980).

We tend to assume that even if geniuses do have to engage in lengthy training in order to master the skills they require, they nevertheless find difficult concepts easier to understand than other people do. So it comes as something of a surprise to discover that a number of geniuses have reported that the sheer intellectual difficulty of what they were trying to achieve was a source of enormous strain. The reports and comments of a number of geniuses suggest that a key difference between them and other people lies not in their finding ideas easier to understand but in their being more determined not to give up and abandon what they are doing when the comprehension fails them.

A number of geniuses have written of becoming exhausted as a result of the sheer strain of having to persist at activities they found especially difficult. Bertrand Russell was made ill by the sheer unrelenting difficulty of the work that he had to do in order to write his *Principia Mathematica* (Russell, 1998). Newton, Darwin, and Einstein all complained about the exhausting mental struggles that their work demanded. In Michael Faraday's case, he literally found himself driven to a halt by the continuous concentration that was necessary. He repeatedly exhausted himself, and on a number of occasions he was forced to stop work for months at a time (Williams, 1965, p. 102).

The determination of a genius to persist even when a task appears to be so impossibly difficult that most people would give up and admit defeat is illustrated by Isaac Newton's response to the experience of finding it impossible to comprehend a difficult book he was trying to master. As a young man, Newton struggled to understand the mathematics in a book that had recently been published, Descartes' *Geometry*. He kept reaching a point at which he could understand no further. But every time he experienced this, he went back a few pages and tried again. He simply refused to be defeated, returning to the struggle again and again and again.

The young Newton, totally determined to master the book despite his apparent inability to comprehend it, "read it by himself when he was got over 2 or 3 pages he could understand no farther than he began again & got 3 or 4 pages farther till he came to another difficult place, than he began again and advanced farther and continued doing so till he had made himself Master of the whole." (Conduit, cited in Westfall, 1980, p. 111.) That degree of determination is rare, of course, but it is easy to see that a person who, like Newton, possesses the doggedness and the self-confidence to persist in refusing to admit defeat, may eventually gain some valuable advantages.

SOCIAL CAPABILITIES

Geniuses need to be focused on particular challenges: the days in which an individual such as Leonardo da Vinci could make major creative achievements in a number of different fields have long passed. But being focused does not mean being narrow, and the majority of geniuses have been people with a range of interests and a number of skills. Everyone knows that

Einstein was a very good amateur violinist: a less widely known fact is that George Eliot was an accomplished pianist.

The possession of just one particular skill or attainment, however impressive or however extraordinary it is, is rarely a sufficient basis for a productive and fulfilling adult life. For many individuals who have produced substantial creative achievements, having possessed a range of skills and interests was not just helpful but essential. In particular, many geniuses had to depend to a marked extent upon social skills and capabilities as well as on intellectual ones. Geniuses are often seen as essentially solitary individuals, but that depiction is not generally correct.

Take the case of Charles Darwin, for instance. Darwin has the reputation of having been something of a recluse. It is true that in the second half of his life he spent most of his time at home, although that was partly because frequent bouts of illness made travel difficult for him. In reality, however, Darwin had impressive social skills, a pronounced gift for making friends, and he was something of a diplomat (Howe, 1999). His social capabilities were immensely important, and without them he would never have achieved what he did.

Because of his powers of diplomacy, Darwin was good at dealing with people, and at certain stages of his life it was essential for him to be able to get along with individuals who were known to be prickly or difficult, beginning with his own father, a loving parent but not an easy one. Darwin was good at forming friendships that endured, and throughout his career he gained benefits from working with other scientists, collaborating with them and regularly sharing information. Darwin was also known to be reliable and he was trusted, and because he combined his positive human attributes with a capacity for friendship other scientists gravitated toward him and stayed loyal to him. It was partly because of his human qualities that he was the (very) young scientist invited to accompany the voyage of *HMS Beagle*. And it was largely because of Darwin's capacity to get on with others that he was able to maintain harmonious relations throughout that voyage with the *Beagle's* notoriously short-tempered captain, Robert Fitzroy. When the *Theory of Evolution* was finally released, it was partly because Darwin was well-regarded as a person as well as a scientist that the personal attacks on him that followed publication of this revolutionary and disturbing new explanation of fundamental matters were, by and large, relatively muted and short-lived.

Of course, it is not hard to think of geniuses who have been solitary, eccentric, or irascible. There have been a few geniuses, such as the late Paul Erdös, the mathematician, who have had few interests outside their area of specialization. The majority of geniuses, however, have not only possessed but also depended on a wide range of capabilities.

CONCLUSION

The lives and experiences of geniuses provide numerous demonstrations of the necessity for human qualities that go beyond the narrowly cognitive. To a considerable extent, in order for a person to acquire and make productive use of impressive skills and capabilities, extracognitive qualities are mandatory.

The experiences and the insights of geniuses suggests that little of enormous significance is achieved in the absence of diligence and the capacity for sustained hard work. Also, at the highest levels of ability, a person who lacks the capacity to keep trying and refuses to give up when difficulties mount will be at a real disadvantage. And someone who does not possess the capacity to get along with other people will encounter serious obstacles at many points in life.

REFERENCES

Barker, J. (1994). *The Brontës*. London: Weidenfeld & Nicolson.
Browne, J. (1995). *Charles Darwin: Voyaging*. London: Jonathon Cape.
Burkhardt, F., & Smith, S. (1985). *The correspondence of Charles Darwin, Volume 1, 1821–1835*. Cambridge, UK: Cambridge University Press.
Cantor, G. (1991). *Michael Faraday: Sandemanian and scientist*. Basingstoke, UK: Macmillan.
Darwin, C. (1958). *The autobiography of Charles Darwin, 1809–1882, with original omissions restored*. (Edited with appendix and notes by Norma Barlow.) London: Collins.
Desmond, A., & Moore, J. (1991). *Darwin*. London: Michael Joseph.
Ericsson, K. A., Krampe, R. Th., & Tesch-Römer, C. (1993). The role of deliberate practice in the acquisition of expert performance. *Psychological Review, 100*, 363–406.
Hamilton, J. (1997). *Turner: A life*. London: Hodder & Stoughton.
Hibbert, C. (1983). *The making of Charles Dickens*. Harmondsworth, UK: Penguin Books.
Hayes, J. R. (1981). *The complete problem solver*. Philadelphia, PA: The Franklin Institute Press.
Howe, M. J. A. (1982). Biographical information and the development of outstanding individuals. *American Psychologist, 37*, 1071–1081.
Howe, M. J. A. (1997). Beyond psychobiography: Towards more effective syntheses of psychology and biography. *British Journal of Psychology, 88*, 235–248.
Howe, M. J. A. (1999). *Genius in the making*. Cambridge, UK: Cambridge University Press.
Jones, B. (1870). *The life and letters of Faraday, Volume 1*. London: Longman, Green.
Russell, B. (1998). *The Autobiography of Bertrand Russell*. London: Routledge.
Sloboda, J. A., Davidson, J. W., Howe, M. J. A., & Moore, D. G. (1996). The role of practice in the development of performing musicians. *British Journal of Psychology, 87*, 399–412.
Smiles, S. (1881). *The life of George Stephenson* (Centenary Edition). London: John Murray. (Originally published in 1857)
Watts, I. (1801). *The improvement of the mind: Or a supplement to the art of logic*. London: J. Abraham.
Weisberg, R. (1999). Creativity and knowledge: A challenge to theories. In R. J. Sternberg (Ed.), *Handbook of creativity* (pp. 226–250). New York: Cambridge University Press.
Williams, L. P. (1965). *Michael Faraday*. London: Chapman & Hall.

Chapter 7

The Development of Talent in Different Domains*

Deborah A. Greenspan
Becca Solomon
Howard Gardner
Harvard University

INFLUENCES ON THE DEVELOPMENT OF YOUNG TALENT

An Olympic gymnast lands a perfect ten on the vault to win gold, a baseball star makes a diving catch to seal a victory, and a violinist, with the final thrust of her bow, brings the audience to its feet. Although we often see or hear such results, we rarely acknowledge the effort preceding the success, including the intense training regimens, year-long competitions, and driven personality required to compete at high levels. Consider now that these athletes and artists have not even reached their fifteenth birthday. Somehow, in a time when a child's attention span is measured by the speed of the television remote control or hours at the local shopping mall, these children have managed to attain tremendous focus and determination. What enables these children to dedicate themselves completely to their activities? How are they able to sustain their intense commitment over an extended period of time?

Some researchers argue that expertise can be attained by a majority of individuals through sustained and "deliberate" practice (Ericsson et al., 1993; Ericsson and Smith, 1991; Simon & Chase, 1973). Ericsson espouses a

---

*This research was made possible by the generous support of the Louise and Claude Rosenberg Jr. Family Foundation. We thank the researchers involved in the Origins of Good Work Study, including Wendy Fischman, Mimi Michaelson, and Kimberly Powell.

"monotonic benefits assumption," in which he claims that an individual's level of expertise is monotonically related to the amount of time she devotes to effortful practice. He further argues that an individual can achieve expertise in a domain through approximately 10 years of practice. Through these assertions, Ericsson implies that expertise is global because an individual is capable of attaining expertise through sufficient and appropriate practice, regardless of the domain.

Many researchers argue, however, that expertise is domain specific (Gardner, 1997; Solomon et al., 1999; Winner, 1996). Individuals possess several distinct and independent intelligences that predispose children to attaining expertise in a particular domain (Gardner, 1983). Indeed, evidence indicates that talented[1] children's proclivities are exhibited at very young ages and in highly specialized realms (Feldman, 1986).

In addition to one's innate capabilities, other factors must be present for talent to come to fruition. An individual's motivation and desire to commit the necessary time and effort to an activity as well as the support received from family, friends, and instructors are essential components in the development of expertise (Bloom, 1985; Csikzentmihalyi, Rathunde, & Whalen, 1993; Gardner, 1997; Winner, 1996).

Motivation encompasses both the individual's personality and the rewards gained through participation in an activity. Researchers have discovered that talented children typically feel passionate about their activities. They do not need constant coaxing to practice, but rather have an obsession or a rage to achieve in their domains (Winner, 1996). Talented children actively direct their own learning experiences by setting personal goals and observing their own development (Zimmerman, Bandura, & Martinez-Pons, 1992). In addition, talented children typically are fiercely persistent, possess a tremendous amount of energy and focus, and welcome activity-related challenges rather than avoid them (Csikzentmihalyi, Rathunde, & Whalen, 1993; Winner, 1996).

Motivation is also engendered by the belief that an individual is receiving something in return for his or her tireless devotion to their activities. Perceived intrinsic or extrinsic rewards are important elements in children's willingness to persist in their work (Csikzentmihalyi, Rathunde, & Whalen, 1993). Intrinsic rewards include the enjoyment and inherent satisfaction that one feels through their efforts and accomplishments. Extrinsic rewards refer to the awards, recognition, and praise garnered through one's participation. Unless children are motivated to participate in an activity through internal or external rewards, it is unlikely that they would dedicate the time and effort necessary to develop expertise.

---

[1] *Talented* and *gifted* are considered synonymous for the purposes of this chapter.

7. DEVELOPMENT OF TALENT

A child's dedication to his or her activity is typically accompanied by great sacrifices for both the child and his or her entire family. Children, then, must be surrounded by individuals who support and nurture their talent. Families, peers, and instructors have all been widely noted in the literature for the important role they play in the development of expertise (Bloom, 1985; Csikzentmihalyi, Rathunde, & Whalen, 1993; Feldman, 1986; Winner, 1996).

Bloom (1985) identified important influences on the development of talented youth using retrospective accounts of accomplished adults. He discovered that the role of families is paramount in nurturing children's talents. The individuals participating in his study defined their families as heavily child-centered in which parents went to great lengths to support their talent development. Parents would work two jobs to pay for private skating lessons, for example, or move large distances in order to be closer to eminent training facilities. Indeed, as Csikzentmihalyi and colleagues note, "When the child's abilities are truly prodigious, parental and social investments need to be prodigious as well" (1993, p. 26).

In addition to their financial and emotional support, parents also tend to set high standards for their talented children (Winner, 1996). Parents help children evaluate the success of their performances and challenge their children to strive for increasingly higher levels of achievement (Bloom, 1985). Zimmerman and Ringle, for example, discovered that the goals parents set for their talented children affected children's personal ambitions and levels of achievement (1981). Thus, challenging and supportive families seem to provide the best environments for cultivating talent (Csikzentmihalyi, Rathunde, & Whalen, 1993).

Parents also influence their children's talent development through the behaviors they model (Bloom, 1985; Winner, 1996). Children closely observe parents and glean parental values from the ways in which parents conduct themselves. Parents can teach children perseverance and industriousness, for example, by working hard themselves. Indeed, researchers found that the duration of an adult model's persistence on a task significantly influenced the length of time children were willing to work on a similar problem (Zimmerman & Ringle, 1981).

Children's peers are also a supportive factor in the development of talent (Bloom, 1985). Talented children often feel isolated from mainstream peers and tend to spend more time alone and with parents than nontalented children (Csikzentmihalyi, Rathunde, & Whalen, 1993; Winner, 1996). The peers that talented children do seek out, moreover, vary according to their social and developmental goals. A child whose central ambition is to pursue her talent development most often seeks peers of similar ability. These children thrive when surrounded by peers that support, challenge, and legitimize their talents and drive toward mastery. On the other hand, talented children whose primary goal is to be sociable or to assimilate into the mainstream population tend to interact more frequently with nontalented children, a proclivity that often results in a diminished desire to achieve (Feldman, 1986).

Instructors also play an important role in the development of talent (Bloom, 1985; Csikzentmihalyi, Rathunde, & Whalen, 1993). Research conducted in the academic context claims that instructional environments can affect the ways in which children are motivated to participate and excel in their activities. Teaching styles characterized by controlled decision-making, explicit rules for achieving excellence, and public performance evaluations foster extrinsic motivation in children. On the other hand, teaching styles that emphasize student involvement in decision-making processes and evaluations of success encourage intrinsic motivation and autonomy (see Eccles, Wigfield, & Schiefele, 1998). Thus, children may be suited for activities in which the instructional styles correspond with their motivational orientations.

In summary, children's talent development is contingent upon a number of factors. In addition to their innate capabilities, children must possess the enthusiasm and drive to commit the effort required to achieve expertise in a domain. The perceived intrinsic and extrinsic rewards obtained for their participation likely contribute to children's willingness to persevere at their tasks. Children also need supportive and challenging social environments, including families, peers, and instructors, in order for their talent to come to fruition. These factors guided our work as we examined the various influences on the development of young talent.

ORIGINS OF GOOD WORK PROJECT

As part of a larger study called the Project on Good Work,[2] we interviewed talented young children. We sought to unravel the complex interpersonal and contextual factors that facilitate their activity-related development. Specifically, we conducted interviews with 43 children aged 10 to 15 in the Boston/Cambridge area: 7 Classical musicians, 8 stage actors, 5 figure skaters, 9 gymnasts, and 14 community service volunteers.

In selecting activities, we focused on areas that demand great amounts of time and effort. Sports such as ice-skating and gymnastics and artistic activities like music and theater emerged early. These domains were selected as a result of domain reputation, a literature review, and personal experiences. We added community service volunteer work to compare the young artists and athletes with a group of students engaged in work more directly focused on social responsibility.

---

[2]Please consult the following website for information regarding this project: http://pzweb.harvard.edu/Research/Create.htm

We chose subject sites based on institutions' reputations and suggestions from expert informants. The age parameters were established based on developmental and domain-based information. In this range, students were usually able to explain details of their interest in their activity, but were still young enough to delay adult work responsibilities.

We sought to include students who were highly committed to their pursuits. Drawing on the input of adult experts in the five activities, we defined highly committed as spending a minimum of ten hours per week devoted to the activity in the case of athletes and artists; at least five hours each week for community service volunteers. Our criteria also required that students be involved in their pursuit for at least one year (mean = 4.5 years, mode = 3 years).

The findings detailed throughout the remainder of this chapter are based primarily on child interview data because our goal was to examine students' perceptions of the influences on their work. In addition, we conducted separate focus groups with the subjects' instructors and their parents, during which we presented our project findings. Both groups of individuals generally concurred with our results. Although the dialogue in these sessions was not systematically examined, the agreement of these consulted adults does serve to bolster our conclusions.

Drawing on the work of Bloom (1985), we identified three stages of talent development through which children progressed: initial participation, perseverance, and mastery. Initial participation included children's first attraction to their activities as well as the initiation of formal instruction. Perseverance encompassed the period in which children acquired basic and intermediate skills. In mastery, children built upon those skills to develop expertise in their activities and to compete at more advanced levels.

The first goal of our research was to examine three realms of influence on children's work: domain-related individuals, non-domain-related individuals and artifacts. Domain-related individuals were those who were involved in the activities in which children participated, such as fellow teammates, adult instructors, and the target audience. Non-domain individuals included parents and peers who did not participate in the activity, such as school friends. Artifacts included media events, books, and films that children described as influential in how they approached their work.

A second goal of our research was to account for variation among the types and amount of influence children described. We examined two possible explanatory factors, domain and stage differences. Drawing on the criteria set forth by Eccles, Wigfield, and Schiefele (1998), we found that instruction in the athletic domains tended to be extrinsic, instruction in theater and community service tended to be intrinsic, and instruction in music contained elements of both intrinsic and extrinsic teaching styles. Likewise, we found that the athletes were extrinsically motivated to participate in sports, theater, and community service students were intrinsically motivated to participate in their activities, and musicians exhibited both types of motivation. Although this was a finding of our study rather than an a priori assumption, it serves as the best way to describe our data and so we will draw on it as needed.

Coaches in gymnastics and skating, for example, unilaterally decided when children were ready to try new moves or to advance to new skill levels. Additionally, the rules for performing successful routines were explicit and rigid, and evaluations often were made public through an assigned point value. Relatedly, children in these domains were extrinsically motivated to participate in their activities and, therefore, relied heavily on external influence and support. In contrast, we found that instruction in theater and community service typically was intrinsic because it relied largely on children's intrinsic motivation rather than on extrinsic cues. Children often directed their learning experiences, in part, by selecting new service projects, for example, or creating their own interpretation of a particular character. In addition, there were few formally established rules by which to judge a successful performance. Unsurprisingly, then, we found that children in these domains were intrinsically motivated to participate and, therefore, relied less on external influences.

Instruction in the music domain contained both extrinsic and intrinsic elements. Instructors directed children's learning of basic skills, but also allowed them the freedom to develop their own interpretations of music. In addition, whereas the athletes practiced primarily under adult supervision, young musicians spent most of their hours practicing independently, which may have fostered intrinsic motivation. Likewise, we found that young musicians exhibited behaviors representing both external and internal motivation.

An equally plausible argument is that variation in children's descriptions of influence is due to their level of expertise. At initial stages in their careers, for example, children likely rely heavily on non-domain individuals, such as parents. Children at more advanced stages are likely to look more frequently to domain experts such as coaches for help in advancing their work. In addition to examining three sources of influence on children's activity-related development, therefore, we also sought to determine whether domain or stage differences could best explain the diverse ways in which children utilized the support of others to develop their talents.

INITIAL PARTICIPATION

Several factors influenced children's decisions to begin participating in their activities, including parents, peers, and media. Through our interviews with young children, we learned that parents were dominant figures

7. DEVELOPMENT OF TALENT   125

in the early decisions in children's careers ($n = 27$). Parents played an overt role in initiating children's participation by informing children of activity-related opportunities or signing them up for lessons. Parents also exerted a more implicit influence by modeling their own involvement, instilling in children either a desire or the expectation to participate. For example, one musician described her initial interest in music: *Well, my mom plays the violin, and my dad plays the piano, my brother was playing the piano and my other brother was playing the piano and the cello. So, it was just kind of like my duty to follow along. But I still thought it was fun because I wanted to be like my mom and play the violin.* Indeed, parents were particularly important for the young musicians in our study. Their initial participation was often related to parental involvement in the activity, and other sources of influence were rarely mentioned.

In examining the remaining sources of influence on gymnasts, skaters, actors, and service practitioners, we discovered that the extent and form of the influence varied according to the domain in which the child participated. Peers, for example, were important for attracting several children to their activities ($n = 11$). The compelling factor within that source of influence, however, varied. The gymnasts in our study frequently participated in order to spend more time with their friends. For example, one gymnast described her early participation: *My grandmother started me in it, but I am thinking a little seriously in it because my friends, my two friends, they did it at a place and they told me that I should come over with them, and so I did, and then it was just fun, and I kept on doing it.*

Actors and community service practitioners, however, tended to describe peer influences on their initial involvement in slightly different ways. In these domains, peers played an important role in *informing* students of opportunities within the activity. The critical factor in their decisions to participate, however, was not to spend more time with their peers but rather their interest in the activity itself.

In addition, media events, which portrayed the glamour and excitement of elite competitions, attracted several gymnasts and skaters to their activities ($n = 6$). Several athletes described their desire to become involved after watching the Olympics or other elite competitions on television. For example, one student explained the origin of her interest in gymnastics: *I always used to watch gymnastics on TV, and that inspired me to do gymnastics.* [Do you remember what you watched?] *I think it was the Olympics . . . I just thought that all of the stuff they did in the air was cool.* Although media played an important early role for children involved in sports, the media rarely were mentioned by the actors, musicians, and community service practitioners in our study.

These findings suggest a trend in the types of relationships children had with their activities. Skaters and gymnasts commonly were drawn to their sports for reasons beyond the activity. They were lured by the glamour portrayed on television and/or the opportunity to spend more time with their peers. Similarly, children in music frequently related their initial participation to parental involvement or expectations. Consequently, early indicators suggest that the athletes and musicians had an extrinsic relationship with their activities. Children in theater and community service expressed a more inherent interest in the activity. They described peers, for example, as a vehicle for getting them involved in an activity in which they were already interested. Therefore, children in these domains seemed to have an intrinsic relationship to their activities.

PERSEVERANCE

The students in our study spoke frequently about what motivated them to remain committed to their activities despite the long and often strenuous hours they devoted each week (Riemberg and Zimmerman, 1992). Children talked about what inspired them to attend practice on days when they would rather watch television or go to a friend's birthday party. They spoke of overcoming the challenges of having little or no free time, balancing the demands of schoolwork and practice, and not being able to go on summer vacations for fear they might fall behind their competitors.

Students gathered many different resources to help them sustain their intense commitment to the activities. The most influential factor in encouraging children to persevere was the moral support that they received from others. Moral support, as defined by children's narratives, constituted various sorts of mental nurturance that allowed children to find the renewed strength needed to continue their work.

Children—gymnasts, skaters, and musicians in particular—garnered a great deal of moral support from their parents to help keep them motivated in their activities ($n = 22$). One way that parents encouraged their children to persevere was by serving as reminders of the sacrifices the entire family had made for their involvement. Parents often paid large sums of money for their children's lessons and equipment. They also spent considerable time driving their children to and from practices and meets as well as observing their children's practice sessions. One skater described how her family's sacrifices inspired her to keep working: *skating is a big part of my family . . .* [Why?] *I don't know, because everyone gives up so much for me to come in and stuff. So it's a big part of everyone's life in my family.* [Does that put any more pressure on you to do well?] *Yes! Because I kind of feel bad sometimes that I'm taking away all their time to come into Boston and then drive back. Because it's an hour both ways, so—basically you're in the car, you're here, and you're in the car. It's a long haul.* [Do you think that keeps you going? Do they want to see you keep going?] *Yeah, I think so. I think that's where I get all my ambition from, to make my parents proud.*

7. DEVELOPMENT OF TALENT

Parents also provided support by sympathizing with their children's demanding schedules and by displaying enthusiasm and pride in their children for their involvement in the activities. Parents attended many of the practices and competitions, providing encouragement and constructive criticism on their children's performances. A gymnast described her father's response to her involvement: *I think my dad is really happy that I do gymnastics. He likes it a lot and he likes going to the meets and watching me, and goes "that's my daughter," you know?*

Finally, parents also fostered their children's commitment to their activities by serving as important role models of hard work and perseverance ($n = 15$). Particularly in the community service domain, children observed their parents' work ethics and claimed that it had an impact on how they approached their own work.

Several of the gymnasts and skaters in our study also described moral support that they received from peers who were not involved in the activity ($n = 6$). Friends from school, for example, sympathized with their activity-related obligations and did not pressure them or make them feel badly for not being able to participate in extracurricular activities such as birthday parties, sleepovers, or trips to the shopping mall. Non-domain peers also supported children by showing enthusiasm for their involvement. They attended students' competitions and expressed excitement and admiration for their skills. Notably, although gymnasts and skaters spoke of their peers' enthusiasm, children in the other domains rarely discussed moral support from non-domain peers as a factor in their willingness to persevere in their tasks.

Children in all domains also spoke often about the friendships they had established *within* their activities ($n = 23$). For many children, domain peers became their closest group of friends. Through frequent contact they came to understand each other well and the commitment and drive that were necessary to pursue the activity at an intense level. Although children in all activities spoke of the ways in which their domain peers helped them persevere in their activities, gymnasts and skaters most often mentioned this source of support.

The children in our study also looked to the audience for which they were performing or serving to garner the motivation they needed to continue their work ($n = 13$). Community service practitioners in particular relied on their target audiences to keep them motivated. They frequently described a deep sense of commitment and obligation toward those they helped.

Although to a lesser extent, children in the remaining domains also mentioned the audience as a reason for their continued participation in their activities. Musicians and actors, for example, enjoyed performing for others and sharing their music and entertainment. Skaters and gymnasts also mentioned the audience as a means of motivating them to persist in the activity, though in a slightly different context. Children in these domains enjoyed the respect and pride of the audience. In contrast to the other groups, however, gymnasts and skaters rarely mentioned the audience in terms of giving or sharing their skills with others.

Finally, children in all domains received moral support from their adult instructors ($n = 17$). The particular messages conveyed, however, varied among the domains. For gymnasts and skaters, moral support often took the form of inciting or motivating children to keep going. Coaches pushed children and helped them envision the possibilities if they continued to work hard. Community service leaders also encouraged children to continue their work by prompting them to consider the consequences of their participation. Unlike athletic coaches who often pressured children to continue working, community service leaders were more likely to engage students in discussion about how their commitment affected the target groups.

Thus, parents, peers, and adult leaders affected many children's decisions and abilities to sustain their commitment to their activities. The quantity and sources of support that children did rely on tended to vary according to the domain in which the child was involved. The athletes gathered support from all three sources—parents, peers, and adult leaders. They frequently commented on the recognition and admiration that they derived from these groups of individuals both for their immediate accomplishments and their long-term goals. Athletes' receptiveness to and the frequency with which they described these types of messages suggest that extrinsic rewards may be a critical factor in sustaining their involvement in sports. As with initial participation, then, children in athletic domains seemed to have an extrinsic relationship with their activities.

Musicians received support primarily from individuals within their domain. Parents, many of whom were involved in music themselves, adult instructors, and domain peers became actively involved in children's efforts to persevere. Thus, although musicians seemed to be extrinsically motivated to persevere in their activities, as indicated by their need for support, they were more discriminating in the types of individuals from which they sought support than were children in the athletic domains. It is possible that the limited media exposure of musical events (particularly of classical music) generates less public enthusiasm for this domain than for sports. Young musicians, then, need to rely more on within-domain individuals for support in sustaining their commitment.

Theater and community service children spoke far less frequently about receiving or seeking moral support from others than did the athletes and musicians. Children in these domains may have needed less support because they were more intrinsically motivated to persist in their activities. Indeed, many community service children spoke of their participation as a moral obligation. One practitioner explained: *It's something—it's a moral duty of mine. We all have—I think that there are a lot of moral duties. And I certainly don't live up to all my moral duties, I don't think anybody does. But we should always try to. Wherever, seeing something that can be fixed, and being able to fix it, is very, very gratifying. I plan to continue it as long as I possibly can.* The need or responsibility to participate described by many community service practitioners and actors further suggests that they are intrinsically related to their activities.

MASTERY

Influential others played a large role in children's efforts to achieve mastery in their domains. For the purposes of this study, mastery was defined as achieving at the highest level of a child's current stage of activity-related development. This definition was developed both because the students in our study were at various stages in their development and because mastery was determined differently across the domains. Thus, mastery for one gymnast might be receiving perfect scores at a local competition while for another gymnast it might mean making the Olympic trials. Likewise, mastery for one actor might mean getting the biggest part in a local production while for another actor it could be receiving national recognition for her performance.

Three components of mastery emerged from children's discussions: technical assistance, evaluations of performance, and risk-taking. Individuals exerted an influence on children's efforts to master their activities by offering them technical assistance on the skills they needed to achieve at high levels, helping them evaluate the success of their performances, and assisting in their decisions about taking activity-related risks. Performance evaluations helped children identify particular weaknesses and ways to improve their overall abilities. Risk-taking also emerged as an important component of mastery because children often needed to push themselves beyond their comfort zone in order to achieve at higher levels. Risk-taking took various forms among the domains, including accepting roles that were out of character for young actors or trying new and highly technical moves for the athletes.

Adult leaders were critical throughout all domains in helping children excel ($n = 27$). Adult instructors in theater and community service, however, more frequently collaborated with children in helping them to achieve mastery than did instructors in the athletic domains. Children in the former groups worked closely with instructors in developing ways to improve their work, in evaluating their performances, and in deciding when it was necessary to take risks. Leaders in these domains helped children generate creative ideas for new projects, for example, implement plans, and develop interpretations of characters. One actor described her instructor's techniques for helping children develop their characters: *And I think Kathy's[3] way of teaching is so unique, and it's so cool to do it . . . at the beginning of the year, we read over whatever play we're doing, like we did the King Stag, or we did A Thousand and One Arabian Nights, or A Midsummer Night's Dream. And we read it over, and then you pick certain scenes and then she assigns people to different roles to try out them, and you improvise them, after you get the gist of it. So you create totally, not new scenes but you create characters out of maybe like a page or two of text, like totally different than normal ones or whatever. And then she takes it and usually she rewrites it using our suggestions in a dance or a fight or whatever. And then we improvise it again, improvising using the new script. And then it's done twice. But it's redone by our improvisations, so it's kind of like we're rewriting it. . . . And it was like we could create the characters instead of doing what some director wanted us to do and stuff.*

In the athletic domains the rules for excellent performances were clearly delineated so children were more likely to rely on coaches' directives regarding how to improve their work. Coaches helped the skaters and gymnasts refine their techniques in accordance with pre-established rules for successful performances. Children also relied heavily on their instructors in determining how well they performed and when to take activity-related risks. When asked how they evaluate their success, the athletes often stated that their instructors told them when they performed well or poorly.

Music instructors used a combination of intrinsic and extrinsic teaching techniques. They provided explicit instruction to children on how to improve particular skills but also encouraged children to develop their own interpretations of musical selections. In addition, the musicians sought their instructors' opinions about their performances but did not consult them about activity-related risks. This mixed relationship may indicate that musicians are moving toward a more intrinsically motivated or autonomous approach to their work.

Parents also were instrumental in helping their children achieve at high levels ($n = 12$). As was the case with respect to perseverance, children in skating, gymnastics, and music relied heavily on their parents. They frequently offered children technical assistance to help them improve their skills. In addition, skaters and musicians were most likely to seek their parents' opinions in judging their performances: this finding likely reflects the greater degree of parental "expertise" in these domains. Parents of skaters and musicians were most likely to have been involved in the activities themselves or to have gained expertise through years of attending children's practices and performances. Interestingly, children in community service and theater rarely spoke of seeking or receiving technical assistance from

---

[3]All names have been changed to preserve confidentiality.

their parents (although parents often helped actors learn their lines). It is likely that the collaborative nature of their projects encouraged children to seek technical assistance from their domain peers rather than their parents.

Children in all domains relied heavily on peer collaborators for improving their skills ($n = 15$). Although they rarely solicited advice regarding the success of their performances or when to take activity-related risks, children in all domains received technical support from their domain peers. Peers provided one another feedback on how to improve their techniques, helped them learn their lines, and discussed innovative and efficient ways of serving the community.

Finally, only children involved in theater discussed how artifacts, and in particular movies and books, helped them improve their skills ($n = 3$). Actors admired stars in both current and classic movies and tried to learn from their performances. Books also provided valuable lessons that helped actors enhance their skills. For example, one young actor explained that the messages of creativity and empathy relayed in her favorite book helped her improve her performances because she believes these qualities are the cornerstone of good acting. It is possible that artifacts like books will become more important to youngsters as they make a transition to career involvement in a domain.

SUMMARY

Our conversations with highly dedicated children revealed various influences on their activity-related development. Three major stages emerged from their descriptions: initial involvement, perseverance, and mastery of the activity. Throughout these stages, children described both the factors that had an impact on their work, including domain individuals, nondomain individuals and artifacts, as well as the mechanisms through which they exerted their influence.

Parents were an extremely significant influence across all stages of children's development. They actively initiated their children's participation, provided moral support to help them sustain their commitment, and offered technical assistance to help children improve their skills. Parents exerted their influence both through providing deliberate and explicit advice as well as by modeling desired behaviors. These findings resonate with previous work that explicates the critical role parents play in nurturing and promoting children's talent (Bloom, 1985; Feldman, 1986; Gardner with Laskin, 1995; Winner, 1996).

Our examination of the impact of adult instructors on talented children also emerged consistent with previous research (Bloom, 1985). We found instructors to be particularly influential during middle and later stages of children's talent development. Coaches helped children stay motivated in their activities by encouraging them to envision the long-term consequences of their commitment. They helped children achieve mastery by providing technical assistance, evaluating children's performances and recommending when to take risks.

We found peers to be important influences on children's talent development as well. Children developed strong relationships with their domain-related peers and provided moral and technical support to one another. Peers who did not participate in children's activities played an equally important role by sympathizing with the lengthy hours children were required to devote to their activities and by demonstrating enthusiasm for their involvement. These findings depart slightly from previous work on talented children's peer relationships. Whereas previous research indicates that talented children tend to gravitate towards either domain *or* non-domain peers, the children in our study successfully navigated and utilized both groups of friends in the development of their talent.

Artifacts had a less consistent impact on children's development. Media events often sparked athletes initial interest in their activities. Movies and books helped the young actors improve their skills in the mastery phase of talent development. Artifacts did not emerge as a factor in children's willingness to persevere in their activities, however.

Multiple groups of individuals facilitated children's participation and commitment to their activities. Each source of influence played a particular role or roles in a child's talent development and in many cases multiple individuals met the same need. For example, children in gymnastics and skating relied heavily on both parents and peers to help them sustain their commitment to sports. This may prove critical for children whose parents or peers may not be supportive of their endeavors. That is, a variety of individuals can serve as supportive influences to assist in children's activity-related development. As we discuss in the final section, however, it is important not only to examine various sources of influence, but also how influences interact with individual motivation and domain instruction.

CONCLUSION

What are the contributing and supportive factors in the development of talented youth? We discovered that there is no ready-made formula for promoting activity-related development. Rather, development is contingent on the interplay among three related factors: the *individual's relationship to the activity, the types of influences* on which he draws, and the *domain* in which the child participates. Our data suggest that development could be enhanced by determining whether an individual is primarily intrinsically or extrinsi-

7. DEVELOPMENT OF TALENT 133

cally motivated to participate in the activity and encouraging support systems and instructional styles that match that tendency.

The athletes in our study were heavily motivated to participate in their activities for extrinsic reasons. They were drawn to, persevered in, and mastered their activities largely for reasons that went beyond the activities themselves. For example, gymnasts and skaters tended to become involved in their sports because of their friends' participation and persevered and excelled because of the rewards and recognition they received. Moreover, the supportive and influential messages to which they seemed most receptive emphasized an admiration for their talents. The coaching styles used in the athletic domains also were extrinsic. Instruction was characterized by controlled decision-making and explicit rules for achievement. We argue that the athletes' activity-related development was enhanced because the supportive networks and instructional practices complemented the extrinsic nature of the athletes.

Children in community service and theater were intrinsically motivated to participate in their activities. Their passion for the activities was the driving force behind their initial participation, their willingness to persevere, and their efforts to achieve mastery. They rarely sought support for maintaining their commitment or described support in extrinsic terms such as the recognition they received through their participation. Children in community service and theater did rely on others but primarily in the context of finding innovative ways to approach their work. In addition, the coaches in these domains tended to use intrinsic instructional styles that emphasized student involvement in decision-making processes and evaluations of success. Again, we believe that talent development for children in community service and theater was enhanced through the coordination of their individual motivational preferences, the types of support they received, and the instructional styles used in their domains.

The musicians in our study described behaviors representing both intrinsic and extrinsic motivation. Their initial participation often was related to parental involvement, and they relied on knowledgeable parents, domain peers, and adult instructors to keep them committed to their activities. Their reliance on these influences during initial participation and perseverance suggests that they were extrinsically related to their activities. They were more selective than were the athletes, however, as they sought support only from domain-related individuals. Instruction in the music domain contained elements of both extrinsic and intrinsic styles as teachers both directed children's early learning and encouraged their input once they had acquired basic skills. In addition, though young musicians continued to rely upon domain experts to help them achieve mastery in their work, they began to show signs of independence. Musicians did not consult others, for example, in deciding whether or not to take activity-related risks.

These findings suggest that it may be best to consider extrinsic and intrinsic motivation along a continuum rather than as discrete categories. Athletes would be located toward the extrinsic end of the continuum, theater and community service children would be located toward the intrinsic end, and musicians, who exhibit both types of behaviors, would be located in the middle of the continuum. Undoubtedly, however, there will be individual variation within these patterns.

Our data also revealed that level of expertise had little impact on the amount of influence on which children relied. Children in community service and theater consistently relied on less support than did children in the athletic domains. However, as they progressed toward mastery, children did tend to utilize the support of domain individuals more and non-domain individuals less. Previous research, which allows us to contextualize our findings within a more extended period of development, reached a similar conclusion. Through interviews with highly accomplished adults, Bloom (1985) discovered that individuals' motivations for participating in their activities evolved over the course of their development. He discovered that attention and recognition tended to be common motivating forces at early stages in one's career, while a sense of competence and an identification with the activity often became predominant in later stages of development. It is possible that the athletes in our study, then, will also become more intrinsically motivated to participate in their activities as they continue to advance in their work.

Although our data revealed strong and distinct trends among the athletic domains and the community service and theater domains, it is important to be aware of variation both within the domains and across time. One should not assume that all individuals within a particular domain are driven by the same factors or that children uniformly rely less on non-domain individuals at advanced stages of their careers. For example, although rare, we did find community service practitioners who volunteered for extrinsic reasons such as improving their chances of being accepted into college. Therefore, while we conclude that activity-related development can be enhanced by aligning an individual's reasons for engaging in an activity with contexts that cultivate those sources of motivation, we caution that each child must be considered individually throughout the course of his or her development.

REFERENCES

Bloom, B. S. (Ed.). (1985). *Developing talent in young people*. New York: Ballantine Books.
Csikszentmihalyi, M., Rathunde, K., & Whalent, S. (1993). *Talented teenagers*. New York: Cambridge University Press.
Eccles, J. S., Wigfield, A., & Schiefele, U. (1998). Motivation to succeed. In W. Damon (Ed.), *Handbook of child psychology* (5th ed.) (pp. 1017–1090). John Wiley & Sons.

Ericsson, K. A., Krammpe, R. T., & Tesch-Römer, C. (1993). The role of deliberate practice in the acquisition of expert performance. *Psychological Review, 100*(3), 363–406.

Ericsson, K. A., & Smith, J. (1991). Prospects and limits of the empirical study of expertise: An introduction. In K. A. Ericsson & J. Smith (Eds.), *Toward a general theory of expertise: Prospects and limits* (pp. 1–38). New York: Cambridge University Press.

Feldman, D. H. (1986). *Nature's gambit: Child prodigies and the development of human potential.* New York: Basic Books.

Gardner, H. (1983). *Frames of mind.* New York: Basic Books.

Gardner, H., with Laskin, E. (1995). *Leading minds: An anatomy of leadership.* New York: Basic Books.

Gardner, H. (1997). *Extraordinary minds.* New York: Basic Books.

Risemberg, R., & Zimmerman, B. J. (1992). Self-regulated learning in gifted students. *Roeper Review, 15*(2), 98–101.

Simon, H., & Chase, W. (1973). Skill in chess. *American Scientist, 61*, 394–403.

Solomon, B., Powell, K., & Gardner, H. (1999). Multiple intelligences and creativity. In M. Runco & S. Pritzker (Eds.), *Encyclopedia of creativity* (pp. 273–283). San Diego, CA: Academic Press.

Winner, E. (1996). *Gifted children: Myths and realities.* New York: Basic Books.

Zimmerman, B. J., Bandura, A., & Martinez-Pons, M. (1992). Self-motivation for academic attainment: The role of self-efficacy beliefs and personal goal setting. *American Educational Research Journal, 29*(3), 663–676.

Zimmerman, B. J., & Ringle, J. (1981). Effects of model persistence and statements of confidence on children's self-efficacy and problem solving. *Journal of Educational Psychology, 73,* 485–493.

Chapter 8

Transforming Elite Musicians Into Professional Artists: A View of the Talent Development Process at The Juilliard School

Rena F. Subotnik
*Esther Katz Rosen Center for Gifted Education Policy,
American Psychological Foundation*

Great performers are a boon to our aesthetic sensibilities and a salve to the weariness that comes with daily routine. The ease and gracefulness of musicians' communication skills mask years of copious study and practice guided by highly expert teachers. This chapter invites readers to explore the environment in which America's finest classical musicians are trained to become professional *artists*, the term used to describe those held in the highest esteem by the field. Data were provided by faculty and staff of the internationally renowned Juilliard School to address the following variables: (a) definitions of elite talent, (b) relationships established between teachers and their students, (c) how curriculum plays a role in transforming talent, and (d) the advent of stars and underachievers among students. The chapter concludes with a list of suggestions for bringing some of the techniques, strategies, and approaches used in the conservatory to undergraduate training in the academic disciplines.

DOES THE CONSERVATORY HOLD SOME LESSONS FOR LIBERAL ARTS INSTITUTIONS?

Mastery of the repertoire in classical music performance is highly sequential, and the values and expectations for transformation from player to artist are steeped in rich tradition. The resulting orderliness of the field makes it an ideal platform from which to view the development of talent, from its beginnings in early childhood through the nurturing of professional careers. Retrospective studies of concert pianists by Bloom (1985) and Sosniak (1985) have delineated the variables that contribute to elite performance in music at various stages in the process. Other scholars (Bamberger, 1986; Gagne, 1999; Haroutounian, 2000; Piirto, 1998; Sloboda & Howe, 1991; Winner, 1996) have also constructed theories or definitions of developing giftedness in music.

A smaller literature looks specifically at the highest level of musical talent development—preparing professionals for concert careers at the conservatory. Two published studies by Kogan (1987) and Kingsbury (1988) characterize American conservatories as monastery like "finger factories." In recent years, however, attention to mental health and broader, more interdisciplinary approaches to training have helped conservatory students and faculty accommodate to shortened audience attention spans, reduced funding for the arts, and the consequent increase in competition within the performing arts world (Olmstead, 1999). What remains undeniable, however, is the success that conservatories have had in transforming elite talent into professional careers.

The most important relationship is with one's private (or studio) teacher, and most teachers who work with advanced students carry a proud lineage of descent from earlier generations of teachers, performers, and composers (Haroutounian, 2000; Kingsbury, 1988; Persson, 1996; Sand, 2000; Shuter-Dyson, 1985; Sosniak, 1985; Subotnik, 2000). In science, Nobel laureates also display a mentor–protege pattern that mirrors the one found in music (Zuckerman, 1996). For example, physicist Baron Rayleigh, who won the Nobel Prize in 1904, was the mentor to physicist J. J. Thompson, who in turn, won the Prize in 1906. One of Thompson's eight laureate proteges was chemist Ernest Rutherford. Rutherford was mentor to no fewer than 11 Nobel laureates in physics and chemistry between 1921 and 1967. Graduate students in science seek a doctoral program based on specific professors who might be good research mentors. Before that point, most science students select their college or university based on the institution's general prestige or location. In contrast, reputation plays a primary role even for a preadolescent's studio teacher. A chance to work with teachers of distinct lineage is what draws many students to a conservatory.

One role that some studio teachers play is career advisor, and the practical or tacit knowledge they provide is instrumental to career success (Sternberg, Hedlund, & Grigorenko, 2000). However, leaving that responsibility solely to studio teachers can be haphazard (Schmidt & Andrews, 1996). Consequently, Juilliard offers its students exposure to many potential sources of professional and practical wisdom.

Another advantage the conservatory offers is access to talented peers who approach, match, or even surpass a student's abilities and ambitions, yet share the passion and commitment needed for sustained effort (Bloom, 1985; Subotnik & Coleman, 1996). Young musicians deal with pressures of competition and the advent of stars and underachievers that contribute to or detract from their growth in artistry or scholarship, to say nothing of their mental health and self-concept (Seymour & Hewitt, 1994). In the end, the student, with the help of his or her teachers and peers, must forge a unique identity as an artist and capitalize on whatever performance opportunities are available.

Talent Development in Science:
A Comparison Leads to the Conservatory

In 1983, I began a 13-year longitudinal study of talented young scientists (Subotnik & Arnold, 1995; Subotnik, Duschl, & Selmon, 1993; Subotnik, Maurer, & Steiner, 2001; Subotnik & Steiner, 1994). Each of the participants was a winner of America's most prestigious high school science award: the Westinghouse Science Talent Search (now called Intel Science Talent Search). To win this award, one had to submit a technical paper describing an original mathematics, life or physical science, or quantitatively based social science investigation, usually under the guidance of an experienced researcher. The judges included Nobel laureates, high-ranking scholars at the National Institutes for Health, the National Science Foundation, and major research universities. In the course of preparing their papers, the winners enjoyed significant participation in the conduct of real science. Although 95% aspired to research or applied science careers, they chose which university to attend based on general prestige rather than on specific faculty members with whom they might study. By the end of their second year in university, two-thirds of the women had dropped their mathematics or science majors, and many of the men were disappointed with their training and preparation. They had been shuttled into classes with several hundred students and received little or no individual attention. If they managed to arrange some affiliation with a laboratory, they were assigned menial tasks. Most of those who survived the weeding out period were eventually able to enjoy relationships with mentors, more cutting edge coursework, and opportunities to contribute significantly in laboratory efforts. Although these brilliant young adults achieved career success in an array of fields, I was dismayed at how blindly they selected an undergraduate institution and how cavalierly our finest universities addressed such outstanding talent at its peak of enthusiasm.

In 1996, as I began my last data collection point in the Westinghouse study, Franz Monks from the University of Nijmegen told me about a fabulously talented young musician he met in his clinic. He asked me to make some inquiries about this student's possible enrollment at The Juilliard School. The Director of Admissions at Juilliard, Mary Gray, graciously answered my questions. In the course of a freewheeling conversation, we discussed my interviews with Midori and Vladimir Feltsman, two internationally renowned artists as part of a series entitled, "Conversations with Masters in the Arts and Sciences."[1] Midori had been a student at Juilliard beginning in early adolescence. Feltsman entered a special full time music school in Moscow at age 6 and completed his elementary and secondary studies there. Both were constantly challenged by teachers and the performance world to surpass the levels of proficiency they had achieved in adolescence. This confluence of experience—the Midori and Feltsman interviews and my visit to The Juilliard School—led me to propose to the Juilliard administration a study of how the Pre-College Program (Subotnik, 2000) and the actual conservatory transform elite musicians into professional artists.

Academically gifted students of comparable promise and career ambition as those found at Juilliard experience fewer opportunities for individualized instruction, cutting edge research positions, or career advice during their undergraduate years. At Juilliard, the unique relationship between studio teacher and student, an abundance of performance opportunities and gifted peers, and scheduled access to explicit, practical information required for the fulfillment of talent are readily available. The objective of this study is to offer insights into restructuring the way that we meet the needs of academically gifted youth based on the success of another educational system.

A STUDY CONDUCTED AT AMERICA'S PREMIERE MUSIC CONSERVATORY

Thirty-four Juilliard faculty and administrators were interviewed in person for this study. Although a little more than 20% of the staff that works in the Music Division participated, the main instrument and voice departments and all levels of administration are represented in the data. Juilliard's Music Division serves only 320 undergraduates, so the full-time staff and faculty are often called on to play many roles. Most of the administrators teach courses or instruct individual students in their own studios. Half of the nonstudio or classroom teachers (in liberal arts, theory, ear training, etc.) hold some kind of administrative position within a department or else serve as coaches to student ensembles or performance groups.

The taped interviews were conducted following a predetermined questioning schedule, with a few unique items included based on the person's role at the institution (see Appendix 1). After the interview session, participants were sent their transcripts so that they could correct errors in musical

---

[1] On occasion, this series appears in the *Journal for the Education of the Gifted*.

terminology, names, or interpretations of an answer and add updates or details to their responses. This method ensures accurate reporting of the data (Hertz & Imber, 1995; Persson & Robsin, 1995).

Six of the ten studio teachers that we interviewed maintain active performance careers as soloists, ensemble players, or principals in major symphony orchestras. All had been recruited by members of their department on the basis of their reputations as teachers and/or performers.

Ten administrators were interviewed including the president, dean, director of admissions, director of student services, head librarian, and key staff associated with organizing student performances. All but one had intensive musical training in their backgrounds. Seven out of the 10 do not perform regularly, devoting most of their energies to administration and some teaching. One continues to perform professionally. All but one of these individuals came into their administrative role either from the ranks of the faculty or after fulfilling a similar responsibility at another well-known conservatory, arts school, or performance group.

Nonstudio instructors and staff ($n = 14$) were categorized under the label of *classroom teachers* for the purposes of this study. This group included professionals who provide seminars on the practical realities of the music world, as well as teachers of theory, ear training, music history, and humanities. This category also encompasses experts in aesthetic education, opera performance, and performance of new music by professional and student composers. All remain professionally active and were recruited by teachers and staff in related departments at the school on the basis of their expertise and reputations in the field.

Defining Elite Talent

A successful audition is the central criterion of the admissions process, and lasts anywhere from 10 to 30 minutes. Approximately 90% of those applying for admission to Juilliard are rejected since there may only be one or two openings for a new student in each department. The challenge of the admissions process is to sort out those who would benefit most from the program from among a large pool of talented applicants.

A team made up of each department's studio teachers sits in the auditions and rates candidates on a list of variables including "chops" or technique (command of the instrument), rhythm, intonation, sound, and style. There are two open questions on the audition form in addition to a space for general comments: *Should this student be accepted? If so, would you take this student in your studio?* Applicants who elicit a more subjective quality like excitement or musicality (how one communicates, the influence of style and emotion on technique) are more likely to succeed, because all applicants are expected to demonstrate high level mastery of the skills listed on the audition grid.

> We're supposed to use a grid with certain criteria and rate people based on that. But it's much more subjective than that. The ones that get in exhibit some sort of really good musical understanding and some sort of identification with the music they're playing. Technically there are a variety of skills they have to exhibit, and if they don't, they're not really going to be considered. There's a subset that has those technical abilities and that feel like they're really making music. When you have the kinds of odds we have, then it's hard to use a set of objective criteria because there are too many people like that. Then it becomes a little more subjective. This person really impressed me because—I'm not sure why. They just really seemed to do something with the music. But as long as it's a committee feeling that way, then I think it's valid. Because that's what music performance is anyhow, on a certain level. (Studio Teacher)

When the faculty, with its varied tastes and values, are in consensus about an applicant, the candidate is viewed as "destined for greatness." However, if there is sufficient space in the program to bring in the next level of candidates, differences in values and tastes held by faculty judges may result in the admission of candidates who are sufficiently pleasing to all, yet not particularly exciting to any.

> Of fifty [applicants to our department], there are about thirty no one is particularly interested in, and there are about two that everyone thought were gods, and then there are about ten that we fight about. If there's only space for two, it's not an issue. But if there were space for four, then people would feel strongly about one candidate as opposed to the other, and about the relative importance of this or that [audition variable]. (Studio Teacher)

Usually the line is clear between those admissible and those who are less qualified. If there is too much disagreement about filling an undergraduate slot, the available opening may be filled by a graduate student. Several years ago, slots in the voice and piano departments were reduced at both the graduate and undergraduate levels for each student to have sufficient performance opportunities.

According to our interviewees, the audition process works well at unveiling "God-given talent" developed by way of intensive focus and hard work. One studio teacher summarized this perspective by saying, "I think the biggest most important part of it is innate. You can recognize it, squelch it, encourage it, develop it, but you can't put it in." Although the results of the audition process are considered satisfactory, some important factors cannot be addressed using a static assessment process. Some departments have introduced a second, dynamic layer of assessment, in-

8. TRANSFORMING ELITE MUSICIANS

cluding an interview and/or a sample lesson to evaluate the "teachability," musicianship, or physical memory of the candidates. A sample lesson would reveal which students can translate given instruction and advice into their musical performance and learn new material quickly by dint of excellent physical memory.

> Musicality is an innate ability. It's something you're born with. You're either musical or you're not. You're not going to be able to teach anybody to be musical. Musicianship is something that you learn, some people more instinctively than others. The best way I can explain it to you is that some people are born with an ability to learn languages very easily, but they don't know the languages. They have to learn them. They just learn them incredibly quickly. It's the same thing with music. You go in with the ability to learn this language, but you have to listen to the music of the composers. You have to know what they were thinking about and what their musical mind worked like in order to become a musician and understand how to bring that music across. Basically as a performer, you are a mouthpiece for somebody who had amazing greatness. So you're entrusted with some stuff that you're supposed to then transmit to others, and it's a tall order. (Studio Teacher)

In the final stages of the talent development process, personality factors tend to outweigh all other variables. Those who are most likely to fulfill their dreams of career success capitalize on charisma and attractive appearance, and apply those qualities to opportunities that come their way. According to the interviewees, greatness results from a *hunger* to express oneself through the medium of musical performance.

> The person who is naturally well turned out is rare; however, those are not always the people that go on to have the careers. A lot of people are given Steinways but never learn to play. Somebody like Maria Callas had a Yamaha and through her tremendous force of will overcame many, many obstacles. (Administrator)

Measuring and quantifying such poorly defined variables as charisma and fortitude remains unfinished business; yet, Juilliard has revealed for us a pattern that may well be mirrored in the more academic environments in which we conduct our work.

Studio Teacher and Student Relationships:
The Basics of Talent Development

A musician's instructional lineage is taken seriously, demonstrating the veneration with which studio teachers are held in the classical music world. Although the only information provided to audition panels is the name of the candidate's hometown, some applicants mention their teacher's name as part of their brief greeting. Even when the name of the teacher is hidden, his or her unique stamp is often evident to the panel. They can figure out the name of the teacher based on the hometown and the quality of the candidate's preparation. In many cases, these teachers were former Juilliard students, "grandchildren" of the department. The close-knit nature of this world is also revealed by the fact that more than 40% of the faculty and administration of the Music Division had some training at Juilliard, either as an undergraduate or graduate student.

When the president approves a new position in a department, a search committee is generated and faculty members make lists of potential candidates. The classical music performance world is small, and most players in it are known, at least by reputation. Consequently, standing in the performance community plays the key role in recruiting studio faculty. Standing is also measured by the success of former students.

Studio teachers are not on full-time contracts. Instead, they are paid according to their prominence and/or the number of students in their Juilliard studio. Each student has to pass a jury examination at the end of the year, judged by all members of the department. How well a teacher's students do on the jury examination may over time affect the esteem in which a teacher is held.

When students apply, they can indicate a first, second, and third choice studio to be admitted to, or else leave the space blank. A few students will turn down admission to Juilliard if their first choice of teacher is not fulfilled.

> We listen to them [at the admission audition] and we mark whether they are material to come into this school—would they fit into the program. Would you accept this student? Yes, no, maybe. Therein lies the tale. And the students coming in might already have a preference for a teacher. He or she might have tried to get in touch with a teacher based on hearsay, or a friend of theirs might have worked with him, and made a connection that way, and say, "That's the one I would really like to work with." Or they've heard, and it's usually the case, the scuttlebutt of whom it is that they'd like to work with. And then they might put down their preferences, or they might say, "I leave that up to the school." So it can happen that a student will say, "I'd like to work with XX on the faculty." XX, not knowing that, might have listened to the audition and might not have liked that particular student and might [have responded to the line on the audition form that says], "Would you take this student?" and if XX says no, that student is not going to make the connection. It has to be agreed on both sides. (Studio Teacher)

According to the admissions office, about 70% of students make their preferences for a studio teacher known; however, the proportion of pre-audition trial lessons that take place varies according to department.

8. TRANSFORMING ELITE MUSICIANS

> We don't recommend that people go around and play for everybody because then it sends the wrong message to faculty, even though finding the right teacher is a very important process. Certainly a lot of our faculty teaches at summer programs and I'm sure many of our best students have come from those kind of connections. We're very clear, however, about sending students a message that it's not essential to have that connection. And it really is not, because the teacher you played for is only one voice on your audition team. No one person can ensure you are admitted. And the faculty tend not to try too hard to push for someone special because there's then going to possibly be a payback with someone for another teacher . . . Teachers let us know whom they'd really like and we do our best to consider the match, while taking all the other factors into consideration. (Administrator)

In the piano and violin departments, where competition for open slots is the most severe, few of the students come in without having "checked out" at least one faculty member. In other departments the proportion of pre-audition interactions may be as small as 20%, especially in voice, where students tend to discover and develop their abilities later than violin and piano students, who apply with at least 7 or 8 years of serious preparation under their belts. The nature of the student–teacher relationship can vary in the degree to which emotional support is given or needed. Although we might idealize the notion of a warm and caring relationship not every student needs or seeks that at this point in his or her career trajectory. Because there are so many variables involved, including personality, values, and teaching and learning style, sophisticated applicants to Juilliard preaudition with various faculty members at summer festivals or in New York. And a few of the faculty members arrange to meet individually with prospective students before committing to take them on to see if enough chemistry is there to work productively together.

In the course of discussing the nature of the teacher–student relationship, two main points emerged. According to our interviewees, no student needs to be subjected to browbeating.

> The stereotype of the classical music teacher as severe and critical is dying away because there's no reason for it. And students are more savvy. In [the old] days students used to be hit by teachers with pencils over their knuckles. Today teachers get fired for that. So students grow up with a knowledge that they have certain rights as individuals, and that they should be afforded a certain respect. And my feeling is that if you feel that a student is good enough for you to work with them, you have to respect them as a human being. And if you need to resort to these kinds of tactics, then you're not really respecting them. I don't see any value in emotional abuse. So I certainly will not subscribe to that. (Studio Teacher)

> I don't think "niceness" is necessarily high on the list of desired teacher characteristics. I'd say a student would rather have a demanding teacher who's go-

ing to make them work and make them better at playing the instrument. They don't enter a school to have a teacher as a friend. That's not the main point. I'd say every student is different in what their needs are. And I would say students are attracted to different faculty on the basis of what their needs are. So there might be a teacher who's more nurturing than another and usually a student who finds that attractive and feels like they learn the best with that kind of a teacher will gravitate there. The selection process occurs partly through summer festivals. Most of our faculty teaches elsewhere during the summer. (Administrator)

Although most high quality teachers say they do not subscribe to the "break down and build up approach," this *maestro* model (Persson, 1996) has been successful in generating world-famous artists. Some students are prepared to undergo whatever is necessary to learn what they need to advance.

It's possible that people are [employing the maestro model], but are not willing to share that about themselves. And I think I might be that way more than I would like to be. I have my own way of being hard on my students. And I think what I get back from them, although they don't tell me so, is that I'm so critical of everything that sometimes they fold under the pressure of trying to please me. And I'm fairly slow to tell them how wonderful I think they are. But it does happen. And I've got a good sense of humor for the most part. But when I lose my patience, I lose it in a very big way.

We have all kinds of students at Juilliard. We have kids [who] would feel very uncomfortable if someone were nice to them. Perhaps the parents or the teachers have also been harsh. It's a really fine and delicate position to be in when you're locked in a room, for, in the case of the undergraduate students, 120 hours over four years, minimum. And no one is watching. And you can develop all kinds of relationships in that setting. And the students very often feel very powerless to protect themselves because the teacher might be vengeful or threaten to be vengeful or to hurt them in some way that they can't control. Also kids are very often in a position where they don't feel it would be proper to stand up for themselves, no matter what they're feeling—unless, of course, they went to Juilliard Pre-College, in which case they know the ropes and they know how to fight for themselves a little bit more because they're used to the situation. If they're from Russia or Israel, they're going to stand up for themselves no matter what, whether they're right or wrong. (Studio Teacher).

Whether the maestro approach is singularly more successful than any others remains to be seen, and with the growing variation in teaching style, a better match can be made to accommodate a wider array of student learning styles. There is no Juilliard philosophy when it comes to instruction. Nor are there professional development seminars for studio faculty. Studio teachers tend to view each student as a puzzle to be analyzed and developed, and, consequently, many strategies are employed, particularly when the performance styles of student and teacher are not compatible. The possibility that students will stop applying to their studio as well as the highly visible success rate of current students in their jury examinations provides accountability for teacher quality.

Classroom teachers, those who serve as instructors for ear training, theory, history, and so on, are also free to choose their instructional strategies at Juilliard, although the instructional goals for these courses are more likely to be discussed in department meetings. Everyone recognizes that there is a need for shared objectives because courses in ear training, music history, and music theory are sequential, and the degree to which students have mastered material in an earlier course will have an impact on their performance in later ones.

Curriculum Matters

Those students who pass the audition but are not sufficiently proficient in the English language or basic academic skills enroll in a provisional 1-year program that focuses entirely on these deficiencies and studio instruction. If a student is unable to pass out of the provisional program after 1 year, he or she has to reapply for admission.

Once a student has been admitted, technique and exposure to an increasingly challenging repertoire continue to be the centerpieces of the curriculum. In the process, emphasis is placed on the unique qualities of each student, with the goal of developing in them a profile of distinctive strengths.

> [Once they are admitted] the teachers will take them a long way even if it means bending fingers and arms and showing them some ways to play without harming themselves and without tension. There's a lot of artistry that remains to be taught. For example, we provide an education that allows them to listen to old performances and classic recordings to understand how people thought about phrases historically, about the context in which writers wrote and painters painted. A certain range of styles is considered "correct," allowing a lot of freedom even within strictly classical music. Once they know what the boundaries are they can soar. But [musical] communication, some of that ability you can't teach. You just try to give lots and lots of tools. (Administrator)

> I would say that someone is talented with only two or three [of the many variables that we look at, namely] physical ease and grace, communicative presence, and technique. Or a strong musical personality which overrides some technical deficiencies. But then it's also possible to have someone who's a klutz on his or her instrument but his intellect and sense of purpose is so

strong that he creates a niche for himself. If a person is developed in two or three areas in a very strong way, and they put that across, they may not say everything you wanted them to say, but what they say is said strongly and clearly. In a way it seems that if you cover too many bases you might not come across as powerfully. (Studio Teacher)

The repertoire for a singer is large in the sense that drama comes into it. In other words, the way your hand of cards adds up is very important. If your voice tells you that you should do light, little perky numbers and you don't look like that, that's a problem. Maybe you're not a light, perky person. All of those things have to add up together, including your language skills, your ability to feel a style and not another style. There are singers who are marvelous at contemporary music, and not really very good at anything else. So what do we do with them? There are so many issues concerning the specific fit of the performer to the repertoire, language, style, personality, drama, range, and volume. (Administrator)

Advanced students are expected to develop their judgment and taste by addressing situations faced by every performer, such as differentiating how one plays as a soloist as opposed to how one plays as a member of an ensemble or an orchestra.

Orchestral playing requires intelligence and discipline, but a person who also has excitement quality can potentially be a big problem in orchestra. . . . They have to know when they are playing second trumpet not first trumpet. But there's also a difference between playing first trumpet on a Mozart symphony where you're an extension of the tympani and you're there to help bring in the cadences occasionally. There's a big difference between that and playing first trumpet on Bartok's Concerto for Orchestra, where there's a solo trumpet part. (Administrator)

How one presents oneself in a public forum—including dress, verbal communication, receiving compliments or criticisms, or recovering from performance errors, requires conscious attention, and according to our interviewees, are better not left to chance.

In traditional European-style conservatories, separate courses are offered in music theory, music history, and ear training, taught by specialists in those fields. The main goal is preparing outstanding performers for the concert stage. Mastery of the repertoire and development of perfect technique are the sole aspirations of the students. These preprofessional vocational programs are nicknamed "finger factories."

The curriculum of the Juilliard School has been broadened beyond the European model since the arrival of the current president, Joseph Polisi. Educated as both a musician and as an academic, Polisi has promoted the expansion of liberal arts requirements as well as services that foster student mental health. The need for change is both philosophical and instrumental in nature, and is conveyed as such to the students. According to Polisi, "We're not a nation that naturally or comfortably supports the so-called classical arts." Whatever music education was offered in the public schools has been cut back in many hard pressed systems, reducing the numbers of potential audience members with a taste for classical arts. Federal funding is hard won by the National Endowment for the Arts, and orchestras without strong public support have struggled to stay alive. The rapid pace of change has also reduced the duration of artists' careers, as audiences seek the "buzz" of the latest phenomenon. All these trends place enormous stress on Juilliard students who see few opportunities to make a mark. In response, faculty and administration have expanded the conservatory curriculum.

The curriculum components for undergraduates include: individual work with one's studio teacher, occasional sessions with other student members of the teacher's studio, performance ensembles and/or orchestra, ear training (solfege), music history, music theory, liberal arts classes, electives that focus on the humanities, and seminars that provide practical information on negotiating a successful music career. In addition, voice students are required to study dramatic arts, movement, diction in four languages (English, French, German, and Italian), and vocal literature and language studies in French, German, and Italian. The number of potential offerings is limited only by the small size of the student body. In addition to attendance and preparation for class, students are expected to practice and rehearse for several hours a day. The philosophical rationale for such a demanding schedule is that a broad education enhances the interpretive abilities of the performer. According to two interviewees:

> Understanding the culture, history, and the psychology of the composers that we play provides an authentic base from which the mode of expression or style of performance can come. This includes having a really good handle on the time and what the composer was interested in. For example, what did he read? Was he a city person? It's different from a musicological or analytical approach. (Studio Teacher)

> I believe that the singers actually need more than they get now, especially in terms of their understanding of art and culture, in relationship to the different periods of music that they're working in. They should know about the history, the philosophy, the art, the culture of the period in which the opera is set. The more they understand that and have a feeling for it, . . . the more they start to understand about things like, "This opera was written when revolution was raging in Italy and this is what the opera is speaking to." Then they have a better way of approaching the character that they're playing in the op-

era. Stretching towards that side has made it harder than being only a pure instrument. It does get in their way at times because people have a hard time stretching towards that, but I think it's something we need to try and do. (Administrator).

Students are encouraged to expand their horizons in the humanities through the curriculum and through their friendships with members of the other Juilliard departments and divisions. Many view this stretching as the path to real artistry. There are also more practical reasons for offering a broad curriculum: (a) accreditation by the Middle States Association requires that Juilliard offer a wider array of courses than one might find at a preprofessional vocational institution, (b) to prepare for interviews and program introductions, students must learn how to speak and write about the music they perform or compose, and (c) accommodating the realities of the performing arts world includes knowing something about teaching and advocating for the arts.

To me, it's abundantly clear that the basic skills of being an educator are part of the kitbag of a twenty-first century artist. I think we're inadequately preparing artists for the world if we haven't introduced at least the basics of these ideas.... I hear rumors of this kind of thinking in other parts of the building, as there's more sense that artists need to know about advocacy. That artists need to be able to speak about their own work. Artists need to know something about education, particularly since over 90% of the graduates end up teaching at some time or other. (Classroom Teacher)

Finally, because music directors are trying to attract and maintain audiences by introducing innovative programs, including crossovers from jazz, pop, and folk music, musicians need to be more flexible. An inclusive approach has its costs, however. Time spent on intellectual or aesthetic pursuits is precious time taken away from practice or relaxation.

The kids tend not to see how important all of this stuff is because they're drowning in the undergraduate program.... One of the problems that we're having right now is this 24–26 unit per semester load which is a lot even if you're not in three and four hours of rehearsal a day. But if you are basically here at school from 9:00 AM to 11:30 PM it's awfully hard to do your academic work. It's even very hard to stay healthy because of a level of physical exhaustion that occurs that you can't afford if you're going to perform.... So at the moment I would have to say that I feel that our academic offerings are a very odd combination of too demanding and not nearly demanding enough.... (Administrator)

How responsive the students are to this [more interdisciplinary] approach varies from student to student. Some are quite taken and excited by this approach, and others patiently wait for me to finish my latest diatribe. I feel we're in a crisis of intellectual curiosity, and people who have mastered systems haven't necessarily learned to think creatively. I don't tolerate that very well. I can't force someone to think creatively, but I keep pressing and it seems to be successful. Juilliard is not the easiest place to do what I want to do [because] I'm limited to the one-hour lesson format. These kids' lives are so full, so sometimes the schedule makes it extremely difficult to do what I want to do with my students. But I do my best. (Studio Teacher)

Students also have to be extremely well organized to fully master the amount of material that is required of them. Some accommodation is made by assigning less writing and reading in academic courses than would be expected at an equivalently elite liberal arts institution. In addition, yoga classes, psychological and counseling services, and a health club help students maintain their physical and mental stamina.

Efforts have also been made to offer a more varied scope and sequence in the required theory and music history classes. Students are exposed to music outside the classical tradition with the purpose of analyzing its structure and how it differs from the repertoire with which the students are most familiar. Additional innovations include taking a creative approach to musical analysis by asking even instrumental students to compose pieces that employ a particular musical structure or style.

> Our curriculum is somewhat untraditional. At the core is the idea that we don't use textbooks but rather study the materials of music by looking at master works of music literature. I'd like to think that my particular spin on it has been to bring more creative opportunities to the classroom, to require faculty members to provide opportunities for improvisation, composition, group work, duo work, performance. Bring in guests that do things that are way outside the classical tradition. West African drummers, North Indian style jazz artists, performance artists. I ask our students to get involved with those people, analyze that style of playing and the music. I'd like them to be part of the global community, to realize that what they do is what artists have done throughout history in all kinds of other traditions. (Classroom Teacher)

Not all classroom instructors employ these new methods, so students tend to have some experience with both approaches and sometimes instruction and learning style are mismatched.

> The strengths of the program are also its weaknesses. In other words, the fact that we don't have a textbook means that students who need to have a really clear through line through four years of theoretical training feel frustrated because they don't get that. They feel it is a little bit too hands-on or vague, not disciplined enough. [We are] trying to remedy that in the next year or two. (Classroom Teacher)

Another relatively new component of the curriculum is the focus on practical knowledge in attaining a successful career in music. Each department conveys this information in its own way. Students learn how to write resumes, conduct themselves in auditions, dress, organize an interesting performance program, and also to consider positions as accompanists, critics, and so on. The most practical creative skill that Juilliard students implement as part of their career is teaching, and far more attention is being paid by studio and classroom teachers than in the past to having students think metacognitively about how they might help another student solve the same musical problem.

Students learn to convey their personal style performing behind a screen, because many auditions for orchestra positions are held in that manner, a process instituted at mid-century to eliminate gender or racial bias.

> [At auditions] you learn how to read the person. I can tell from the minute they walk in. I learn something about them by the way they are dressed. Then I will learn something about them before they even play the first note, how they're holding the instrument, and what are they doing to collect themselves before they start. That is what I hate about audition behind the screen for orchestra. You are not getting a sense of the whole person. It becomes quite antiseptic in a way. That's another thing they have to learn how to do, how to play behind the screen, how to project themselves and be true to themselves behind the screen. (Studio Teacher)

Over the course of the baccalaureate program, particularly in seminars and elective courses designed to address career matters, students are encouraged to seek a psychological balance. They need to acquire a thick skin to tolerate the frustration of rejection in such a highly competitive performance world. At the same time, they must be able to display composure and be a good colleague. Students are reminded that their classmates may be future ensemble or orchestra colleagues, be in positions to recommend hiring you, and may also serve as competitors. In any small community, it is best to neither hold grudges nor to be the subject of them. These lessons are discussed explicitly in departmental seminars.

How Student Stars Are Accommodated

The participants in the study were asked to consider how a talent development program for elite performers should accommodate individual differences in a rarified environment. Every Juilliard student, having advanced through a rigorous and selective admissions process, can surely be labeled as highly talented. They have bypassed other young people with equal preparation and commitment who were unsuccessful at winning a coveted spot

8. TRANSFORMING ELITE MUSICIANS

in the studio of a legendary teacher at a world-renowned conservatory. Having achieved the goal of admission to Juilliard, however, new goals and aspirations are generated and some students stand out as extraordinary, even among their gifted peers.

The institution has moved significantly beyond its earlier reputation of exclusive attention to stars. Despite serious efforts at making talent development opportunities more equitable, some individuals persist in being more visible and generate more excitement than do their peers. At this stage of training, much of the basic technique preparation is in place and conservatory teachers focus on identifying students' strengths expressly to exaggerate individual differences. Variation increases with exposure to the curriculum and instruction offered at Juilliard.

Over the years, Juilliard has added significantly to the number of performance opportunities available to all students. Singers can be featured in art songs or in arias, whereas instrumentalists and composers can play in chamber music and orchestra venues. In the course of this exposure, some students stand out as having distinct star power.

The reality of star power forces certain choices on the institution and its students. First, the school must strike a balance between its responsibility to fulfill each student's need for some public exposure and the need that developing stars have for exercising increasingly challenging repertoire. In contrast to an earlier era when stars were featured at the expense of other students, the current ethos is one of "paying dues." Students who have been in the program longest get first "dibs" on performance opportunities whenever possible. Rules have also been instituted whereby winners of a concerto competition may not compete again during their degree program at Juilliard. Efforts to make performance opportunities more equitable are offset for the stars by the reality that many of them perform regularly both inside and outside the school in a variety of venues.

Studio teachers tailor their lessons for stars to include more advanced material and more directed career advising, such as what opportunities are out there and when to go for them. Classroom teachers accommodate student stars by enrolling those who pass placement examinations into more advanced sections of theory and ear training, and may arrange for tutoring or coaching students who miss sessions because they are "concertizing."

Teachers must also weigh the degree to which public exposure is healthy or even wise for long-term career development. Most teachers are proud of their students' success in achieving recognition both inside and outside of the institution. Others are concerned that the work required to prepare for a competition or performance, such as an intense focus over several months on mastering a program of work selected with ticket sales in mind, is not a good investment of time. Also, many instruments have limited solo repertoire, and featuring one's ability as an excellent team player may be a better way to ensure future employment. Still others claim that winning a competition has little predictive validity when it comes to future career eminence. And in late-developing talent domains like voice, there is some debate as to whether an undergraduate is wise to strain his or her still-immature instrument.

> We were talking about what happens to these very prodigious talents among singers. They can go out and work early. Some of the young artists at the Met are singing roles in their early 20s. And so in a sense we're competing with that. And we have to be realistic and give them enough to do while they're here because at this point, they can be out working. On the other hand, it can be very beneficial to them, over the long run, to nurse themselves along a little slower, and perhaps get a couple of opportunities, and yet still have a safe place to explore, and to grow, and not just suddenly expect to be full-fledged at a tender age. So with stars and singing, it's a very tricky thing. (Classroom Teacher)

> These particular gentlemen [in my studio] are going to be stars, but emotionally they are not ready. They are not mature enough. I've seen incredible transformations of people in four years. (Studio Teacher)

The general consensus of the participating faculty and administration was that the student stars tended to be among those most committed to their entire program of study. Matriculating students must meet attendance quotas (no more than 2 weeks' absence at a stretch or 8 classes in a semester) and notify the school about extended absences for outside performance obligations (a special form is completed and signed by classroom and studio teachers). Any missed classroom material must be made up, and teachers or coaches are available to help those who do not abuse the attendance policy.

> We have an excused absence form so that everybody knows [the student is] gone, so they know [the student has] to do the work in order to pass the class. Teachers do have limits beyond which will earn the student an insufficient attendance grade, so it's partly my job to persuade the student not to be gone that much and [persuade] the teacher to give the kid credit for the class if he knows the material. The tension there is that we devise classes so that class participation is a substantial part of the grade so they don't have to write tons of papers, they don't have to read tons of books each semester, a lot of the learning happens in the classroom. If they're not in the class then they do miss a large part of the value of the class. . . . But if they're going to graduate from this school it means something, and they may have to defer some of those concerts until after they have graduated, so they can satisfy the requirements, which I think are very flexible. We try to be flexible; we try to let people do what they want to do. (Administrator)

Curtis Institute of Music admits the number of students they need to fill an orchestra, and that's it. They don't have any extras and so they really don't permit people to go out and concertize because the orchestra can't function without everyone there. At Juilliard we have more students in orchestra than we need so that people can take off. We design the orchestra schedule so that no one student would ever be required to do the entire orchestra schedule. It would be inhumane. We have, let's say, 50% more than we need in one of the orchestras, so they rotate throughout. (Administrator)

How Students Respond to Student Stars

According to the administrators and teachers that we interviewed, students respond to peers in the limelight with a mixture of envy and awe, especially when cast lists or orchestra positions are posted or when students discuss whether to attend a peers' recital. Some undergraduates (one or two a year) have numerous concert engagements and powerful managers. Others are visibly active in student or faculty productions. From the perspective of faculty and staff, the degree to which students experience negative rather than positive emotion when comparing themselves to their peers is related to their maturity, self-confidence, and social skills.

> The only ones who get jealous are those that are getting left behind. There are kids who try to keep up and try to keep up, but they have bad luck, they get sick or something [else] that prevents them from practicing, or they get tendonitis. Prestige comes from having a really well rounded sense of who you are and knowing that you're valuable and having your friends love you for it. (Classroom Teacher)

> Not being a star doesn't usually lead to very great joy, unless you are the kind of person whose joy comes from being inundated by music. If the music is its own reward you can be happy [playing] in a cocktail lounge, or on a cruise ship. If the music itself is not its own reward you are going to get in trouble if you are not a star. And if you are a star you can get into trouble too. Stars do break a hand. (Classroom Teacher)

> But isn't it like that in baseball, or basketball? The team members know who are the gifted ones. And they're all good. They all can make the game happen. They can all get together and do a sing-in or an opera or something, but they know who the really gifted ones are. (Studio Teacher)

> I do sense that even though this a competitive place, those people who are on top really do earn a lot of respect from the other students, from their peers. The lesser lights are going to feel some sense of envy of that kind of accomplishment. But I think there's also a sense that those people are there because

they really are good and you have to respect what's good. It really elicits a gamut of emotions. (Administrator)

If envy or jealousy does get in the way of a student's productivity, Juilliard has a comprehensive support system in place. Professional psychological services, yoga classes, a workout room, and more informal counseling are all available. This is especially important given the competitiveness of the music world, particularly in New York City.

Those students who handle comparisons with stars the best tend to view them as peer teachers and sources of stimulation.

> I learned much more from my peers than from any of my teachers here because you really get a sense of the top level of excellence in your own age group, and that's invaluable. And the students who have the right attitude here benefit the same way. We have the Itzhak Perlmans of the future in this school right now. If you look at it as something to fear or to shun or to resent, then you're cheating yourself out of a fantastic educational opportunity. (Studio Teacher)

Even under the best circumstances some stars may feel isolated. Although stars advance beyond their peers, they still seek their peers' company. A soloist who is willing to play second violin for a student composition or serve as a dependable ensemble member is less likely to elicit negative feelings. The faculty commented on how it is smart for stars to be good citizens to maintain a positive reputation, solid friendships, and support.

Being labeled a star does not mean that you are simply a really great player. According to the interviewees, there are other factors like drive and charisma that enter into the picture as well. According to several of our participants, acquiring the label of star comes from capitalizing on whatever opportunities are made available to them, like performing with members of other departments or divisions or introducing themselves to visiting artists.

> Stars probably get some opportunities to play because they have become well known around school, having won a concerto competition, for example. Also they tend to be very motivated students who participate in a lot of projects with other students, and thus get asked to play in special performances, such as a Tully Hall chamber music program. It's not that they're necessarily given special opportunities, but they wind up taking some of the important roles. (Administrator)

There are students who come in that are obviously at a much higher level to begin with. In my class this year, there is a student who is far and away above the others. Do they envy him? For sure. They also admire him and look to him for advice and help. And he, I must say, is a great colleague and a lovely sweet kid, who's also looking to learn something there. He doesn't have an attitude, at least that I'm aware of. I've seen the other kind too. Usually the kind that is stuck up and is not quite as gifted somehow, or as interested in what's going on. It seems to me that the people who are the top achievers, the people at the very, very top tend to be so because they are interested in learning and taking advantage of any and every opportunity that crosses their path. (Studio Teacher)

These top achieving students have their goal set on moving beyond the label of *star*, toward the much-desired label of *artist*.

Dealing With Underachievers

Just as stars emerge from a cohort of talented students, so do underachievers. According to the Juilliard administration, there are one or two individuals a year who have special arrangements made to accommodate their burgeoning public concert careers. There are also one or two individuals a year that are dismissed from the program. Between these extremes, there are stars whose brilliance is recognized within the school community but not yet by the public at large and there are underachievers who become increasingly invisible to their classmates, teachers, and the administration.

> As a composer, you have to pound the pavement. You have to be a go-getter. If you are not, most likely your compositions are not going to be heard. And there are certain composers whom I haven't really heard from much all year. I encourage people to come up to me at any time, knock on the door, show me a score. I want to see all their stuff. Maybe I can point them in the right direction. I just got a call from someone who needs a composer to do a short film. I will think about it tonight and give a number out and someone will get a gig out of it. As in anything, there are hierarchical levels, even among students, about who are the foremost leaders of their group. And maybe these composers will change one day and maybe they won't. (Administrator)

Underachievement can be exhibited in either the performance dimension of the curriculum or in the classroom component (including liberal arts, ear training, and theory). Students who come unprepared for their lessons or rehearsals, do poorly on juries or orchestra auditions, or engage in difficult relationships with their studio teacher or coaches are often advised to seek another type of higher education or career path. Poor communication with a studio teacher can be devastating for the talent development process, but on occasion, a switch to another teacher has alleviated the problem.

When students fail to fulfill their classroom obligations they are recommended for tutoring by a student coach. If there is no improvement and a pattern of failure is established in either studio or classroom, a four-step process is put into place: a letter of concern, formal warning, probation, and finally, dismissal.

> We might say an underachiever is a person who doesn't belong here. So if in their jury examinations or their orchestral auditions their grades are very much at the bottom we try to encourage them to think about doing something different with their life. A friend once told me that . . . it's a whole lot easier to be a mediocre lawyer than to be a mediocre violinist, and so he became a lawyer, still plays, enjoys music. That's the kind of counseling that I try to do with people who might be described as underachievers. However, there are very talented kids who get in by playing a wonderfully intuitive audition, who don't develop once they're here. They don't work so we either have to light a fire or kick them out, and sometimes the best way to light a fire is to kick them out. Then they come back realizing that they have to do the work or else they're not going to survive. I'm the heavy. It's a task that I am pleased to do because I don't think it's unkind to make a person confront reality. I think it's the kindest thing that I can do, and if the talent isn't there it may result in them crying. I want them to know that they really need to do something else because it is going to be a frustration for the rest of their lives. I think it's immoral to allow them to go through four years of school knowing that when they graduate they are not going to be able to get a job. (Administrator)

A less dramatic display of underachievement that frustrates the faculty comes in the form of insufficient intellectual curiosity. They speculate that the problem develops from preoccupation with performance goals, or from a kind of mental inertia that precludes stretching into other disciplines, although it might better inform musical performance.

> Lots of faculty members are saying the same thing. They'll say that the standard of playing is higher than it's ever been. Chamber ensemble sounds better than it ever did. The orchestra sounds better than it ever did, but they're not intellectually curious or imaginative. We have lots of classes filled with students for whom the idea of going out and experiencing on your own is not part of the learning experience. (Classroom Teacher)

> I told the students to meet me at the gallery the next week instead of in the classroom. Out of a class of 24 people, only 4 of them had ever been to SoHo [a district in New York with many art galleries]. Mind you, these are kids who are 22 years old and have lived in New York for at least four years. Most of this class had never been below 57th street, because 57th street is where Carnegie Hall is. (Classroom Teacher)

Unlike student stars, underachievers may not introduce themselves to a guest artist visiting a class, or grab any opportunity to make some kind of connection. Nor are they hungry to capture one of the few performance dates available for optional and extra student performances in the various halls in the building.

Our interviewees expressed the opinion that underachievers who persist in their behavior by the second year jury examination, despite intervention, should be counseled out of the school. However, the school ethos is that if a student was sufficiently talented to be accepted, every effort should be made to help that person be successful.

Students' Reactions to Underachieving Classmates

The long hours and high stress of a rigorous conservatory curriculum can enhance the bonds among students. Although stars can elicit feelings of envy and awe, the underachievers do not appear to be held in contempt, according to the faculty and staff. The line is drawn, however, when behavior disrupts the learning or performance quality of other students. Disturbance can come in various forms, even with inconsiderate dormitory conditions.

> I think they get frustrated with each other when they feel like someone's being disruptive and interfering in terms of their achievement. For example, over in the residence hall we try to maintain an environment that's conducive to performance excellence and academic success, which means that we have quiet hours and visitation hours. We don't want an environment where the students can't get enough sleep because people are being loud and being disrespectful. And when that kind of thing happens, they do lose their patience with their peers. They expect their peers to be understanding that, "Look, I've got a major performance tomorrow, and I need some peace and quiet. I expect you to give it to me, because you, of all people, should understand what I'm going through because you're a performing artist too." They do confront each other, or come and talk to us about somebody's not being cooperative, or somebody's being disruptive and how it's affecting them. (Administrator)

In nonstudio classes, students expect that standards for class are maintained even when one is not interested. In studio class, some students resent listening to students who have not prepared, and ensemble members do not appreciate a participant who has not rehearsed his or her part.

> If you are in a [university] classroom and you are not prepared, you are the only one who suffers the consequences, but if you are part of a debate team, that is an entirely different situation. If you are in an ensemble and you do not know your part, you may compromise the performance of the ensemble. In the worst case, if the ensemble is canceled because of this, no one gets to per-

form. We have a small department and may not have someone able to replace the person who is ill prepared. These situations come up, and we are trying to find ways to deal fairly with the issues created by them. A consequence might be loss of coaching privileges, not being able to participate in special events, etc. We want to keep the good will of the students who are prepared and help the others meet their responsibilities by finding out the reasons for the problem, offering help, setting standards, and having consequences for certain actions. (Studio Teacher)

Our interviewees believe that poor performance in the classroom or studio can result from excess stress, a change of heart about one's life goals, an inappropriate match with a teacher, or a mismatch between the values of the student and the institution. Put into perspective, however, the incidence of underachievement is small and must be viewed relative to the enormous achievement motivation of the student body.

APPLICATIONS OF THE CONSERVATORY MODEL TO THE EDUCATION OF ELITE TALENT IN THE ACADEMIC DISCIPLINES

As a world-renowned conservatory with a long history of preparing elite musicians, the philosophies and practices of Juilliard raise important questions regarding the preparation of elite talent in other domains. The purpose of this study was to explore the critical variables that contribute to the transformation of extraordinary talent in music into professional artistry. The study follows in the footsteps of explorations conducted in the sciences with Westinghouse Science Talent Search winners (Subotnik & Steiner, 1994), with high-IQ children grown up (Subotnik, Kassan, Summers, & Wasser, 1993), and with the Juilliard Pre-College Program (Subotnik, 2000). In each case, an argument is made for more rigorous and individualized teaching and learning based on extraordinary strengths and deep interests. The conservatory model would be inappropriate for most undergraduate students. Only a select few commit themselves to a particular career path on entry and stay involved in preparing for that career by investing a large proportion of their adolescence to furthering these pursuits. The proposed adaptations are offered for working with undergraduate students who meet the following two criteria: *talent of sufficiently high caliber to be judged equivalent to the talent exhibited by Juilliard students and a desire to pursue an academic discipline deeply, possibly as a life's work.* I argue that patterned after the success of the conservatory with equally gifted students of the same age, academically gifted students should receive doctoral type instruction during their undergraduate years. Some suggestions for implementation follow.

8. TRANSFORMING ELITE MUSICIANS

Employ Some Form of Audition for Purposes of Admission

Auditions have advantages and disadvantages. Their primary advantage is that candidates are asked to display skills and talents directly related to the program for which they are applying. Second, there are no secrets about the preparation that is involved, because the requirements are made explicit. Most teachers who work with advanced students develop their instruction around this repertoire. There are no surprises, and no real way to cheat.

For example, Juilliard requires its undergraduate violin applicants to prepare the following for their audition:

- A fast and slow movement from any concerto in the standard repertoire.
- Any movement from a Bach unaccompanied sonata or partita. No repeats please, unless ornamented. A dance section and its double constitute one movement.
- Two contrasting brilliant concert pieces.
- One Paganini Caprice and one study from Rode, Gavinies, Dont Op. 35, Wieniawski Op. 10, or Paganini Op. 1.
- Major and minor scales and arpeggios in three octaves with double stops.
- One piece of the preceding must have been composed since 1939. Memorization of music since 1939 is encouraged but optional. All other compositions must be memorized except for duo sonatas. Please minimize piano accompaniment interludes (application supplement to the Juilliard School Viewbook, p. 10).

In preparation for the audition, there are certainly many decisions to be made by both teacher and student about which pieces to choose to highlight a person's strengths. This process of selection can be of vast learning value.

Auditions also have drawbacks. They are certainly subjective. Candidates can be disregarded if their appearance or manner seem off-putting. Biases against certain groups can also come to the fore with little accountability for the decisions made. Second, once the top candidates are selected, audition teams may fill open slots with those who are sufficiently pleasing to most but not necessarily exciting to any.

Juilliard has dealt with these drawbacks in the following ways: One is to deliver clear messages from the administration that a supremely talented yet diverse student body is welcome and desired. The other is to limit the number of undergraduates that are admitted to those who are sufficiently talented and prepared to benefit from the program. If any available slots remain in a department, they are filled with a qualified graduate student.

Students who are mathematically or scientifically gifted, who have been participating in research projects, summer institutes, and camps, could be invited to "audition" with department members at universities, rather than or in addition to interviews conducted with the admissions staff. Modeled after the Intel Talent Search, students who are extraordinarily talented in academics could be admitted to an institution on the basis of a two-step process. First, submit samples of their work to the faculty in the discipline they hope to pursue. Second, provide a brief oral presentation to the faculty on what they have been learning and problems they would like to tackle. This approach is used regularly with doctoral students and is especially helpful in matching students with professors who are working in related areas. In evaluating a student's submitted work and presentation, the department would need to consider what resources are available in the program to fortify student weaknesses and develop unique strengths.

**Each Student Is Viewed as a Unique Challenge
With Their Own Profile of Skills, Talents, Personality, and
Intellectual Acuity and Interests**

Too much energy, emotion, and time can be wasted on competition with others within a teacher's studio or a professor's laboratory. Comparisons are inevitable, but self-flagellation is not. Two aspects of the Juilliard program that help to alleviate this difficult situation include individualizing instruction in the studio and offering seminars geared to inculcating practical intelligence. The studio teachers interviewed for this study say they love to teach. They view each student as a challenge, and they are held accountable for their students' success by way of juries, concerto competitions, job placements, and the number of new students that wish to join their studio. They are motivated to help nurture the artistry of their students so their students can be successful in the deeply competitive music performance world.

Professional critics, managers, tax lawyers, and performers meet with students in each department by way of explicit practical knowledge seminars. As described in the interviews, students are reminded that their classmates are to be treasured. They are current and future friends, supporters, and teachers. They may also someday be a source of employment. Learning to be gracious at all times and under all circumstances is a goal that students are asked to consider.

In the academic world, individualization would be welcome to undergraduates. The elite group of Westinghouse Science Talent Search winners that I studied encountered large and anonymous classes in mathematics and science at their universities of choice. By the end of the sophomore year, a third had left science and mathematics. Some were attracted by other disciplines, and have pursued rewarding careers in those areas. Others might have left because they were not able to keep up with the material. Yet, to win the Westinghouse Science Talent Search, they had spent their high school summers and afternoons in close contact with professors and graduate students, often on the frontiers of a science subspecialty. Once they got to college, a distinct number of winners were turned off by the inaccessibility of meaningful laboratory opportunities until they were juniors, seniors, or even graduate students.

As for the practical knowledge gained from the explicit seminars on career related topics, Sternberg et. al. (2000) has provided ample support for how this knowledge contributes to the success of individuals in different fields. Certainly the socialization process could be made more consistently available to gifted students. It is especially healthy for students to understand the growing role played by personality, charisma, and drive in creating stars, not only at Juilliard but in every field. Specific practice in interviewing, making presentations, networking, teamwork, problem selection, solution selection, and time management would be invaluable to young scholars. Too often in the university setting this information is provided haphazardly by mentors. Access to this information is too important to career success to be left to chance.

Regular Opportunities for Public Demonstration of Learned Skills and Creative Work Should Be Available

Young talented scholars should be able to display their skills publicly in a variety of venues. There is no reason why institutional research seminars and roundtables should be solely in the purview of graduate students and postdocs. Every opportunity to speak publicly about one's work helps to clarify one's own thinking and to inform others about new and exciting ideas. Student stars should be encouraged to make co-authored or even single authored conference presentations and follow up with publication.

Annual juries are one way that student skills are displayed at the conservatory. The entire faculty from the department attends these examinations and gives a grade to the student. Novice scholars could benefit from an annual jury of their skills and ideas evaluated by all the members of the department. The institution would also benefit by the "cross-pollination" bound to result from hearing what is developing in the labs and the classrooms within a department. An even better idea, particularly in the academic realm, would be to provide written feedback on those presentations. Students who have poor juries for 2 years in a row, who cannot keep up even after receiving coaching and assistance, disrupt the learning of others, or show a lack of commitment should be counseled out of the program. Stepping back into a broader liberal arts program might be more suitable for an academically gifted student who is not yet ready to focus on one area in such depth.

Focusing on one area should not preclude creative and meaningful interactions with talented students and their professors in related disciplines. The enrichment and insights that can be gained from interdisciplinary projects parallel the path musicians make to achieve artistry. The path to transformational scholarship would also be enhanced by such exposure.

Broadcast the Talents and Creative Productivity of the Faculty and Encourage Students to Apply to Programs Based on That Information

Our colleges and universities need to promote the talents of their faculty to undergraduates considering their programs. Students should be coming to higher education with a sophisticated knowledge of their professors' work. College teachers appear in public forums, and their work is available in libraries and on the Web. I have often wondered why there were so few guides and Web sites that offer background information about faculty to prospective undergraduate students who have clear career goals. The internet provides an opportunity for highly talented mathematics and science students to read the work published by various potential faculty mentors, and to contact other students who have interacted with them in the labs. Academic faculty at undergraduate institutions share intriguing lineages just like their conservatory peers; they are also entitled to the veneration that accompanies the special relationship between student and teacher in the performing arts world.

In the course of this research, I was especially fascinated with the terminology tagging the different stages of talent development in the music world: one moved from being an instrumentalist to being a *musician*. If one's performance and contributions were truly transformational, then one could be called an *artist*. In the academic world, the parallel might go from *student*, to *academic*, to *scholar*. The goal of this chapter was to highlight some features of the process of talent development in classical musical performance so that we might consider adapting them to our academic settings. After my immersion in the world of Juilliard, I will never again hear a performance without thinking of the effort, time, and passion that went into it. Nor will I advise a gifted student without remembering the lessons learned from the conservatory.

APPENDIX 1: INTERVIEW QUESTIONS:

- How did you end up at Juilliard?
- What are your responsibilities?
- What is your primary mission in fulfilling your responsibilities?
- Please provide some commentary on the curriculum beyond the traditional conservatory offerings.
- How much freedom do teachers have in instructional style and strategies?
- How are faculty recruited?
- What factors make up elite level musical talent?
- Which of those factors do you consider to be trainable at Juilliard?
- Please provide some comments about the audition process including anything you know about outreach.
- Please provide comments about placement of new students with studio teachers.
- How are "stars" accommodated at Juilliard?
- In your experience, how do students respond to the "stars?"
- How are underachievers dealt with?
- In your experience, how do students respond to the underachievers?

REFERENCES

Bamberger, J. (1986). Cognitive issues in the development of musically talented children. In R. J. Sternberg & J. E. Davidson (Eds.), *Conceptions of giftedness* (pp. 388–413). New York: Cambridge University Press.

Bloom, B. S. (1985). Generalizations about talent development. In B. S. Bloom (Ed.), *Developing talent in young people* (pp. 507–549). New York: Ballantine.

Gagne, F. (1999). Nature or nurture: An examination of Sloboda and Howe's (1991) interview study on talent development in music. *Psychology of Music, 27*, 38–51.

Haroutounian, J. (2000). The delights and dilemmas of the musically talented teenager. *Journal of Secondary Gifted Education, 12*, 3–16.

Hertz, R., & Imber, J. B. (1995). *Studying elites using qualitative methods.* Thousand Oaks, CA: Sage.

Kingsbury, H. (1988). *Music, talent, and performance: A conservatory cultural system.* Philadelphia, PA: Temple University Press.

Kogan, J. (1987). *Nothing but the best: The struggle for perfection at The Juilliard School.* New York: Random House.

Olmstead, A. (1999). *Juilliard: A history.* Urbana: University of Illinois.

Persson, R. S., (1996). Studying with a musical maestro: A case study of commonsense teaching in artistic training. *Creativity Research Journal, 9*, 33–46.

Persson, R. S. & Robsin, C. (1995). The limits of experimentation: On researching music and musical settings. *Psychology of Music, 23,* 39–47.

Piirto, J. (1998). *Understanding those who create* (2nd ed.) Scottsdale, AZ: Gifted Psychology Press.

Sand, B. L. (2000). *Teaching genius: Dorothy DeLay and the making of a musician.* Portland, OR: Amadeus.

Schmidt, C. P., & Andrews, M. L. (1996). Case study of a first year university voice major: A multidisciplinary perspective. *Psychology of Music, 24,* 237–243.

Seymour, E., & Hewitt, N. M. (1994). *Talking about leaving: Factors contributing to high attrition rates among science, mathematics, and engineering undergraduate majors.* Boulder: Bureau of Sociological Research, University of Colorado.

Shuter-Dyson, R. (1985). Musical giftedness. In J. Freeman (Ed.), *The psychology of gifted children* (pp. 159–183). Chichester, UK: Wiley.

Sloboda, J. A., & Howe, M. J. A. (1991). Biographical precursors of musical excellence: An interview study. *Psychology of Music, 19,* 3–21.

Sosniak, L. (1985). Phases of learning. In B. S. Bloom (Ed.), *Developing talent in young people* (pp. 409–438). New York: Ballantine.

Sternberg, R. J., Forsythe, G. B., Hedlund, J., Horvath, J. A., Wagner, R. K., Williams, W. M., Snook, S. A., & Grigorenko, E. (2000). *Practical intelligence in everyday life.* New York: Cambridge University Press.

Subotnik, R. F. (1995). Conversations with masters in the arts and sciences: Midori. *Journal for the Education of the Gifted, 18,* 339–351.

Subotnik, R. F. (1997). Conversations with masters in the arts and sciences: Vladimir Feltsman. *Journal for the Education of the Gifted, 20,* 306–317.

Subotnik, R. F. (2000). The Juilliard model for developing young adolescent performers: An educational prototype. In C. F. M. van Lieshout & P. G. Heymans (Eds.), *Developing talent across the lifespan* (pp. 249–276). Hove, UK: Psychology Press.

Subotnik, R. F., & Arnold, K. D. (1995). Passing through the gates: Career establishment of talented women scientists. *Roeper Review, 18*(1), 55–61.

Subotnik, R. F., & Coleman, L. J. (1996). Establishing the foundations for a talent development school: Applying principles to creating an ideal. *Journal for the Education of the Gifted, 20,* 175–189.

Subotnik, R. F., Duschl, R., & Selmon, E. (1993). Retention and attrition of science talent: A longitudinal study of Westinghouse Science Talent Search winners. *International Journal of Science Education, 15*(1), 61–72.

Subotnik, R. F., Kassan, L., Summers, E., & Wasser, A. (1993). *Genius revisited: High IQ children grown up.* Norwood, NJ: Ablex.

Subotnik, R. F., Maurer, K., & Steiner, C. L. (2001). Tracking the next generation of the scientific elite. *Journal of Secondary Gifted Education, 13,* 33–43.

Subotnik, R. F., & Steiner, C. L. (1994). Adult manifestations of adolescent talent in science: A longitudinal study of 1983 Westinghouse Science Talent Search winners. In R. F. Subotnik & K. D. Arnold (Eds.) *Beyond Terman: Contemporary longitudinal studies of giftedness and talent* (pp. 52–76). Norwood, NJ: Ablex.

Winner, E. (1996). *Gifted children: Myths and realities.* New York: Basic Books.

Zuckerman, H. (1996). *Scientific elite: Nobel laureates in the United States* (2nd ed.). New Brunswick, NJ: Transaction.

Part IV

EXTRACOGNITIVE ASPECTS OF HIGH ABILITY AND THE IDEAL ENDS OF DEVELOPMENT

Chapter 9

Wisdom and Giftedness*

Robert J. Sternberg
Yale University

Some people are never forgotten. What they are remembered for is not their gifts, but the gifts they gave to the world. If we ask what distinguishes four such extremely gifted individuals of the twentieth century—Mahatma Gandhi, Mother Teresa, Martin Luther King, and Nelson Mandela—we could safely conclude that it is not the kind of giftedness measured by conventional tests of intelligence. The kind of wisdom these individuals share is not even captured by broader theories of intelligence. For example, these individuals may all have been high in interpersonal intelligence (Gardner, 1983), but so was Adolph Hitler. Hitler was certainly able to understand crowds and was masterful at imposing his will on people. Wisdom also is different from social intelligence (Cantor & Kihlstrom, 1987) and emotional intelligence (Goleman, 1995; Salovey & Mayer, 1990). Like practical intelligence, these kinds of intelligence may be used to further one's own interests to the exclusion of or even systematically against the interests of others.

My own triarchic theory of intelligence and intellectual giftedness (Sternberg, 1984, 1985, 1997, 1999) equally fails to capture what distinguishes the four individuals. They all may have been analytically gifted, in

---

*Preparation of this article was supported by Grant REC-9979843 from the National Science Foundation and by a grant under the Javits Act Program (Grant No. R206R950001) as administered by the Office of Educational Research and Improvement, U.S. Department of Education. Grantees undertaking such projects are encouraged to express freely their professional judgment. This article, therefore, does not necessarily represent the position or policies of the National Science Foundation, Office of Educational Research and Improvement or the U.S. Department of Education, and no official endorsement should be inferred.

the sense that they would achieve high scores on IQ tests. But probably they would hardly compare in IQ with analytical geniuses like Sir Isaac Newton, John Stuart Mill, or Albert Einstein. They all may have been creative (showing signs of what Renzulli [1984] has called "creative-productive giftedness"). But there is, again, no sign that they would compare with Chaucer or Dante in the field of literature, Mozart or Tchaikovsky in the field of music, or Pasteur or Darwin in the field of science. They did not leave behind stunning works of literature, music, science, philosophy, or similar achievements. They were enormously practically gifted, but so have been Saddam Hussein and Mobutu Sese Seku, wily men who devised ways to stay in power and to maintain absolute control in the face of enormous odds. These examples point out that practical intelligence can be used to further exclusively one's own ends or the ends of those with whom one is intimately connected. Wisdom never can be used in this way. High-level practical intelligence may lead to success in life according to traditional standards, but wisdom may be a key to satisfaction and contentment in life according to one's own standards, although certainly it is not the only key. Practical intelligence and wisdom are related: It will be argued here that practical intelligence is necessary but not sufficient for wisdom.

Most importantly, these people were probably not, in their careers, at the top of the IQ scale, and *no one cared*. No one pretended that what made them gifted was their stellar IQs. Finding out that Mother Teresa's IQ was high, medium, or low would give us no real insight into what it was that made her gifted in what she had to offer to the world. And to the extent that we view giftedness as not only a gift received, but also, as a gift one has to bestow upon the world, IQ seems woefully incomplete as an index of who is gifted in some important sense.

The kind of giftedness people like Mahatma Gandhi, Mother Teresa, Martin Luther King, and Nelson Mandela have in common, then, appears to be one of wisdom, rather than of intelligence either as traditionally defined or as defined in more modern theories. Indeed, human intelligence has, to some extent, brought the world to the brink. Intelligence has brought us many good things, but also has brought us the nuclear weapons that have the power to destroy the world several times over as well as the addictive designer drugs that are destroying the lives of millions of people—young and old— around the world. Human intelligence has brought us where we are. It may take wisdom to help us find our way out of a trap of our own making.

THE NATURE OF WISDOM

Wisdom can be defined as the "power of judging rightly and following the soundest course of action, based on knowledge, experience, understanding, and so forth" (*Webster's New World College Dictionary*, p. 1533), but dictionary definitions usually do not suffice for psychological understanding. In the case of the dictionary definition of wisdom, it is not even clear what it means to judge "rightly." A number of scholars have attempted to approach wisdom in different ways, both philosophical (see Robinson, 1990) and psychological. Alternative approaches are summarized in Sternberg (1990, 1998) and in Baltes and Staudinger (2000). Some theorists of intelligence and learning, such Guilford (1967) and Bloom (1985), have discussed the importance of evaluative skills in high or gifted levels of intelligence, and these skills may provide one kind of link between intelligence and wisdom.

The approach to wisdom proposed here is taken by Sternberg (1998). This notion of wisdom starts with the construct of tacit knowledge (Polanyi, 1976) about oneself, others, and situational contexts. Tacit knowledge comprises the lessons of life that are not explicitly taught and that often are not even verbalized (Sternberg et al., 2000; Sternberg, Wagner, Williams, & Horvath, 1995). Tacit knowledge thus has three main features:

1. it is procedural;
2. it is relevant to the attainment of goals people value; and
3. it typically is acquired through experience or mentoring rather than through direct classroom or textbook instruction.

An example of tacit knowledge is one's procedural knowledge of how to write and present a book chapter such as this one in an effective way. Most people never learn such skills in a course: They pick up the skills from experience.

Tacit knowledge forms an essential component of practical intelligence, and indeed, the particular notion of tacit knowledge used here derives from the triarchic theory of intelligence (Sternberg, 1985, 1997, 1999). An advantage of the proposed theory is that it is linked to a theory of intelligence (the triarchic one) at the same time that it makes explicit how wisdom is different from the triarchic (analytical, creative, and practical) aspects of intelligence as they typically are encountered.

Although tacit knowledge is acquired within a domain, it more typically applies to a field—a distinction made by Csikszentmihalyi (1988, 1996). Csikszentmihalyi refers to the domain as the formal knowledge of a socially defined field. So, for example, knowing how to construct, conduct, or analyze the results of experiments would be knowledge important to the *domain* of experimental psychology. But knowing how to speak about the results persuasively, how to get the results published, or knowing how to turn the results into the next grant proposal would constitute knowledge of the *field*. Thus, academic intelligence would seem to apply primarily in the domain, whereas practical intelligence, in general, and wisdom, in particular, would seem to apply primarily in the field. Because the field represents the social organization of the domain, it is primarily in the field that intrapersonal, interpersonal, and extrapersonal interactions take place.

The greater importance of the field rather than of the domain to wisdom helps to clarify why tacit, informal knowledge rather than explicit formal knowledge is the main basis of wisdom. Formal knowledge about the subject matter of a discipline is certainly essential to expertise in that discipline (Chi, Glaser, & Farr, 1988; Hoffman, 1992) but domain-based expertise is neither necessary nor sufficient for wisdom. All of us know domain-based experts who seem unwise. At least some of us also know very wise individuals who have little formal education. Their education is in the "school of life," which is in the acquisition of tacit (informal) knowledge.

The argument, then, is that intelligence, broadly defined, is important for giftedness, but so is wisdom. One needs creative abilities to come up with ideas. One needs analytical abilities to decide whether one's own ideas (and those of others) are good ideas. One needs practical abilities to make ideas functional and to persuade other people of the value of these ideas. But one needs wisdom to balance the effects of one's ideas not just on oneself, but on others and on institutions as well, both in the short and the long terms.

Even an intuitive analysis suggests that wisdom is separate from analytical, creative, and practical abilities. By all accounts, Richard Nixon was extremely intelligent in a traditional sense, but so unwise was he that he ended up having to resign his presidency. Bill Clinton, a graduate of Yale and Oxford (as a Rhodes Scholar), also came close to losing his position. Joseph Mengele, the Nazi physician, was certainly creative, in an extremely perverse sense, but was unwise by any reasonable standard. Less extreme, William Shockley was creative enough to win a Nobel Prize for his invention of the transistor, but nevertheless, he was a foolish racist with hare-brained theories that no responsible behavioral scientist took seriously. And Fidel Castro has outlasted Nixon, Clinton, and everyone in-between (not to mention Kennedy and Johnson), and yet, he seems less than wise. Wisdom is something different, and perhaps, something more.

THE BALANCE THEORY OF WISDOM

Wisdom as Tacit Knowledge Used for Balancing Interests

The definition of wisdom proposed here (see Fig. 9.1) draws both on the notion of tacit knowledge, as described earlier, and on the notion of balance, a notion going back at least to Aristotle. In particular, wisdom is defined as the application of tacit knowledge as mediated by values toward the

9. WISDOM AND GIFTEDNESS 173

Goal

```
                    ┌─────────────┐
                    │ Common Good │
                    └─────────────┘
                           ⇧

                       Adaptation
Balance of Responses to        ╱╲
Environmental Context         ╱  ╲                  V
                             ╱    ╲         ⇐       A
                            ╱      ╲                L
                           ╱        ╲               U
                    Shaping  ⇧  Selection           E
                                                    S
                       Extrapersonal       ⇐

                           ╱╲
Balance of Interests      ╱  ╲
Over the Short- and      ╱    ╲
Long-term               ╱      ╲
                       ╱        ╲
                Intrapersonal ⇧ Interpersonal

                ┌──────────────────────────┐
                │ Tacit Knowledge Underlying│
                │   Practical Intelligence │
                └──────────────────────────┘
```

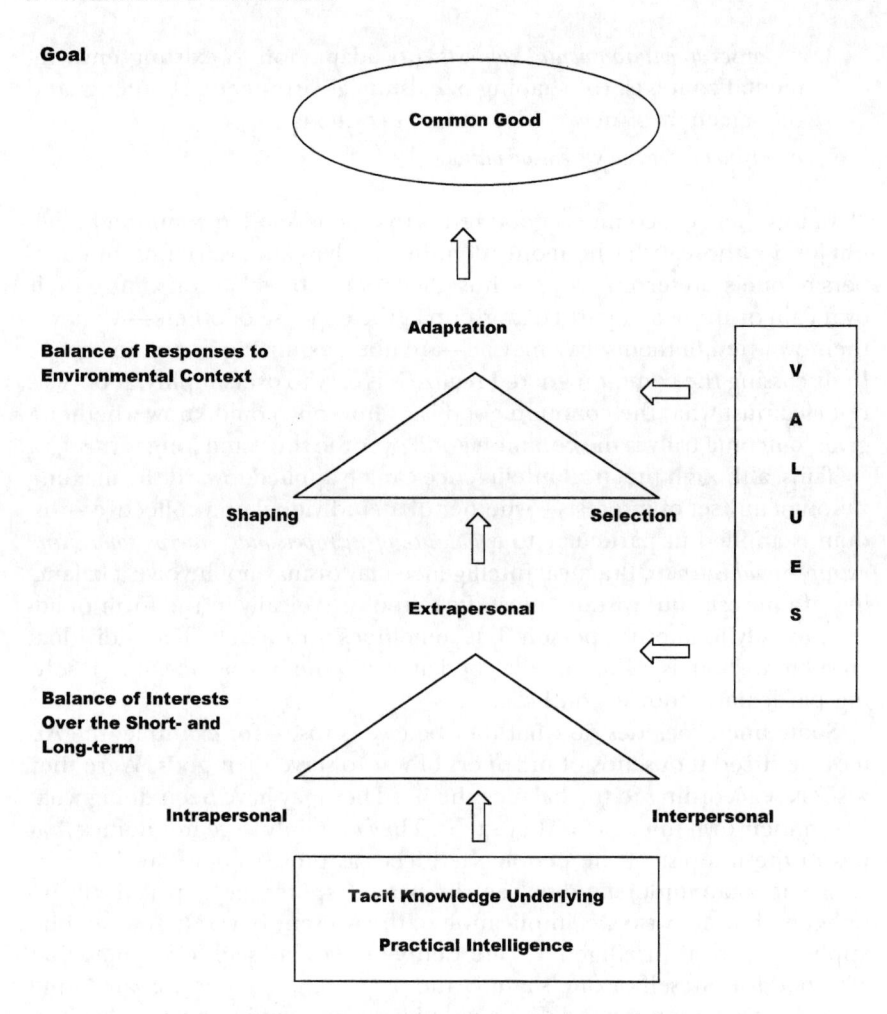

FIG. 9.1. A balance theory of wisdom. Tacit knowledge underlying practical intelligence is applied to balance intrapersonal, interpersonal, and extrapersonal interests to achieve a balance of the responses to the environmental context of adaptation to, shaping of, and selection of environments in order to achieve a common good. Values mediate how people use their tacit knowledge in balancing interests and responses.

goal of achieving a common good. This good is achieved through a balance among multiple

1. *interests:* (a) intrapersonal, (b) interpersonal, and (c) extrapersonal in order to achieve a balance
2. *over time:* (a) short-term and (b) long-term, among

3. *responses to environmental contexts:* (a) adaptation to existing environmental contexts, (b) shaping of existing environmental contexts, and (c) selection of new environmental contexts
4. *as influenced by a system of values*

In this theory, a common good refers to what is good in common for all, not just for those with whom one identifies, such as family, friends, or members of one's preferred group. Thus, dictators who seek to maximize their own gain or those of a particular group at the expense of others—whatever their own view of themselves may be—are not maximizing a common good. In discussing the common good, I realize it is easy to oversimplify: It often is not clear just what the common good is or how one could know whether a given outcome truly is the common good over the short and long terms.

Thus, although practical intelligence can be applied toward the maximization of any set of interests—whether of an individual or a collective—wisdom is applied in particular to a *balance of intrapersonal, interpersonal, and extrapersonal interests.* Practical intelligence may or may not involve a balancing of interests, but wisdom must. Its output is typically in the form of advice, usually to another person, but sometimes for oneself. The individual gifted in wisdom is exceptionally good at giving the best advice or at resolving particularly thorny conflicts.

Sometimes, societies do what they believe is wise—for example, the Aztecs sacrificed thousands of prisoners of war to serve their gods. Were they wise? Not according to the balance theory. They may have been doing what was in their own interest, as they saw it. They certainly were not doing what was in the interest of the people sacrificed, as those people saw it.

We now can understand better why cruel despots may be practically intelligent, but not wise. An implication of the present view is that when one applies practical intelligence, one deliberately may seek outcomes that are good for oneself or one's family and friends that may at the same time be bad for a common good. For example, despots exhibit practical intelligence by managing to control an entire country largely for their own benefit. Hitler or Stalin may have balanced factors in their judgments, but *not* for a common good. Their policies may have been in support of a common good for a preferred group (e.g., supposed "Aryans"), but were not in support of the common good for those outside their preferred group (e.g., Jews, Gypsies, people with physical disabilities) as these others saw things.

One also may apply practical intelligence to maximize someone else's benefit, as does a lawyer. In the subset of practical intelligence that is wisdom, one certainly may seek good ends for oneself (intrapersonal interests), but one also seeks to balance them with good outcomes for others (interpersonal interests) and with the contextual factors (extrapersonal

9. WISDOM AND GIFTEDNESS

interests) involved. The balance among interests determines adapting, shaping, and selecting environments.

Problems requiring wise solutions always involve at least some element of intrapersonal, interpersonal, and extrapersonal interests, although the weights may be different in different instances, just as they may be different for adaptation, shaping, and selection. The gifted individual weighs interests especially well. Thus, although traditional concepts of giftedness emphasize amounts on one or more scales, the concept of giftedness in wisdom emphasizes balance in judgment. For example, one might decide that it is wise to go to college, a problem that seemingly involves only one person. Yet many people are affected by an individual's decision to go to college—parents, friends, significant others, children, and the like. The decision always has to be made in the context of what is the whole range of available options.

Might wisdom involve total dedication to just one pursuit, such as the pursuit of truth, justice, God, or whatever? According to the balance theory, it can if such a pursuit balances one's self-interest with the interests of others and extrapersonal factors (which can include, truth, justice, and God). A risk in such pursuits is that one loses such balance, as seems to occur in the case of religious and other extremists who kill others in the belief that they are somehow serving truth, justice, or God. In this case, the extremists have lost focus on the need to take others' interests into account as well.

In making the decision, one selects a future environment, and in doing so, adapts to and shapes one's current environment, as well as the environments of others. Similarly, a decision about whether to have an abortion requires wisdom because it involves not only oneself, but also the fetus that will not be born, others to whom one is close such as the father, and the rules and customs of the society. One is profoundly adapting to, shaping, and selecting the environment, both for oneself and for a potential infant. In each case, one might make a practically intelligent decision for oneself without balancing interests. But for the decision to be wise, it must take into account other interests and seek a common good.

The ultimate test of whether a judgment is wise is how the judgment is made, as much as in what the judgment is. Two individuals can come to different conclusions but both be wise if they fulfill the criteria specified by the balance theory in their judgmental information processing. For example, religious leaders of different faiths may have different belief systems and yet be comparably wise. At the same time, for the decisions to be wise, they must truly represent the common good.

It is worth emphasizing that interpersonal and extrapersonal values *never* disappear in the theory—they are always weighted in the balance, no matter how difficult or stressful a situation may be. The balance is part of why people give their lives for their countries, their religious beliefs, their children, or whatever. According to the balance theory, thinking is *unwise* when, due to expediency, one removes from the balance others and institutions. Once this door to removing others or institutions is opened, people quickly find reasons to consider only their self-interest.

Consider further the nature of adaptation, shaping, and selection. In adaptation, the individual tries to find ways to conform to the existing environment that forms his or her context. Sometimes adaptation is the best course of action under a given set of circumstances. More typically, one seeks a balance between adaptation and shaping, realizing that fitting into an environment requires not only changing oneself, but changing the environment as well. When an individual finds it impossible or at least implausible to attain such a fit, he or she may decide to select a new environment altogether, leaving, for example, a job, a community, a marriage, or whatever. Again, balance rather than sheer amount is crucial to wisdom.

Finally, wise decisions are always made in the context of a set of values. In studying wisdom, one is studying an integration of mental abilities with values. This integration is, in part, why it is impossible to specify objectively "wise" decisions. Should one sacrifice one's family for one's country, or one's life for one's family, or one's country for one's ideology? These questions can only be addressed within the context of a system of values. Historically, it has been a major purpose of the world's religions to teach systems of values. Although there is much correspondence among these systems of values, the correspondence is not complete, so that people may come to wise decisions in the context of one set of values that seem unwise in the context of another.

Processes Underlying Wisdom

Underlying wisdom is a series of processes. Among these processes are what I have referred to as "metacomponents" (Sternberg, 1985, 1999), including

1. recognizing the existence of a problem,
2. defining the nature of the problem,
3. representing information about the problem,
4. formulating a strategy for solving the problem,
5. allocating resources to the solution of a problem,
6. monitoring one's solution of the problem, and
7. evaluating feedback regarding that solution.

In deciding about whether to fight one's boss on a matter of principle, for example, one has to recognize that something is wrong with the situation in the workplace, define the problem (such as the boss allowing unethical behavior), represent information (such as exactly what it is that is unethical, and according to whom), and so forth. Deciding whether to fight such behavior can be a matter requiring wise judgment: Is the perceived offense worth the battle (shaping of the environment): to oneself, to others, and to the organization?

The use of these metacomponents is a hallmark of thinking, in general (Sternberg, 1985), and they are used in all of analytical, creative, and practical thinking. What distinguishes their use in wisdom is that these processes are applied to balancing their impact on interested parties.

The balance theory suggests that wisdom is at least partially domain specific, in that tacit knowledge is acquired within a given context or set of contexts. It typically is acquired by

1. selectively encoding new information that is relevant for one's purposes in learning about that context;
2. selectively comparing this information to old information in order to see how the new fits with the old; and
3. selectively combining pieces of information in order to make them fit together into an orderly whole (Sternberg, Wagner, & Okagaki, 1993).

These processes are referred to as *knowledge-acquisition* components in the triarchic theory of intelligence (Sternberg, 1985). Again, the processes are used in all aspects of intelligence (analytical, creative, and practical). However, there is nothing peculiar to wisdom in the uses of these components, other than that the knowledge may later be used for wise purposes.

The use of metacomponents, and knowledge-acquisition components in wisdom or any other kind of practical intelligence, points out a key relationship between wisdom and intelligence (as conceptualized by the triarchic theory). All aspects of intelligence—analytical, creative, and practical—involve utilization of metacomponents for executive processing and of knowledge-acquisition components for learning. What differs is the kind of context in which they are applied. Analytic intelligence is called on for relatively familiar decontextualized, abstract, and often academic kinds of situations. Creative intelligence is called on for relatively unfamiliar, novel kinds of situations. Practical intelligence is called on for highly contextualized situations encountered in the normal course of one's daily life. Wisdom applies *only* to highly contextualized situations. It does not apply to all of the kinds of abstract situations to which one might apply one's intelligence (e.g., in the context of ability-test or achievement-test problems) or one's creativity (e.g., in formulating original, high-quality, but abstract ideas). On intelligence tests, there may be better and worse answers in the sense of certain answers being more justifiable on logical or other grounds. But there are not answers that are wiser or less wise. The concept simply does not apply.

Consider a concrete, if extreme example of the difference between practical intelligence and wisdom. An individual becomes a government official with the hope of financial gain from his position. He quickly learns how by accepting contributions from wealthy supporters; he quickly can become rich, thereby achieving his goal of financial gain. He is at the edge of what is legal but, through expensive legal advice, always manages to stay within the dictates of the law. He is pleased to see how politics can be mixed with financial success. During his term in office, he shows up for the necessary meetings but does little else. He leaves office having contributed little to his country but a lot to his bank account. This individual has been practically intelligent, in that he has found a way to manipulate the environment to achieve his own goals. But he has not been wise, because he has used his position only to advance his own interests and not those of his constituents. Thus he has achieved his goals at the expense of their legitimate hopes that he would work for their benefit. Although he has done nothing illegal, he has deprived his constituents of representation that would have benefited them. He has looked out for his own interests, but not those of others or of his country. In terms of the balance theory, he has emphasized intrapersonal interests at the expense of interpersonal and extrapersonal ones.

People who acquire wisdom in one context may be those who would be well able to develop it in another context, but the tacit knowledge needed to be wise in different contexts may differ. For example, the wise individual in one society may be able to give useful advice in the context of that society. But the same advice might be suicidal in another society (e.g., to criticize a governmental policy as it applies to a particular individual). Thus, the ability to be wise may transfer, but the actual content of wise advice may vary. A wise person will therefore know not only when to give advice, but when not to (see Meacham, 1990), because the individual will know the limitations of his or her own tacit knowledge. Giftedness in wisdom is thus a function of how one makes judgments rather than of the particular judgments one makes.

The Role of Values

In discussing wisdom (as well as practical intelligence, in general), there is no escape from values. As shown in the model, values always play a major role—in terms of what constitutes a common good, in terms of what constitutes an acceptable balance among interests, and in terms of what constitutes an adequate balance among adaptation, shaping, and selection of environments. Anyone's examples of the exercise of wisdom or its absence will reflect his or her own values. Those individuals who wish a construct that is value free would do best to look elsewhere. At the same time, many psychological constructs—intelligence, creativity, beauty, judgment, personality—

involve a valuing system, whether the valuing system is explicit or not. The value system must be one that seeks a common good.

It truly is impossible to speak of wisdom outside the context of a set of values, which in combination may lead one to a moral stance, or in Kohlberg's (1969, 1983) view, stage. Behavior is viewed as wise as a function of what is valued in a societal/cultural context. Values mediate how one balances interests and responses, and collectively contribute even to how one defines a common good. Wisdom is in applying processes of thought in combination with values to achieve solutions to problems that take into account a common good within a societal/cultural context, which may be as narrow as a family or as broad as the world. Although different societies may hold to different values, certain values seem to stand out as being endorsed across a whole spectrum of societies—values such as truth, honesty, sincerity, mercy, and compassion for others. Where there are conflicts between societies due in part to differences between values, part of wisdom—involving balancing interpersonal and extrapersonal interests—can involve reaching viable judgments regarding how to balance the value system of one culture with that of another.

Wisdom intersects with the moral domain and the notion of moral reasoning as it applies in the two highest stages (4 and 5) of Kohlberg's (1969) theory. At the same time, wisdom is broader than moral reasoning. It applies to any human problem involving a balance of intrapersonal, interpersonal, and extrapersonal interests, whether or not moral issues are at stake.

Sources of Developmental and Individual Differences in Wisdom

The balance theory suggests a number of sources of developmental and individual differences in wisdom. These sources determine who will be gifted with wisdom and who will not be. Of course someone may be gifted in wisdom but not so in other ways (such as in drama), or someone may be gifted in other ways but not in wisdom. There are two kinds of sources of individual differences in wisdom—those directly affecting the balance processes and those that are antecedent.

Individual and Developmental Differences Directly Affecting the Balance Processes. There are five sources of individual differences. Gifted people would have to master most or all of them.

1. *Goals.* People may differ in the extent to which they seek a common good and thus in the extent to which they aspire to wisdom. The seeking of a common good does not apply to intelligence in general, however. One

could be analytically, creatively, or even practically intelligent without looking out for the interests of others.

2. *Balancing of Responses to Environmental Contexts.* People may differ in their balance of responses of adaptation to, shaping of, and selection of environmental contexts. Responses always reflect an interaction of the individual making the judgment and the environmental context, and people can interact with contexts in myriad ways. Balancing is needed adequately to achieve one's goals.

3. *Balancing of Interests.* People may balance interests in different ways. This balancing is unique to wisdom and does not necessarily apply to analytical, creative, or common practical intelligence. Again, balancing is needed adequately to achieve one's goals.

4. *Wisdom as Deriving from Tacit Knowledge.* People bring different kinds and levels of tacit knowledge to judgmental situations, which are likely to affect their responses.

5. *Values.* People hold different values that mediate their utilization of tacit knowledge in the balancing of interests and responses.

These sources of variation differentiate how well people can apply their wisdom in different kinds of situations. Wisdom is associated with greater intellectual and even physical maturity, presumably because the development of tacit knowledge and of values is something that unfolds over the course of the lifespan, and not just in childhood or even in early years of adulthood.

Although the goal of this chapter is to express a theory rather than to present empirical data, the theory as it stands is testable and we are currently testing it. For example, it suggests that judgments made about interpersonal conflicts or organizational negotiations should be rated as more wise to the extent they take into account a common good of all stakeholders and to the extent they balance intrapersonal, interpersonal, and extrapersonal interests. Such outcomes often are *not* sought, as when parties to a divorce try only to maximize their own self-interest or when management–union negotiations are between negotiators looking out for the interests only of one party to the negotiations. The theory predicts that judgments will be rated as wise by experts to the extent they take into account these parameters of the theory.

Problems Used in Measuring Wisdom

If one looks at the kinds of problems that have been used to measure wisdom empirically, one can evaluate the degree to which they measure wisdom according to the balance theory. In our own work, we are using intrapersonal, interpersonal, and organizational-conflict situations. A life-planning task (Baltes, Staudinger, Maercker, & Smith, 1995) is also an excellent task for measuring wisdom. It involves one's own interests, but usually will take into account the interests of others about whom one cares deeply as well as the context in which one lives and in which one may live in the future. A task in which one must decide what to do when a good friend calls and says he or she wants to commit suicide (Staudinger & Baltes, 1996) would also involve the interests of the other, one's own interest in getting involved, the consequences of not being successful in persuading the individual not to commit suicide, and also the difficulty of acting in the context of an unexpected telephone call. Similarly, counseling a 14-year-old girl who is pregnant or a 16-year-old boy who wants to marry soon (Baltes & Smith, 1990) both involve balancing of the interests of the individuals to be counseled, the other people in their lives, and the costs of giving the wrong advice. But adults are not the only ones who possess wisdom. According to Harris (1998), most of the advice children receive is from other children. In their plans, children take into account other children at least as much as they take into account adults. Hence, it is all the more important for children to acquire wise ways of thinking.

Wise people recognize the limitations of plans. There is a saying that if one wishes to make God laugh, one should tell God one's plans. People who are gifted in wisdom recognize the limitations and fallibility of their own thinking.

Perhaps the ideal problems we could pose for measuring wisdom are complex conflict-resolution problems involving the formation of judgments, given multiple competing interests and no clear resolution of how these interests can be reconciled (see, e.g., Sternberg & Dobson, 1987; Sternberg & Soriano, 1984). Given the relevance of such problems, it makes sense that Baltes and his colleagues (Smith, Staudinger, & Baltes, 1994) would have found that clinical psychologists would do particularly well on wisdom-related tasks. Another group who might be expected to do well would be experienced foreign-service officers and other negotiators who have helped nations reach resolutions of their disagreements.

The wisdom of problem posing and problem solving cannot be measured adequately through some kind of objective multiple-choice or short-answer test. Rather, it can be measured by people who recognize wisdom using the balance theory as a basis for judging the wisdom of how people reach judgments. Like creativity, wisdom is in the interactions among a person, a task, and a situation, not simply in the head of a person (see Csikszentmihalyi, 1996). But wisdom differs from creativity in that wisdom need not represent a novel idea, and creativity need not be directed toward a common good.

Development of Wisdom

Wisdom may sound like a construct relevant only to adults. We need to start developing wisdom in children, and my group currently has a project to devise a curriculum to do just that. We begin by developing a valuing and appreciation of wisdom and what it can bring to society. The devaluing of older people in many societies reflects as well a devaluing of the wisdom that elders can bring to the societies.

Wisdom as a form of giftedness can be developed in a number of ways. Seven of these ways are particularly important.

First, provide students with problems that require wise thinking. Such problems might be problems requiring negotiations between parties, giving of advice to others, or dealing with ethical or moral dilemmas. For example, such a problem might involve giving advice to another student on how to deal with a substance-abuse problem.

Second, help students think in terms of a common good in the solution of these problems. For example, what would happen if everyone had a substance-abuse problem? How would such a situation affect the moral, health-related, and even economic situation of the society? Clearly, the common good would be diminished.

Third, help students learn how to balance their own interests, the interests of others, and the interests of institutions in the solution of these problems. For example, how might the substance-abuse problem destroy the individual's life in the long term, if not the short term? What effects is it likely to have on the individual's loved ones and others who care about the individual? And what will it do to the individual's ability to contribute to society?

Fourth, provide examples of wise thinking from the past and analyze them. Provide examples of people who have overcome substance abuse problems and have gone on to make important contributions to society. And provide examples of people who have not overcome such problems and who have gone on to ruin (e.g., actors and athletes who have destroyed their careers).

Fifth, role model wisdom for the students. Show them examples of wise thinking you have done and perhaps not so wise thinking that has taught you lessons. You might take decisions you have made or now are making and show them how you do what you are asking the students to do.

Sixth, help your students to think dialectically. Wisdom probably best is developed through the incorporation of dialectical thinking (Hegel, 1807, 1931) into one's processing of problems (Basseches, 1984; Labouvie-Vief, 1990; Pascual-Leone, 1990; Riegel, 1973; Sternberg, 1999). The essence of dialectical thinking is that most problems in the world do not have right or wrong answers, but better or worse ones, and what is seen as a good answer can vary with time and place. With respect to time, it involves the recognition that ideas evolve over time through an ongoing, unending process of thesis followed by antithesis followed by synthesis, with the synthesis in turn becoming the next thesis (Hegel, 1807/1931). When dialectical thinking occurs with respect to place (or space), it involves the recognition that at a given point in time, people may have diverging viewpoints on problems that seem uniquely valid or at least reasonable to them. The values we espouse today or in the United States cannot immediately be applied to other times or other places without considering the context in which others live and have lived.

Seventh, show your students that you value wise information processing and solutions. Without rewards for wise behavior, whatever wisdom children show may be extinguished quickly. If one wants children to act wisely, one must show them how by doing it oneself. It is essential that students feel that they are not only being told to think wisely, but also will be rewarded for doing so.

Finally, carry what you learn and encourage students to carry what they learn outside the classroom. The goal is not to teach another "subject" that will serve as the basis for an additional grade to appear on a report card. The goal is to change the way people think about and act in their lives.

CONCLUSION

The theory of giftedness in wisdom proposed here has a number of possible strengths. First, it is formulated in at least some detail. Second, the theory and, I hope, the exposition of it clarify how wisdom is both similar to and different from related constructs, such as intelligence. Third, the theory is formulated in a way that it can be tested—for example, by determining whether solutions to problems that balance intrapersonal, interpersonal, and extrapersonal interests are indeed perceived as wiser than solutions that do not. We currently are conducting such tests. Finally, the theory seems to capture intuitive conceptions of what giftedness in wisdom should be.

At the same time, there are weaknesses that will need to be corrected. First, there is a need for explicit instructional techniques to help develop wisdom. Second, the theory is new and empirical work is already under way but not completed. Without empirical validation, the theory remains speculative. Third, there is a need to show that higher levels of wisdom as conceptualized by this theory lead to behavior in everyday life that is demonstrably wise.

There is no unique form of giftedness that a society should reward, but one could legitimately ask whether there is any more fundamentally important form of giftedness than wisdom. One also might ask whether there is any form of giftedness that societies today ignore more than wisdom? Many countries, even the United States, seem to separate themselves from the wisdom that could help individual development, societal development, and the interaction between the two.

Wisdom is not the same as intelligence. There is one source of evidence that suggests that, as individual-difference variables, wisdom and academic intelligence might be rather different "kettles of fish." We know that IQs have been rising substantially over the past several generations (Flynn, 1987; Neisser, 1998). The gains have been experienced both for fluid and for crystallized abilities, although the gains are substantially greater for fluid than for crystallized abilities. Yet it is difficult for some to discern any increase in the wisdom of the peoples of the world. Levels of conflict in the world show no sign of de-escalating, and even have intensified in many parts of the world. So maybe it is time that psychologists, as a profession, take more seriously the formulation of theories of wisdom and of theory-based measures of wisdom. Educators need to take seriously identifying and developing giftedness in wisdom. Although there has been some scholarship in the area, the amount is dwarfed by work on intelligence. We even need to create experiences that would guide people to develop wisdom, much as we have done with respect to the development of intelligence (see, e.g., Perkins & Grotzer, 1997).

Ironically, Luis Alberto Machado, former Minister for the Development of Intelligence in Venezuela, argued that the key to a better society is intelligence. In the 1980s, he oversaw massive intervention programs in Venezuela to improve the intelligence of Venezuelan school children. His political party lost the next election, and with that loss went the intervention programs. Rising IQs have provided a natural experiment: Intelligence as defined in the traditional sense has gone up. Yet the conditions of the world have not improved as much as many people would like, at least with respect to the elimination or severe reduction of poverty, crime, and other societal scourges. Perhaps the answer is not and never was increased intelligence, but increased wisdom.

The United States and many other countries have created a "game" in schools whereby certain skills are rewarded and others are not. The question we must ask ourselves is whether the skills that are rewarded in school are those that later will matter in life. To some extent, certainly the answer is yes. But these academic skills are a beginning, not an end. Knowledge has no use when it is accumulated for its own sake. It becomes useful when it is used to good ends. Wisdom is what enables people to use knowledge to good ends.

With a world in turmoil, perhaps we need to turn our attention in schools, not only to the identification and development of knowledge bases, nor even of giftedness in intelligence, narrowly or broadly defined. Perhaps we need to turn our attention to the identification and development of giftedness in wisdom. If there is a key to a better world, this may be it.

REFERENCES

Baltes, P. B., & Smith, J. (1990). Toward a psychology of wisdom and its ontogenesis. In R. J. Sternberg (Ed.), *Wisdom: Its nature, origins, and development* (pp. 87–120). New York: Cambridge University Press.

Baltes, P. B., & Staudinger, U. M (2000). Wisdom: A metaheuristic (pragmatic) to orchestrate mind and virtue toward excellence. *American Psychologist, 55,* 122–135.

Baltes, P. B., Staudinger, U. M., Maercker, A., & Smith, J. (1995). People nominated as wise: A comparative study of wisdom-related knowledge. *Psychology and Aging, 10,* 155–166.

Basseches, J. (1984). *Dialectical thinking and adult development.* Norwood, NJ: Ablex.

Bloom, B. S. (1985). *Developing talent in young people.* New York: Ballantine.

Cantor, N., & Kihlstrom, J. F. (1987). *Personality and social intelligence.* Englewood Cliffs, NJ: Prentice-Hall.

Chi, M. T. H., Glaser, R., & Farr, M. J. (Eds.). (1988). *The nature of expertise.* Hillsdale, NJ: Lawrence Erlbaum Associates.

Csikszentmihalyi, M. (1988). Society, culture, and person: A systems view of creativity. In R. J. Sternberg (Ed.), *The nature of creativity* (pp. 325–339). New York: Cambridge University Press.

Csikszentmihalyi, M. (1996). *Creativity.* New York: HarperCollins.

Flynn, J. R. (1987). Massive IQ gains in 14 nations. *Psychological Bulletin, 101,* 171–191.

Gardner, H. (1983). *Frames of mind: The theory of multiple intelligences.* New York: Basic Books.

Goleman, D. (1995). *Emotional intelligence.* New York: Bantam Books.

Guilford, J. P. (1967). *The nature of intelligence.* New York: McGraw-Hill.

Harris, J. R. (1998). *The nurture assumption: Why children turn out the way they do.* New York: Free Press.

Hegel, G. W. F. (1931). *The phenomology of the mind* (2nd ed.; J. D. Baillie, Trans). London: Allen & Unwin. (Original work published 1807)

Hoffman, R. R. (Ed.). (1992). *The psychology of expertise: Cognitive research and empirical AI.* New York: Springer-Verlag.

Kohlberg, L. (1969). Stage and sequence: The cognitive-developmental approach to socialization. In G. A. Goslin (Ed.), *Handbook of socialization theory and research* (pp. 347–380). Chicago: Rand McNally.

Kohlberg, L. (1983). *The psychology of moral development.* New York: Harper & Row.

Labouvie-Vief, G. (1990). Wisdom as integrated thought: historical and developmental perspectives. In R. J. Sternberg (Ed.), *Wisdom: Its nature, origins, and development* (pp. 52–83). New York: Cambridge University Press.

Meacham, J. (1990). The loss of wisdom. In R. J. Sternberg (Ed.), *Wisdom: Its nature, origins, and development* (pp. 181–211). New York: Cambridge University Press.

Neisser, U. (1998). *The rising curve.* Washington, DC: American Psychological Association.

Pascual-Leone, J. (1990). An essay on wisdom: Toward organismic processes that make it possible. In R. J. Sternberg (Ed.), *Wisdom: Its nature, origins, and development* (pp. 244–278). New York: Cambridge University Press.

Perkins, D. N., & Grotzer, T. A. (1997). Teaching intelligence. *American Psychologist, 52,* 1125–1133.

Polanyi, M. (1976). Tacit knowledge. In M. Marx & F. Goodson (Eds.), *Theories in contemporary psychology* (pp. 330–344). New York: Macmillan.

Renzulli, J. S. (1984). *Technical report of research studies related to the revolving door identification model* (rev. ed.). Storrs: Bureau of Educational Research, University of Connecticut.

Riegel, K. F. (1973). Dialectical operations: The final period of cognitive development. *Human Development, 16,* 346–370.

Robinson, D. N. (1990). Wisdom through the ages. In R. J. Sternberg (Ed.), *Wisdom: Its nature, origins, and development* (pp. 13–24). New York: Cambridge University Press.

Salovey, P., & Mayer, J. D. (1990). Emotional intelligence. *Imagination, Cognition, and Personality, 9,* 185–211.

Smith, J., Staudinger, U. M., & Baltes, P. B. (1994). Occupational settings facilitating wisdom-related knowledge: The sample case of clinical psychologists. *Journal of Consulting and Clinical Psychology, 66,* 989–999.

Staudinger, U. M., & Baltes, P. M. (1996). Interactive minds: A facilitative setting for wisdom-related performance? *Journal of Personality and Social Psychology, 71,* 746–762.

Sternberg, R. J. (1984). Toward a triarchic theory of human intelligence. *Behavioral and Brain Sciences, 7,* 269–287.

Sternberg, R. J. (1985). *Beyond IQ: A triarchic theory of human intelligence.* New York: Cambridge University Press.

Sternberg, R. J. (Ed.). (1990). *Wisdom: Its nature, origins, and development.* New York: Cambridge University Press.

Sternberg, R. J. (1997). *Successful intelligence.* New York: Plume.

Sternberg, R. J. (1998). A balance theory of wisdom. *Review of General Psychology, 2*(4), 347–365.

Sternberg, R. J. (1999). The theory of successful intelligence. *Review of General Psychology, 3,* 292–316.

Sternberg, R. J., & Dobson, D. M. (1987). Resolving interpersonal conflicts: An analysis of stylistic consistency. *Journal of Personality and Social Psychology, 52,* 794–812.

Sternberg, R. J., Forsythe, G. B., Horvath, J., Hedlund, J., Snook, S., Williams, W. M., Wagner, R. K., & Grigorenko, E. L. (2000). *Practical intelligence in everyday life.* New York: Cambridge University Press.

Sternberg, R. J., & Soriano, L. J. (1984). Styles of conflict resolution. *Journal of Personality and Social Psychology, 47,* 115–126.

Sternberg, R. J., Wagner, R. K., & Okagaki, L. (1993). Practical intelligence: The nature and role of tacit knowledge in work and at school. In H. Reese & J. Puckett (Eds.), *Advances in lifespan development* (pp. 205–227). Hillsdale, NJ: Lawrence Erlbaum Associates.

Sternberg, R. J., Wagner, R. K., Williams, W. M., & Horvath, J. A. (1995). Testing common sense. *American Psychologist, 50,* 912–927.

Webster's New World College Dictionary (3rd ed.). (1997). New York: Simon & Schuster.

Chapter **10**

High Abilities and Excellence:
A Cultural Perspective

Jin Li
Brown University

ZHUGE LIANG—A CHINESE IDEAL OF HIGH ABILITY AND EXCELLENCE

When Chinese people find themselves having to rack their brains to solve a challenging problem, they often say to each other, "Remember, three cobblers with their wits combined equal one Zhuge Liang!" whereby they gather their strength and courage to embark on the task. By frequent usage of this saying, the Chinese subscribe to the idea that it takes several ordinary folks to replace a highly intelligent, able, wise person.

In a recent survey on who may be regarded as the most creative Chinese individual of the past and present by college students from mainland China, Taiwan, and Hong Kong (Yue, 2000), Zhuge Liang again ranked among the top nominees. Who is this Zhuge Liang who requires three ordinary people to be his equivalent and who also won the high regard of today's Chinese?

Zhuge Liang (or Chukeh Liang) was a real person (A.D. 181–234) who lived during the period of the Three Warring States (A.D. 220–280). Despite his humble background, Zhuge Liang was said to be extremely bright; he pursued knowledge and learning on his own and became a highly esteemed scholar in politics and military studies in his time. His writing is among the permanent anthologies of Chinese literature, and his debates are studied and held in awe by his admirers. He also knew how to observe and forecast weather, invented new weapons, and built vehicles that could transport larger cargoes. Clearly, Zhuge Liang fitted the image of the encyclopedic man. But most admirable of all was the ability and wisdom that enabled him to assist a royal offspring in establishing an equally powerful kingdom from scratch. Zhuge Liang accomplished this by persuading others to join his force and by using creative strategies (e.g., winning many battles without losing a single man). However, his long-lasting influence cannot be fully understood without considering the extracognitive side: his moral character and virtue. Legend has it that, being a person of integrity with lifelong dedication to his cause, Zhuge Liang worked until the moment he stopped breathing, handled public affairs with fairness and prudence, appeased conflicts between different ethnic minorities, treated people with respect, sincerity, and humility, and served his country without regard for fame and personal gain. What Zhuge Liang did was so unimaginable that he became an eternal source of inspiration to the Chinese in virtually every area of life for nearly two millennia. Every Chinese adult and child knows who Zhuge Liang is and knows, to varying degrees, what he stands for because his stories are in the classics, in textbooks, and in contemporary media. His image may have been idealized and idolized, but when it comes to what Chinese people think high ability and excellence are, it is predictable that Zhuge Liang will emerge as the definition.

Is this image of high ability and excellence universally acclaimed? Or is it culturally based and therefore uniquely Chinese? These are complicated questions to which no straight answers can be found. In this chapter, I present an argument that, although high ability and excellence assume universal foundations, culture also has a role to play in how these human qualities are conceptualized and developed. Culture's role is also indispensable in delineating the general realm of what these models might be (LeVine, 1999) and in making these models available to its members. To proceed with this argument, I first discuss what aspects might be considered common across cultures. Then, I use primarily Chinese notions and examples from recent empirical data against their well researched and described Western counterparts to discuss possible differences in conceptualization and development of high ability and excellence. I conclude by suggesting some implications for future research in this area.

COMMON VIEW OF HIGH ABILITY AND EXCELLENCE

Any discussion of high ability and excellence in any domain necessarily requires that one first examine the notion of ability and achievement in general. In the West, the most discussed and researched area pertaining to ability and achievement is the notion of intelligence, generally understood to be a person's general mental capacity. This capacity is typically determined by a measured IQ score (Hernstein & Murray, 1994; Spearman, 1927; Terman, 1925). For several decades, though, IQ as a singular concept has been challenged as being limited to logico-mathematical and verbal skills (leaving out other intelligences such as musical and spatial, Gardner, 1983), academic ability (leaving out the practical and the creative, Sternberg, 1985a), and measured individual level (leaving out the cultural, Vernon, 1969). However, despite these different delineations of intelligence, there is hardly any doubt that intelligence is understood as a property of the human mind that enables humans to do many things that are impossible for other species to accomplish (Pinker, 1997).

However, the scholarly debate pertaining to intelligence is, for the most part, not centered around differences between species, but among individuals and the often problematic comparisons among cultures and groups (Irvine & Berry, 1987; Lynn, 1987; Neisser et al., 1996; Rushton, 1989). Thus, the notion of high ability inevitably involves different levels of intelligence on a hierarchy, however it might be defined (e.g., a higher IQ score and a larger or faster memory). Moreover, the existence of giftedness, prodigies, talents, and extraordinary abilities that are recognized across cultures (Feldman, & Goldsmith, 1991; Gardner, 1983, 1993; Winner, 1996) makes it difficult to ignore individual differences in intelligence.

The concept of achievement, especially academic achievement, is also intimately related to the notion of intelligence because schooled knowledge both requires and further results in adept mental functioning as valued in the West (e.g., abstract reasoning, which underlies much of the decontextualized learning in school, Gardner, 1991; Olson, 1994; Perkins, 1981). It is no wonder why the idea of "ability" (used largely interchangeably with "intelligence") is so much an integral part of research on academic achievement (Bempechat & Drago-Severson, 1999; Covington, 1992; Dweck, 1999; Nicholls, 1976, 1984; Ogbu, 1981; Stevenson, Hofer, & Randel, 2000; Stevenson & Stigler, 1992; Stipek, 1988). Naturally, for some level of achievement to be regarded as excellent, it has to rank high on the achievement continuum of established measures such as various school achievement tests, aptitude tests, and other similar tools used to determine local or national honors.

To be sure, high ability and excellence in the West are not limited to the school context. In fact, there is a large body of research on individuals who have extraordinary achievements in various fields of expertise such as art, music, science, and technology as well as professions of practice such as business, education, and institutional leadership (Gardner, 1993; Csikszentmihalyi, 1988, 1994; Gruber, 1981; Simonton, 1984, 1988). Here, in addition to intelligence, we encounter a great deal of attention also to individuals' personality traits. Research on creativity, for example, is replete with analyses of personal characteristics such as risk taking, iconoclasm, high motivation, perseverance, even one's need to be in solitude (Barron, 1969; Gardner, 1993; Ghiselin, 1963; Guilford, 1959; Storr, 1989; Torrance, 1962).

The social environment in which high ability and excellence occur has also been examined. Here, scholars study the nature of social support (micro-level) that children receive from their homes, school, and other adults (Amabile, 1983; Arnold, 1995; Csikszentmihalyi & Rathunde, 1998; Gottfried, Fleming, & Gottfried, 1998; Wachs, 1992). For example, Csikszentmihalyi documents Nobel laureates in various fields reporting that as children they lived in intellectually stimulating homes where their parents encouraged them to explore the world (Csikszentmihalyi & Rathunde, 1998). A related approach is to the larger sociohistorical milieu (macro-level) that helps to shape environments such as scientific or other intellectual paradigms, political climate, and zeitgeist (Gardner, 1993; Holton, 1973; Kaplan, 1963; Kuhn, 1970; Li, 1997; Taylor & Barron, 1967). Scholars generally agree that the social environment does play an important role in providing the opportunity for high ability and excellence to flourish.

Taken together, there seem to be three main foci of the Western view of high ability and excellence. The first and the foremost is the attention to the mental, the cognitive, where the mind assumes supremacy over other domains of the human existence such as the affective, the social/moral, or the purposive. Research concentrates on human mental capacities and their functions in human lives. The second focus is on personality traits. The superior mental capacity and its prowess coupled with unique personality profiles enable individuals to develop high ability and to achieve excellence in whatever domain they choose to pursue. The third, perhaps relatively less contemplated, is the sociohistorical setting necessary for fostering individuals' high ability and excellence (Csikszentmihalyi, 1988, 1994; Gardner, 1993). These three areas may turn out to be universally necessary for developing high ability and any genuine achievement across cultures. On the one hand, every human being, regardless of his or her culture, possesses a certain degree of intelligence, is a unique person with his or her personality profile, and lives in a web of social settings and contexts (Bronfenbrenner, 1979; Cooper & Denner, 1998). On the other hand, there are domains where standards for determining high ability and excellence are also commonly shared across cultures, such as Nobel Prizes, international Olympic math achievement, and other international evaluations for human achievements. These common aspects must also be examined.

However, the mind, personality traits, and the general sociohistorical context do not fully explain the phenomenon of Zhuge Liang, particularly his time-honored acclaim among and inspirational effect on the Chinese. Nor would he be likely to qualify for an international prize of any sort. Throughout Chinese history, there have been numerous individuals that are regarded as equally if not more intelligent when viewed from the tradition of the West. These include recorded prodigies as well as accomplished individuals, not to mention the renowned contemporary of Zhuge Liang, the 6-year-old Cao Pi, who proposed a remarkable solution to the problem of weighing an elephant without a giant scale (by having the beast stand on a boat in order to mark the water level first, then filling up the boat with pebbles to the same water level, and weighing the pebbles a sack at a time with a regular scale last!). Zhuge Liang's versatile talent was matched by many others such as the poet Su Dong Po, who not only stands on the pedestal of Chinese literature, but who invented new methods to produce ink and created new gourmet food that is still widely popular today. Sociohistorical contexts provided opportunities for even more individuals to emerge as honored personages in countless fields. These other people with superior intelligence and accomplishments may be admired by many Chinese, but they do not represent cultural ideals of high ability and excellence as comprehensively and singly as Zhuge Liang does. To fully appreciate the phenomenon of Zhuge Liang, the specifics of the culture must be considered.

Thus, even though culture is related to sociohistorical aspects, it is not identical to them. It may offer a unique window for understanding the topic under discussion.

THE CULTURAL LENS

Research on cultural differences with regard to high ability and excellence is regrettably scarce. But within the research on the general notion of ability and achievement, one encounters predominately *etic* research perspectives, that is, theories and research methods based on Western subjects but applied directly to subjects in other cultures without consideration of their own views. Attempts have been made, for example, to identify among preliterate cultures indicators of children's formal cognitive ability from their daily activities (Munroe & Munroe, 1971; Nerlove, Roberts, Klein, Yarbrough, & Habicht, 1974). Similarly, indigenous conceptions of intelligence have been scrutinized in order to advance the argument that non-Western cultures such as the Chinese can measure up to the West (Chan, 1996). Achievement motivation, another concept from the West, has been claimed to be less present in many non-Western cultures (e.g., the Latino, the Indian, and the Chinese). This has been attributed to their lack of the sense of individual independence that was once regarded as the determinant of achievement motivation (McClelland, 1961, 1963; Suárez-Orozco & Suárez-Orozco, 1995).

Admittedly, the etic perspective is bound to occur because it is inevitable and perhaps also desirable when cross-cultural research is to be conducted

(Munroe & Munroe, 1971, 1997; Romney, 1994). However, this research orientation alone, while possibly uncovering some universal trends, may be limited in that it neglects significant cultural differences (D'Andrade 1990, 1995; Harkness & Super 1996; Quinn & Holland, 1987; Shweder, 1997; Shweder & Sullivan, 1993). This widespread etic tendency has been challenged by anthropologists and cultural psychologists (D'Andrade, 1995; Goodnow 1976, 1998; Li, 2001, 2002, 2003a, 2003b; Serpell, 1993; Super, 1983). These scholars argue that in order to do full justice to cultural differences, it is equally important to include *emic* perspectives, that is, indigenous or folk views from the members of the culture under study (Sternberg, 1985b; Yang & Sternberg, 1997).

Research tapping emic understandings not only addresses validity problems that may be associated with many cross-cultural research findings, but it also shows how they tend to be inveterate, not easily subject to alteration despite extensive exposure and study of more scientific ways of thinking (Bruner, 1996; Gardner, 1991; Strauss, Ravid, Magen, & Berliner, 1998). Because of their deep-rooted nature, such beliefs have been shown to guide reliably and systematically people's behavior, including the very childrearing and socialization processes that foster competence and achievement (Bruner, 1996; Chao, 1996; Harkness & Super, 1996; Strauss et al., 1998).

Still, rather than viewing these emic models as inadequacies or impediments categorically, it may be important to distinguish two types of emic understandings. The first is the widely noted "naïve theories" of children about various domains (e.g., scientific phenomena, DiSessa, 1982; Gardner, 1991; Perkins, 1995), to which beliefs held by illiterate adults (e.g., classification of objects by people's daily activities instead of a scientific taxonomy, Luria, 1976) may arguably belong. These are labeled naïve because they run counter to tested scientific knowledge, which, as dictated by educational aspirations, we would hope, will be altered as children are schooled further (Gardner, 1991, 1999).

However, the second type of emic understandings, or folk models, concern accumulated cultural experiences, ways of thinking, feeling, and behaving, and wisdom (Sternberg, 1985b, this volume) into which children are, to varying degrees, enculturatred (LeVine, 1990). Folk models of this type are not well researched in general (with perhaps the exception of parental beliefs about childrearing, Chao, 1996; Harkness & Super, 1996; Hollos, 2002). Unlike naïve views about scientific phenomena, folk models of many areas in child development are likely to have varied functions with some not so adaptive but with others highly advantageous within particular cultures (e.g., U.S. and Chinese cultural conceptions of learning, Li, 2001, 2002, 2003a). High ability and excellence may be one such area where emic models may be crucial in illuminating how children develop and achieve these abilities and levels of excellence.

Thanks to anthropological research, folk models of intelligence have indeed been shown to differ from culture to culture. Rather than the more cognitive and mental notion and verbal skills typically emphasized in the West, African conceptions of intelligence, for example, emphasize wisdom, trustworthiness, social attentiveness, and responsibility (Dasen, 1984; Serpell, 1993; Super 1983; Wober, 1974). Differences also exist among various ethnic groups within the United States. For instance, Sternberg (1985b) documented differences between "implicit theories" (a similar notion to folk models) of intelligence, creativity, and wisdom versus formal notions of these concepts. Moreover, Okagaki and Sternberg (1993) further showed that Latinos emphasized more social competence in viewing intelligence than their Anglo counterparts. These exemplary efforts have charted new territories in research on cultural models of high ability and excellence.

In what follows I draw on existing literature and my own research on Chinese cultural conceptualization of high ability and excellence to show what these culture-specific meanings might be and how they may guide children in developing these skills.

RESEARCH ON CHINESE CONCEPTIONS OF INTELLIGENCE AND EXCELLENCE

Even though much research has recently been done to explain the phenomenon of higher academic achievement among Chinese school children than their Western peers (Biggs, 1996; Stevenson et al., 2000; Stevenson & Stigler, 1992), little research exists on Chinese high ability and excellence beyond school performance in math and science. An earlier attempt to explore the Chinese concept of intelligence reported (Keats, 1982) that Chinese view an intelligent person to be one who is "responsible, pragmatic, socially oriented . . . who gets things right. He observes and memorises but he is not an enquiring mind nor a critical faculty" (p. 73, cited in Berry, 1984). However, a more recent study (Zhang & Wu, 1994) collected a set of Chinese attributes of intelligence such as logical reasoning, accepting new things, creativity, independence, and even a sense of humor. Most recent research examining conceptions of intelligence among Taiwanese Chinese by Yang and Sternberg (1997) found additional notions: Chinese people think that an intelligent person seeks knowledge and learning while cultivating his or her moral character. These latter dimensions of intelligence have not been well tapped in previous research on any cultural groups.

In an attempt to examine emic perspectives on Chinese views of intelligence in the domain of learning (rather than in general) and its origin, as well as Chinese views of excellence of learning and its origin, I collected written descriptions of these respective ideas from 62 Chinese college seniors (Li, 2002). By using established prototype research methods (Horowitz, Wright, Lowenstein, & Parad, 1981; Shaver, Schwartz, Kirson, & O'Connor, 1987), I tallied frequencies higher than 20% across the subjects (see details of analysis in Li, 2002). Out of all the possibilities, the following five attributes were named as the core ideas about intelligence in learning: personal effort (32%), inherent ability (23%), possession of knowledge (21%), thinking ability (21%, e.g., good mind, reasons well), and mental agility (20%, e.g., think and react fast). Subjects' conceptions of excellence in learning also converged on four ideas: application of knowledge to solving problems (42%), high academic achievement (37%), mastery of knowledge (32%), and creativity/breakthroughs (28%).

When asked to reveal their thoughts on where one's intelligence originates, subjects identified "factors after birth" (42%, e.g., home and other social environment) and a combination of inherent ability and factors after birth (28%). However, 84% of subjects' responses with regard to origin of excellence referred to diligence, hard work, and perseverance on the one hand and use of effective learning methods (24%, e.g., read newspapers) on the other.

Recently, my colleague and I (Li & Yue, forthcoming) are conducting a follow-up study with a sample of 1806 Chinese children aged 10 through 18 (5th- through 10th-graders from six regions of China living both in the city and rural areas) on how they think about intelligence and excellence of learning. Based on analysis of 80 subjects' responses thus far, we found similar themes in general. For example, with respect to intelligence, the most frequently named conception was a well-functioning mind or mental agility (54% of all subjects, e.g., a clear or quick mind), followed by a high IQ level (18%), thinking ability (17%, e.g., being reflective), application of knowledge to solving problems (16%), insight, wisdom, and originality (15%), and good learning attitudes (14%, e.g., diligence and conscientiousness). Moreover, these conceptions did not seem to show any developmental trend across the age range examined. The only exception was the "ability to understand things" (28%), where more children named this conception the older they were (i.e., although no 5th-graders mentioned it, the number of children mentioning it increased with age: 18%, 21%, 31%, and 46% corresponding to 6th-, 7th-, 8th-, and 10th-graders, respectively).

When explaining where one's intelligence originates (causal attribution), children also gave responses similar to adults. Again "one's personal effort" (e.g., everyday hard work) ranked as the top cause (71%) followed by a "combination of inherited potential and influence after birth" (43%) and "social engagement in learning" (19%, e.g., interaction with people and observing social activities). Very few children named inherited ability alone as a cause (4%). Developmentally, although "personal effort" seemed to be a shared understanding across the ages, the number of children expressing the combination view (of inherited potential and influence after birth) increased with age (18%, 30%, 45% 29%, and 64% in the previously mentioned grades respectively). In addition, whereas children below 7th grade did not mention "social engagement" at all, their peers above this grade level recognized it similarly in frequency across the remaining ages.

With regard to excellence of learning, three similar (to adult notions) main conceptions again emerged: High academic achievement (90%), mastery (in breadth and depth, and good judgment) and application (including creative application) of knowledge (23%), and high moral and virtuous character (21%). Moreover, neither "high academic achievement" nor "high moral and virtuous character" showed any developmental trend, indicating that these conceptions of excellence may be well understood among these children of different ages. However, "mastery and application of knowledge," although not mentioned by 5th- and 6th-graders at all, showed a steady increase starting with the 7th grade (20%, 31%, and 76% in 7th, 8th, and 10th grade, respectively).

In terms of origin of excellence, we also saw the repeated nomination of a set of eight related ideas termed "essentials of learning attitude" by 90% of subjects:

1. self-resolve,
2. love for learning,
3. diligence,
4. endurance of hardship,
5. practice,
6. perseverance,
7. conscientiousness, and
8. humility.

Among these component ideas, diligence and endurance of hardship were most frequently named (48% of all entries). These ideas did not seem to differ across the age groups.

These research findings indicate that Chinese adults and children see intelligence for the most part as a domain of mental functioning, with some also viewing the ability to apply knowledge and to solve problems as a component of it. In addition, older children endorse the idea of the ability to understand things. However, the vast majority name high academic achievement as the definition of excellence of learning, although a number of them also include mastery of knowledge and insight/wisdom/creativity on the one hand and high moral character on the other. Furthermore, these same people also attribute the origin of intelligence and excellence mostly to one's personal effort with the elaborated essentials of learning attitude and behavioral implications. Finally, inherited potential, albeit not singularly but in combination with environmental influences after birth, is also viewed as a part of intelligence, but rarely a part of excellence.

Interestingly, these findings do not seem to correspond well to the descriptions by Keats (1982), especially his assertion that the intelligent Chinese person "observes and memorises but he is not an enquiring mind nor a critical faculty." One then wonders about the notions of the "ability to understand," "application of knowledge," and "insight, judgment, and wisdom" found in the present study and remains puzzled as to how these abilities and their manifestations in real life are possible without an inquiring mind and a critical faculty. Additionally, although some of our findings do seem to overlap with a few attributes of intelligence derived by Zhang and Wu (1994) more recently (e.g., logical reasoning, and accepting new things), "a sense of humor" was never present in our data.

However, juxtaposing these findings on intelligence with Western implicit views such as those documented by Sternberg (1985b), one can actually see more overlap (than the results from the above research designed to investigate Chinese conceptions of intelligence). For instance, both Americans and Chinese share the mental dimension (e.g., thinking, IQ level, understanding), "practical problem solving," and "contextual intelligence" (Chinese ideas in the dimension of "insight/judgment/wisdom" and of "social engagement" are similar to this American category). It is therefore warranted to conclude that these conceptions may be the ones likely to be regarded by people from at least these two cultures as the essential dimensions of intelligence.

Despite these similarities, there are dimensions on both cultures' lists that do not seem to resemble each other. For example, American "verbal ability" rarely, if at all, came up in the Chinese conceptions. Likewise, the Chinese "essentials of learning attitude," a largely self-as-agent and affective dimension as a cause for both intelligence and excellence, and the peculiar emphasis on factors after birth being the off-setting force (for inherited potential) in the formation of one's intelligence are absent from Sternberg's comprehensive list. The most striking difference of all is perhaps the presence of the Chinese "high moral and virtuous character" as one of the three core conceptions of excellence. Even though these dimensions were not part of Sternberg's (1985b) American implicit theories of intelligence, our latter finding did confirm one key result in the most recent research by Yang and Sternberg (1997): Chinese people think that an intelligent person seeks knowledge and learning to cultivate his or her moral character.

These differences may be the more culturally specific dimensions that are also a constituent part of each culture's core conceptions without which our understanding of intelligence would be incomplete. These undoubtedly need further analysis. For the purposes of this chapter, I focus on aspects of the Chinese understanding of intelligence in the next section, instead of delving into that of the United States in order to illustrate how we might continue the examination of culture regarding the topic under discussion.

WHY ZHUGE LIANG MATTERS TO THE CHINESE

As stated earlier, the mental dimension may be shared widely across culture, but in the ethos of this volume, culture-specific aspects of high ability and excellence may be best characterized as factors of "extracognition" that are interwoven with the mental. In the case of Zhuge Liang, it is perhaps these Chinese "extracognitive" values and processes that nurtured Zhuge Liang in the first place as well as ensured his impact throughout Chinese history.

The findings on "seeking knowledge," "cultivating one's moral character," and the "essentials of learning attitude" from our research (Li, 2001, 2002, 2003a; Li & Yue, forthcoming) as well as those of Yang and Sternberg (1997) reflect interrelated aspects of both life purposes and developmental processes of Chinese lives. These are core notions that Confucius and his admirers used to guide their lives (Tu, 1979; Wu & Lai, 1992). Accordingly, the highest purpose of life is self-perfection (therefore "cultivating one's moral/virtuous character"). Human perfectability can be sought by everyone so long as one seeks it through the process of self-cultivation. Learning or "seeking knowledge," broadly construed, is of paramount importance in the process of self-perfection because it is seen as the only way self-perfection is possible (Lee, 1996; Li, 2002, 2003b; Tu, 1979; Wu & Lai, 1992). However, because there is no end to self-perfection, learning becomes a lifelong dedication and is to be pursued with all effort humanly possible, thus the "essentials of attitude toward learning" (Li, 2001, 2002, 2003a).

This particular construal of life and its developmental processes are understood in common folk parlance as *zuoren* (做人), literally, becoming a person. Based on the analysis by Tu (1979), an esteemed scholar on Confucian thought, the "person" here is not merely a human in the biological sense but a fully encultured and cultivated existence. In the Confucian aspiration, this person is one who is always in the process of becoming the most genuine, sincere, and humane (*junzi*, 君子) as he or she can be. Instead of reaching an endpoint of maturity, this person is, at any point of life, capable of further maturing and ideally strives to do so. In short, seeking *zuoren* (engaging oneself in the process of self-perfection) is in fact tantamount to *junzi*. Even though this Confucian ideal of a person is an ancient idea, research attests to its unfailing appeal to today's Chinese (Li, 2002; Li & Yue, forthcoming).

In order to provide a sense of what *zuoren* means to today's Chinese children, we performed a preliminary analysis on the responses to our probing in the same study being conducted by Li and Yue (forthcoming). We have identified seven categories of meanings of *zuoren*:

1. Pursuing fulfillment of life,
2. self-strengthening without ever stopping,
3. developing high moral/virtuous character,
4. seeking knowledge,
5. maintaining harmonious social relations,
6. striving for a successful career, and
7. contributing to society.

Under the umbrella of "pursuing fulfillment of life" (1st category), our subjects also expressed ideas such as searching for happiness, finding meaning, and doing things one enjoys. Traditionally, this category is understood as going beyond the satisfaction with meeting one's basic survival needs, to taking an interest in the larger world. This outlook includes all areas that the world has to offer such as the arts, science, social sciences, philosophy, current affairs, traveling to places, and so forth whereby one finds a niche to connect one's life to the larger universe (Liu, 1973).

"Self-strengthening without ever stopping" (*ziqiang buxi*, 自强不息, 2nd category) is a phrase that Chinese people take from *I Ching* (*The Book of Changes*, one of the *Five Classics*,[1] all scholars were traditionally required to study) to draw inspirations for lifelong self-cultivation. The meaning of this phrase charts the course of life a *junzi* (the most genuine, sincere, and humane person one can be) shall take. Chinese have long sought to draw strength from the natural universe and to regard one's existence similarly to the unceasing process of renewal of nature. As the *Book of Changes* (Wang, Li, & Zhang, 1998) states: "The universe is strong, renewing itself ceaselessly; a *junzi* shall follow it, self-strengthening without ever stopping." The Chinese embrace of this self-strengthening process is quite sensible considering that the ultimate purpose of one's life is to self-perfect.

---

[1] The other four are *The Book of Songs*, *The Book of History*, *The Book of Rites*, and *The Spring and Autumn Annals*. The authors of these books have been subject to historical debates for centuries. Many scholars agree that these ancient classics were not written by single but numerous authors throughout Chinese history. See Wu and Lai (1992) for an introduction and complete translation of these books into modern Chinese.

The next category (3rd category), "developing high moral/virtuous character," pertains to the Confucian emphasis on character building. To be sure, what constitutes a person's moral/virtuous character in this context is not the same as any free-standing set of universal moral rules such as those proposed by Kohlberg (1976), but a set of values specific to Chinese culture. A person with moral/virtuous character, accordingly, possesses not only the fundamental ability to discriminate right from wrong; but also a broad set of virtues. The cardinal virtues—sense of propriety, justice, integrity, sense of honor and shame, loyalty, filial piety, love and respect for one's siblings, and trust for friends—address the basic elements of moral conduct (Mencius, 1970; Tu, 1979; Wu & Lai, 1992). The notion of virtue is also extended to include prudence, frugality, diligence, a heart and mind for wanting to learn, and one's daily words and deeds, such as not holding an old grudge, going out of one's way to help others, and so on. Self-perfection is defined in these terms and dimensions (Tu, 1979; Wu & Lai, 1992).

As stated earlier, "seeking knowledge" (4th category) is part and parcel of Confucian life purpose and process (Lee, 1996; Li, 2001, 2002; Wu & Lai, 1992). My recent study on Chinese and U.S. learning models reveals large differences in how members of these two cultures view learning (Li, 2003a). Briefly, although the U.S. model seems to stress a "mind" orientation, the Chinese model favors a "person" orientation. Because seeking knowledge is so central to the lifelong personal endeavor toward self-perfection for the Chinese, there is little wonder why Chinese adults and children time and again nominate this aspect as an essential part of their lives (Li, 2001, 2002, 2003a, 2003b; Li & Yue, forthcoming; Yang & Sternberg, 1997).

As can be seen in the discussion of "developing high moral/virtuous character," much of the Confucian value system stresses "maintaining harmonious social relations" (5th category) as a major life task. Inevitably, to pursue self-perfection also means to develop the understanding and skill required for harmonious social interactions within one's family as well as one's larger social world. Individuals who succeed in cultivating themselves in this regard respect their parents (filial piety), admit their weaknesses and the need to further self-improve instead of pretending to be more than what they are (humility), are sincere in their dealings with others, hold high standards of bringing honor to the collective (gratitude for their nurturance) while possessing the heightened sense of correcting their wrong doings (shame), and reciprocate (have empathy) with others. These and many other areas of social relations are areas for self-improvement in daily life (Tu, 1979; Yu & Yang, 1994).

Related to the *junzi* ideal is "striving for a successful career" (6th category). Here also lies a deep Chinese sense of personal agency and personal accomplishment. Unfortunately, previous research has produced the widespread claim that Chinese individuals lack the notion of self as an individual and a sense of agency, due to the so-called collectivist orientation of Chinese culture (Hui, 1988; Hui & Triandis, 1986). This one-sided emphasis on collectivism may make Chinese "striving for a successful career" appear to be antithetical to Chinese social orientation of selves. However, our current (Li & Yue, 2002) as well as previous research (Li, 1997) tapping emic views has enabled us to discover many indigenously Chinese conceptions of self that unequivocally point to oneself striving for a successful career (e.g., individual effort, 个人努力). *Junzis* do not only own their independent inner voices of morality and virtue (*shendu*, 慎独), but they also exert their utmost effort to be self-sufficient socioeconomically. Even though as a principle *junzis* seek to maintain their deep roots in their social world, their sense of honor, respect, and gratitude for the social support (that nurtured their development) prevent them from becoming a burden to family, friends, community, and society. This self-sufficient emphasis is also reflected in the notion of "self-strengthening without ever stopping" where giving up on oneself is not a real option.

Finally, "contributing to society" is an unambiguously resounding goal throughout the history of Chinese people. Contributing one's knowledge and skill back to society has been a consistent call of the Confucian *junzi*, which is the ultimate purpose of self-perfection. A person is not regarded as a true *junzi* without understanding his or her need to contribute to society what his or her people gave him or her in the first place. In light of this purpose, individual efforts toward self-perfection are not just recycled within the individual but are tied to the commonwealth for all (Lee, 1996; Li, 2001, 2002, 2003a, 2003b; Tu, 1979; Wu & Lai, 1992; Yu & Yang, 1994).

It is surprising how similar these purposes and processes are to the age-old articulation of a *junzi*'s life course as stated clearly in the *Book of Great Learning*:[2] "cultivate oneself, organize one's family, order the affairs of the state, and bring stability and piece to the world" (Wu & Lai, 1992). Accordingly, the Confucian ideal image of a person starts out with him or her developing aspirations, learning, working hard, doing all he or she needs to do in order to self-cultivate. The next task is to understand and obtain the most fundamental human relationships, those found in each individual's family, between husband and wife, between parents and children, between siblings, and between the core members of the family and their extended

---

[2] This is one of the four books that are also part of the traditionally required readings for Chinese scholars: *The Great Learning, The Doctrine of the Mean, The Analects of Confucius,* and *Mencius.* Like the Five Classics, the authors of the books were most likely not single individuals but many who participated in writing, editing, and compiling them throughout Chinese history (Wu & Lai, 1992).

10. HIGH ABILITIES AND EXCELLENCE

relatives. Having accomplished these two tasks, one is to be entrusted to serve one's community. As a final goal, the person is to take on the greatest task of serving humanity as a whole. It is believed in Confucian persuasion that those who lack self-cultivation may have great difficulties in developing satisfying relationships within their families. Those who fail to maintain harmonious social relationships are also unlikely to have the moral strength and dedication to serve people in the larger community. In the end, those who are deficient in all of these major life areas cannot stand up to the task of serving humanity as a whole despite their superior mental skills and charming personalities. Even though the specific wordings differ, the essential gist of the Confucian *zuoren* resonates in the beliefs of today's Chinese children, suggesting that these goals are very much alive and are likely to be actively pursued by them.

The Confucian *junzi* has been an inspirational guidepost for Chinese people throughout history, perhaps because it offers something profound in the face of the limitations of human existence. Because it encourages them to search for meanings beyond their individual and small social worlds (family) into the larger world via the process of lifelong self-perfection, individual lives may be fulfilled, thus allowing people to experience a sense of psychological and spiritual extension. Therefore, it is not too far-fetched to suggest that the ultimate appeal of the Confucian *junzi* and *zuoren* may reside in the delicate symbiosis between a sense of self as an agent and a deep social connection; together they may serve to prolong one's physical and psychological existence (Tu, 1979; Wu & Lai, 1992).

Although these are deeply held aspirations of Chinese people, their attainment is by no means automatic. In fact, as Chinese history shows, very few individuals have been deemed to have reached all of these goals. And those few individuals, including Confucius himself, are undoubtedly esteemed as displaying excellence of the highest order and are thus upheld as models called "sages" for younger generations to learn about and to emulate.

It is against this background that Zhuge Liang, or the idealized image of him, must be seen. His image is one that first and foremost represents the full realization and embodiment of these Chinese life goals and processes. He was indeed an exemplar in every life task as envisioned by Chinese sages. To highlight the particular balance between his superior intelligence and creativity and his exemplary moral courage, one of Zhuge Liang's feats is worth retelling: Upon learning that a general from his enemy kingdom known for his indecisiveness was approaching a town which Zhuge Liang was guarding with only a few men, Zhuge Liang suddenly came up with a strategy for repulsing the enemy. He ordered to have the town deserted, leaving the town gate widely open with only a few old men pretending to clean the streets. He himself sat atop the town wall playing a calm tune on his harp. When the general with his army arrived, he indeed became suspicious of the tranquillity of the town. Instead of charging into the town, he retreated. This "strategy for repulsing one's enemy" became known as the "empty town strategy" and became a legend because Zhuge Liang used his brilliant mind to find a creative solution to an impossible situation. He succeeded in saving the town without losing a single man. But there was no doubt that he also put the lives of his people and men above his own life and displayed moral courage as well as a high sense of duty.

Zhuge Liang represents the best possible combination of the cognitive and the "extracognitive," turning the once imagined Chinese ideal into a reality. This reality, once born, not only reaffirms the value of self-perfection, but it also sets a specific model for what the actual process of self-perfection looks like. This existence undoubtedly illuminates what the Confucian *junzi* and *zuoren* together with one's mental power can be. Perhaps, this is how Chinese culture retains its vitality as a whole and how its people continue to strive forward despite frequent social, political, economical, and other incomprehensible challenges throughout its history.

CONCLUSION

In this chapter I have reviewed literature on intelligence and excellence and argued, as have many cultural psychologists, that the etic perspectives alone may fall short of explaining the nature of human high ability and excellence. Emic perspectives are equally important for any empirical research and theory on this topic. Without a doubt, the universal factors such as the biological existence of the brain, the basic functions of the human mind, personality traits, and the general social context need to be examined. However, culture also has an indispensable role to play in shaping the conceptions and the development of high ability and excellence, and therefore its role must be investigated as well. To illustrate how we may be better informed about the role of culture, I presented some new data from my own research as well as drew on related findings from other studies on indigenously Chinese conceptions about intelligence, ability, and excellence. I concluded that, in the case of Chinese culture, the existence of high ability and excellence cannot be sufficiently understood without considering the fundamental life purposes and processes of the culture (Lee, 1996; Li, 2001, 2002, 2003b; Yu & Yang, 1994).

As a general implication from the analysis previously mentioned, I hope to suggest that individuals in particular cultures who develop high ability and achieve excellence are, far from popular belief, not isolated phenomena or results of mere individual brilliance and processes. Like the magical Zhuge Liang, these great individuals do not arise above their culture but are deeply embedded in the cultural values and processes that nurtured them and allowed them to flourish in the first place. Their accomplishments, if deemed essential to their culture, will continue to nurture and shape younger generations.

Despite a growing consensus regarding emic perspectives, there is, regrettably, still a dearth of empirical investigations on cultural differences in this area. To begin thinking about how we might fill this gap, I venture to discuss a few directions. First, I would argue that emic meanings shall remain essential in any research on cultural differences. As research in anthropology, cultural psychology, and in some circles of mainstream psychology has shown, members of different cultures not only think differently about intelligence and excellence, their conceptions are often intricate and complex (Azuma & Kashiwagi, 1987; Okagaki & Sternberg, 1993; Serpell, 1993; Super, 1983; Yang & Sternberg, 1997; Wober, 1974). Moreover, these folk models have also been shown to influence people's actual behavior (Strauss et al., 1998). Our own studies also confirm this general finding (Li, 2001, 2002, 2003a, 2003b; Li & Yue, forthcoming). If our goal is to explain intelligent behavior and excellence and to foster such optimal outcomes of development (Csikszentmihalyi & Rathunde, 1998), we also need to include the actual context in which such behaviors occur. Unequivocally, culture is an essential part of the context.

Second, while investigating a single culture has unquestionable value, comparative perspectives are also needed. Many researchers (e.g., Markus & Kitayama, 1991; Shweder, Mahapatra, & Miller, 1990; Yang & Sternberg, 1997) have demonstrated the advantage of these perspectives in that they generate more informative research results. My own research examined Chinese conceptions first, but without analyzing the data against Western findings. Under comparative scrutiny, many more ideas and processes have emerged, better illuminating the similarities and differences between the two cultures.

Third, intelligence and excellence have traditionally been studied more as domain-general phenomena that can be applied to all human activities and areas of human endeavor. Research of this orientation has produced and will continue to produce important knowledge. However, recent advancement in research also points to the importance of domain-specific high ability and excellence (Csikszentmihalyi, 1994; Feldman & Goldsmith, 1991; Gardner, 1993; Gruber, 1981; Li, 1997; Winner, 1996). A balance of the two somewhat opposing research orientations may be more beneficial. It is difficult to maintain, for example, that general, integrated mental capacity and functioning are not worthy of research. Moreover, our own as well as others' research on cultural views has shown that people do share beliefs and ideas about the general notion of intelligence and excellence (Li & Yue, forthcoming; Sternberg, 1985b). Consider the notions of "versatility" of talent and the "encyclopedic" mind that exist in both the West and other cultures such as China. These shared notions are indicative of the wide recognition and appreciation of an integrative view of intelligence and excellence by people from different cultures. Still, despite this fact, there is no reason why specific values and processes associated with common domains (science, art, literature) as well as culturally specific domains (e.g., Guatemalan weaving, Greenfield, 1984, and martial arts in the East) should not also yield unique insight into human high ability and excellence.

Finally, the area that is probably most uncharted is the development of high ability and excellence. From existing research, it appears that cultures the world over recognize and value individuals with these qualities however they may be defined in their own cultural contexts. It also appears to be the case that cultures make an effort to foster these qualities in their young. Therefore, it is crucial to examine how such abilities and qualities are developed from childhood to adulthood or from the novice-state to expertise within various domains regardless of age. In light of this volume's focal theoretical frame, research has indeed much to gain from investigating the "extracognitive" aspects in terms of development.

With these and other possible directions, we can better hope to narrow the gap of knowledge in this area, to foster deeper understanding and appreciation among cultures, and ultimately to help our young to realize their potential in full, perhaps becoming the Zhuge Liang of their own culture.

REFERENCES

Amabile, T. M. (1983). *The social psychology of creativity*. New York: Springer Verlag.

Arnold, K. D. (1995). *Lives of promises: What becomes of high school valedictorians*. San Francisco, CA: Jossey-Bass.

Azuma, H., & Kashimagi, K. (1987). Descriptors for an intelligent person: A Japanese study. *Japanese Psychological Research, 29*, 17–26.

Barron, F. (1969). *Creative person and process*. New York: Holt, Rinehart & Winston.

Bempechat, J., & Drago-Severson, E. (1999). Cross-national differences in academic achievement: Beyond etic conceptions of children's understanding. *Review of Educational Research, 69*, 287–314.

Berry, J. W. (1984). Toward a universal psychology of cognitive competence. *International Journal of Psychology, 19*, 335–361.

Biggs, J. B. (1996). Western misperceptions of the Confucian-heritage learning culture. In D. A. Watkins & J. B. Biggs (Eds.), *The Chinese learner* (pp. 45–67). Hong Kong: Comparative Education Research Centre (CERC) & The Australian Council for Educational Research Ltd. (ACER).

Bronfenbrenner, U. (1979). *The ecology of human development*. Cambridge, MA: Harvard University Press.

Bruner, J. (1996). *The culture of education*. Harvard University Press.

Chan, J. (1996). Chinese intelligence. In M. H. Bond (Ed.), *The handbook of Chinese psychology* (pp. 93–108). Hong Kong: Oxford University Press.

Chao, R. K. (1996). Chinese and European American mothers' views about the role of parenting in children's school success. *Journal of Cross-Cultural Psychology, 27,* 403–423.

Cooper, C., & Denner, J. (1998). Theories linking culture and psychology: Universal and community-specific processes. *Annual Review of Psychology, 49,* 559–584.

Covington, M. V. (1992). *Making the grade.* New York: Cambridge University Press.

Csikszentmihalyi, M. (1988). Society, culture, and person: A system view of creativity. In R. Sternberg (Ed.), *The nature of creativity* (pp. 325–340). New York: Cambridge University Press.

Csikszentmihalyi, M. (1994). The domain of creativity. In D. H. Feldman, M. Csikszentmihalyi, & H. Gardner (Eds.), *Changing the world* (pp. 135–158). Westport, CT: Praeger.

Csikszentmihalyi, M., & Rathunde, K. (1998). The development of the person: An experiential perspective on the ontogenesis of psychological complexity. In R. M. Lerner (Ed.), *Handbook of child psychology. Vol 1: Theoretical models of human development* (5th ed., pp. 635–684). New York: Wiley.

D'Andrade, R. (1990). Some propositions about the relations between culture and human cognition. In J. W. Stigler, R. A. Schweder & G. Herdt (Eds.), *Cultural psychology: Essays on comparative human development* (pp. 66–129). New York: Cambridge University Press.

D'Andrade, R. (1995). *The development of cognitive anthropology.* New York: Cambridge University Press.

Dasen, P. R. (1984). The cross-cultural study of intelligence: Piaget and the Baoulé. *International Journal of Psychology, 19,* 407–434.

DiSessa, A. (1982). Unlearning Aristotelian physics: A study of knowledge-based learning. *Cognitive Science, 6*(1), 37–76.

Dweck, C. S. (1999). *Self-theories.* Philadelphia, PA: Psychology Press.

Feldman, D. H., & Goldsmith, L. T. (1991). *Nature's gambit: Child prodigies and the development of human potential.* New York: Teachers College Press.

Gardner, H. (1983). *Frames of mind.* New York: Basic Books.

Gardner, H. (1991). *The unschooled mind: How children think and how schools should teach.* New York: Basic Books.

Gardner, H. (1993). *Creating minds: An anatomy of creativity seen through the lives of Freud, Einstein, Picasso, Stravinsky, Eliot, Graham, and Gandhi.* New York: Basic Books.

Gardner, H. (1999). *The disciplined mind: What all students should understand.* New York: Simon & Schuster.

Ghiselin, B. (1963). The creative process and its relation to the identification of creative talent. In C. W. Taylor & F. Barron (Eds.), *Scientific creativity: Its recognition and development* (pp. 355–365). New York: Wiley.

Goodnow, J. J. (1976). The nature of intelligent behavior: Questions raised by cross-cultural studies. In L. B. Resnick (Ed.), *The nature of intelligence* (pp. 169–188). New York: Lawrence Erlbaum Associates.

Goodnow, J. J. (1998). Contexts of achievement. In S. G. Paris & H. M. Wellman (Eds.), *Global prospects for education: Development, culture, and schooling.* Washington, DC: APA.

Gottfried, A. E., Fleming, J. S., & Gottfried, A. W. (1998). Role of cognitive stimulating home environment in children's academic intrinsic motivation: A longitudinal study. *Child Development, 69,* 1448–1460.

Greenfield, P. M. (1984). A theory of the teacher in the learning activities of everyday life. In B. Rogoff & J. Lave (Eds.), *Everyday cognition: Its development in social context* (pp. 117–138). Cambridge, MA: Harvard University Press.

Gruber, H. (1981). *Darwin on man* (2nd ed.). Chicago, IL: University of Chicago Press.

Guilford, J. P. (1959). Three faces of intellect. *American Psychologist, 14,* 469–479.

Harkness, S., & Super, C. M. (Eds.). (1996). *Parents' cultural belief systems: Their origins, expressions, and consequences.* New York: Guilford Press.

Hernstein, R. & Murray, C. (1994). *The bell curve.* Chicago: Free Press.

Hollos, M. (2002). The cultural construction of childhood: Changing conceptions among the Pare of Tanzania. *Childhood, 9*(2), 167–189.
Holton, G. (1973). *Thematic origins of scientific thought.* Cambridge, MA: Harvard University Press.
Horowitz, L. M., Wright, J. C., Lowenstein, E., & Parad, H. W. (1981). The prototype as a construct in abnormal psychology: A method for deriving prototypes. *Journal of Abnormal Psychology, 90,* 568–574.
Hui, C. H. (1988). Measurement of individualism-collectivism. *Journal of Research in Personality, 22,* 17–36.
Hui, C. H., & Triandis, H. (1986). Individualism and collectivism: A study of cross-cultural researchers. *Journal of Cross-Cultural Psychology, 17,* 225–248.
Irvine, S. H., & Berry, J. W. (1987). *Human abilities in cultural context.* New York: Cambridge University Press.
Kaplan, N. (1963). The relation of creativity to sociological variables in research organizations. In C. W. Taylor & F. Barron (Eds.), *Scientific creativity: Its recognition and development* (pp. 195–205). New York: Wiley.
Keats, D. (1982). Cultural bases of concepts of intelligence: A Chinese versus Australian comparison. *Proceedings of Second Asian Workshop on Child and Adolescent Development* (pp. 67–75). Bangkok: Behavioral Science Research Institute.
Kohlberg, L. (1976). The psychology of moral development: The nature and validity of moral stages. In T. Lickorn (Ed.), *Moral development and moral behavior* (pp. 170–205). New York: Holt, Rinehart & Winston.
Kuhn, T. S. (1970). *The structure of scientific revolutions.* Chicago, IL: University of Chicago Press.
Lee, W. O. (1996). The cultural context for Chinese learners: Conceptions of learning in the Confucian Tradition. In D. A. Watkins & J. B. Biggs (Eds.), *The Chinese learner* (pp. 45–67). Hong Kong: Comparative Education Research Centre (CERC) & The Australian Council for Educational Research Ltd. (ACER).
LeVine, R. A. (1990). Enculturation: A biosocial perspective on the development of self. In D. Cicchetti & M. Beeghly (Eds.), *The self in transition: Infancy to childhood* (pp. 99–117). Chicago: University of Chicago Press.
LeVine, R. (1999). An agenda for psychological anthropology. *Ethos, 27,* 15–24.
Li, J. (1997). Creativity in horizontal and vertical domains. *Creativity Research Journal, 10,* 107–132.
Li, J. (2001). Chinese conceptualization of learning. *Ethos, 29,* 1–28.
Li, J. (2002). A cultural model of learning: Chinese "heart and mind for wanting to learn". *Journal of Cross-Cultural Psychology, 33*(3), 248–269.
Li, J. (2003a). US and Chinese cultural beliefs about learning. *Journal of Educational Psychology.*
Li, J. (2003b). The core of Confucian learning. *American Psychologist.*
Li, J., & Yue, X.-D. (2002). Self in learning: Personal and social goals and agency among Chinese adolescents. Manuscript submitted for publication.
Li, J., & Yue, X.-D. (forthcoming). Learning conceptions, desires, actions among Chinese school children.
Liu, Z. (1973). *Shi dao* [Principles of teacherhood]. Taipei, Taiwan: Chung Hwa Book Company.
Luria, A. R. (1976). *Cognitive development.* Cambridge, MA: Harvard University Press.
Lynn, R. (1987). The intelligence of the Mongoloids: A psychoactive, evolutionary and neurological theory. *Personality and Individual Differences, 8,* 813–844.
Markus, H. J., & Kitayama, S. (1991). Culture and the self: Implications for cognition, emotion and motivation. *Psychological Review, 98*(2), 224–253.
McClelland, D. C. (1961). *The achieving society.* New York: Van Nostrand.
McClelland, D. C. (1963). Motivational pattern in Southeast Asia with special reference to the Chinese case. *Journal of Social Issues, 19*(1), 6–19.

10. HIGH ABILITIES AND EXCELLENCE

Mencius. (1970). *Mencius.* (D. C. Lao, Trans.). Harmondsworth: Penguin Books.
Munroe, R. H., & Munroe, R. L. (1971). Effect of environmental experience on spatial ability in an East African society. *Journal of Social Psychology, 83,* 15–22.
Munroe, R. L., & Munroe, R. H. (1997). A comparative anthropological perspective. In J. W. Berry, Y. H. Poortinga, & J. Pandey (Eds.), *Handbook of cross-cultural psychology: Vol. 1. Theory and method* (pp. 171–214). Needham Heights, MA: Allyn & Bacon.
Neisser, U., Boodoo, G., Bouchard, T. J., Jr., Boykin, A. W., Brody, N., Ceci, S. J., Halpern, D. F., Loehlin, J. C., Perloff, R., Sternberg, R. J., & Urbina S. (1996). Intelligence: Knowns and unknowns. *American Psychologist, 51,* 77–101.
Nerlove, S. B., Roberts, J. M., Klein, R. E., Yarbrough, C., & Habicht, J. P. (1974). Natural indicators of cognitive ability. *Ethos, 2,* 265–295.
Nicholls, J. G. (1976). Effort is virtue, but it's better to have ability: Evaluative response to perceptions of effort and ability. *Journal of Research in Personality, 10,* 306–315.
Nicholls, J. G. (1984). Achievement motivation: Conceptions of ability, subjective experience, task choice, and performance. *Psychological Review, 91*(3), 328–346.
Ogbu, J. U. (1981). Origins of human competence: A cultural ecological perspective. *Child Development, 52,* 413–429.
Okagaki, L., & Sternberg, R. J. (1993). Parental beliefs and children's school performance. *Child Development, 64,* 36–56.
Olson, D. R. (1994). *The world on paper: The conceptual and cognitive implications of writing and reading.* New York: Cambridge University Press.
Perkins, D. (1981). *The mind's best work.* Cambridge: Harvard University Press.
Perkins, D. N. (1995). *Smart schools.* New York: Free Press.
Pinker, S. (1997). *How the mind works.* New York: Norton.
Quinn, N., & Holland, D. (1987). Introduction. In D. Holland & N. Quinn (Eds.), *Cultural models in language and thought* (pp. 3–40). New York: Cambridge University Press.
Romney, A. K. (1994). Cultural knowledge and cognitive structure. In M. M. Suárez-Orozco, G. Spindler, & L. Spindler (Eds.), *The making of psychological anthropology II* (pp. 254–283). Fort Worth, TX: Harcourt Brace.
Rushton, J. P. (1989). Evolutionary biology and heritable traits: With reference to Oriental-White-Black differences. Paper presented at the Annual Meeting of the American Association for the Advancement of Science. San Francisco, CA.
Serpell, R. (1993). *The significance of schooling: Life journeys in an African society.* New York: Cambridge University Press.
Shaver, P., Schwartz, J., Kirson, D., & O'Connor, C. (1987). Emotion knowledge: Further exploration of a prototype approach. *Journal of Personality and Social Psychology, 52,* 1061–1086.
Shweder, R. (1997). The surprise of ethnography. *Ethos, 25,* 152–163.
Shweder, R. A., Mahapatra, M., & Miller, J. G. (1990). Culture and moral development. In J. Stigler, R. A. Schweder, & G. Herdt (Eds.), *Cultural psychology: Essays on comparative human development* (pp. 130–204). New York: Cambridge University Press.
Shweder, R. A., & Sullivan, M. A. (1993). Cultural psychology: Who needs it? *Annual Review of Psychology, 44,* 497–523.
Simonton, D. K. (1984). *Genius, creativity, and leadership.* Cambridge, MA: Harvard University.
Simonton, D. K. (1988). Creativity, leadership, and chance. In R. J. Sternberg (Ed.), *The nature of creativity* (pp. 386–426). New York: Cambridge University Press.
Spearman, C. E. (1927). *The abilities of man.* New York: Macmillan.
Sternberg, R. J. (1985a). *Beyond IQ: A triarchic theory of human intelligence.* New York: Cambridge University Press.
Sternberg, R. J. (1985b). Implicit theories of intelligence, creativity, and wisdom. *Journal of Personality and Social Psychology, 49,* 607–627.
Stevenson, H. W., Hofer, B. K., & Randel, B. (2000). Mathematics achievement and attitudes about mathematics in China and the West. *Journal of Psychology in Chinese Societies, 1,* 1–16.

Stevenson, H. W., & Stigler, J. W. (1992). *The learning gap.* New York: Simon & Schuster.
Stipek, D. J. (1988). *Motivation to learn: From theory to practice.* Englewood Cliffs, NJ: Prentice-Hall.
Storr, A. (1989). *Solitude: A return to the self.* New York: Ballantine.
Strauss, S., Ravid, D., Magen, N., & Berliner, D. (1998). Relations between teachers' subject matter knowledge, teaching experience and their mental models of children's minds and learning. *Teaching and Teacher Education, 14,* 579–595.
Suárez-Orozco, C., & Suárez-Orozco, M. (1995). *Trans-formations: Immigration, family life, and achievement motivation among Latino adolescents.* Stanford, CA: Stanford University Press.
Super, C. M. (1983). Cultural variation in the meaning and uses of children's intelligence. In J. B. Deregowski, S. Dziurawiec, & R. C. Annis (Eds.), *Expisications in cross-cultural psychology* (pp. 199–212). Lisse: Swets & Zeitlinger.
Taylor, C. W., & Barron, F. (Eds.). (1967). *Scientific creativity: Its recognition and development.* New York: Wiley.
Terman, L. M. (1925). *Genetic studies of genius.* Stanford, CA: Stanford University Press.
Torrance, E. P. (1962). *Guiding creative talent.* Englewood Cliffs, NJ: Prentice Hall.
Tu, W. M. (1979). *Humanity and self-cultivation: Essays in Confucian thought.* Berkeley, CA: Asian Humanities Press.
Vernon, P. E. (1969). *Intelligence and cultural environment.* London: Methuen.
Wachs, T. D. (1992). *The nature of nurture.* Newbury Park, CA: Sage.
Wang, Q., Li, L.-J., & Zhang, W.-G. (1998). *Interpretation of the Book of Change in modern Chinese.* Xian, China: Sanqi Press.
Winner, E. (1996). *Gifted children: Myths and realities.* New York: Basic Books.
Wober, M. (1974). Towards an understanding of the Kiganda concept of intelligence. In J. W. Berry & P. R. Dasen (Eds.), *Culture and cognition: Readings in cross-cultural psychology* (pp. 261–280). London: Methuen.
Wu, S.-P., & Lai, C.-Y. (1992). *Complete text of the Four Books and Five Classics in modern Chinese.* Beijing, China: International Culture Press.
Yang S.-Y., & Sternberg, R. J. (1997). Taiwanese Chinese people's conceptions of intelligence. *Intelligence, 25,* 21–36.
Yu, A. B., & Yang K. S. (1994). The nature of achievement motivation in collectivist societies. In U. Kim, H. C. Triandis, C. Kagitcibasi, S. C. Choi, & G. Yoon (Eds.), *Individualism and collectivism: Theory, method, and applications* (pp. 239–250). Thousand Oaks, CA: Sage.
Yue, X.-D. (2000). Who are the most creative people in Chinese history and at present times: A comparative study among university students in Beijing, Guangzhou, Hong Kong, and Taipei and its implications for education. Unpublished paper.
Zhang, H., & Wu, Z. (1994). People's conceptions of intelligence: A study of Beijing residents' conceptions of intelligence [in Chinese]. *The Science of Psychology, 17,* 65–69, 81.

Part V

CONCLUSION

V

CONCLUSION

Chapter 11

Educating Selves to Be Creative and Wise

Michel Ferrari
*Ontario Institute for Studies in Education/
University of Toronto*

My task in this concluding chapter is—to the extent possible—to integrate the accounts of extracognitive aspects of high ability encountered in the preceding chapters into a single story. I hope that readers, and the authors themselves, will forgive me if I fail to address some of the subtleties in their work, or if I bend their views to fit into my own story of how these ideas fit together. This is especially true of the detailed case studies provided by Subotnik and by Shutte, Soloman, and Gardner. Let me begin by making a basic point endorsed by all the authors of the volume: Human flourishing and all exceptional achievement requires more than just expert knowledge.

HUMAN FLOURISHING REQUIRES MORE THAN INTELLECT

Creativity Advances Intellectual Knowledge

Creativity, Simonton tells us, differs from expertise in that developing expertise involves refining one's performance until it achieves remarkable levels of skill, whereas creativity involves generating new knowledge, and this necessarily requires guesswork and chance. The notion that new ideas depend on chance, advanced by Simonton, seems directly at odds with the claims of several other authors that creativity depends on the intuitions or metacognitive abilities of individual creators. I would like to advance the following formula for reconciling these two positions: Chance proposes, judgment disposes. What I mean by this becomes clear in the next section.

Chance Proposes

Chance combinations of ideas propose possible advances to existing knowledge that many individuals trained in a domain have acquired. In other words, each creator's set of ideas, acquired through training, may indeed be freely recombined so as to occasionally generate original and useful permutations. (This seems a good reason why ideas imported from other disciplines can sometimes be so powerful; new elements are there to enter the combination.) On a superficial reading of Simonton, exceptional creativity is thus totally a function of accumulative advantage due to chance, and is not a result of psychological ability at all. Indeed, similar ideas are sometimes arrived at by very different methods and from different conceptual starting points by multiple inventors. This Darwinian mechanism for generating new ideas, proposed by Simonton, seems eminently plausible; it suggests that there is a large part of chance and luck in what are proposed as new and potentially fruitful ways to advance knowledge in a domain.

Creativity in this sense necessarily concerns the *internal history* of a knowledge domain; that is, how ideas develop and are transformed given their origins (Lakatos, 1978; Piaget & Garcia, 1983). As Kuhn (1964/1981; see also Latour, 1999, 2000) said, creative solutions that advance knowledge in a domain allow us to grasp "the finer structure of reality," and often requires a paradigm shift that inaugurates a radical conceptual change in how we understand that reality. An example is how Galileo replaced Aristotle's (~300 B.C./1984) views on motion with a more sophisticated theory.[1]

> [Aristotle's concept of speed] functioned so successfully that potential conflicts with observations went entirely unnoticed. And while [it] did so—until, that is, the potential difficulties in applying the concept began to become actual—we may not properly speak of the Aristotelian concept as confused. [However,] we may say that because the concept was false, the men who employed it were *liable to become confused*.... But we cannot, I think, find any intrinsic defect in the concept by itself. Its defects lay not in its logical consistency, but in its failure to fit the full fine structure of the world to which it was

---

[1] As Simonton notes—and here he agrees with Latour (1999, 2000)—what enters the combinatorial process (and what gets invented) are not merely symbolic or physical artifacts, but also practices and techniques for creating and doing things. These lead to ways of improving on existing social knowledge, artifacts, tools, or practices to fill recognized niches, or to create new ones. So in the example mentioned here, Galileo designed new techniques and equipment for observing moving bodies, the most famous being his use of the telescope to observe the moons of Jupiter.

expected to apply. That is why learning to recognize its defects was necessarily learning something about the world as well as about the concept. (Kuhn, 1964/1981, p. 21)

Of course it is equally true that the most insightful of individuals working in a field will notice similar defects in existing theories and try (perhaps through random recombination of existing ideas, but perhaps also through targeted reflection to explain anomalies) to remedy that deficiency. If so, it is the conceptual deficiency that allows them to notice when a particular recombination is apropos (a lesser mind might chance upon the same new idea but dismiss it without realizing its implications). And so, although Simonton criticizes earlier work on creativity as a personal activity, the work of researchers such as Herb Simon (1982) is not so easily dismissed because even if the experimenters did know the solution to the problems they had subjects try to solve, the subjects they examined did not. In fact, Simon's approach seems entirely consistent with Simonton's own presupposition that all of the elements must be in the intellectual environment before individuals working in a field can creatively solve a problem; the question then becomes, how do people organize existing elements into a creative solution.

A close reading of Simonton notes that he introduces the idea of *serendipity* at the end of his chapter, agreeing with Pasteur, that "chance favors the prepared mind." Indeed, there is a great difference between a role for chance that capitalizes on serendipity and one that sees chance as "blind luck." Serendipity is not blind; it requires better than 20/20 vision. People who are well-trained appreciate the implications of chance combinations of ideas when they stumble on them. They recognize that a particular idea is what they have been looking for all along: this is serendipity (Eco, 1998; Roberts, 1989).

Judgement Disposes

Many would agree with Simonton and Runco in saying that method and logic are not irrelevant to creativity, but are only applied at the end. (Was it Hegel who said, "The owl of Minerva only flies at night" to make just this point?) Randomness may be integral to the generation of ideas, but logic is key to determining their internal coherence and importance to a particular knowledge domain. And it is in this sense that creativity also requires judgement. Chance proposes, but judgement disposes creators to pursue certain randomly generated recombinations as particularly fruitful. Individual creators, regardless of the source of their ideas, judge which to pursue on the basis of intuition as well as logical analysis.

Helmholtz (1898, cited in Simonton, this volume) seems to be making this point when he writes about being able to show others a shorter path to the top of a mountain as soon as one has reached its summit and can get a clear view to the bottom. There are different paths up a mountain, as Helmholtz said, and several people can discover the same or different paths to scale the same mountain, but there was never any doubt that these individuals were scaling that particular mountain.

I also admire Simonton's innovative support and refinement of the work of Quételet (1835/1968), in particular, his showing that career age—not physical age—is one of the determinants of peak creativity. But it is worth stating the obvious: capacity is still a prerequisite for engaging in some kinds of activity, and that this may take a few years to acquire. According to developmentalists who follow Piaget—like Robbie Case (1991, 1998) and Kurt Fischer (1980; Fischer & Biddell, 1998)—children have difficulty thinking in terms of abstract systems before adolescence. And some people are just unable to ever acquire certain key ideas or techniques: To take a limit case, someone with an IQ of 60 will not be able to access many intellectual ideas understood by most adults in a culture; likewise, perhaps a certain minimum level of giftedness is needed to grasp the most difficult cultural ideas that might serve as the basis for creativity in a field.

Of course, creativity is not merely a matter of intellectual strength. Although keen judgement allows such individuals to discern between good and bad ideas, Pauling (cited in Shavinina, this volume) agrees with Simonton that one needs a lot of such ideas, and that quantity comes from great effort. The greatest minds also are drawn to deep problems that require great effort as well as creativity to solve (see Feyerband, cited in Shavinina, this volume). Many authors in the volume reiterate the claims of Nobel Laureates, among others, who emphasize the value of hard work and mental effort in exceptional achievement. In this vein, it is striking that Howe shows that many great minds exhausted themselves with the effort involved in developing their radically new ideas, and had to pace themselves, sometimes taking months of rest.

Runco emphasizes that creativity is at heart a process of analogy, with creative genius being defined by the interestingness and the breadth of one's ability to form analogies where others do not see any relationship. Runco mentions a variety of heuristics that exceptional individuals use to give chance a helping hand in fostering creativity. For example, creative individuals seek to generate analogies, particularly local analogies (Dunbar, 1995), and use borrowing strategies to marshal knowledge from other domains in service of new tasks.

What is more, exceptional thinkers proceed *metacognitively*, by planning, monitoring, and evaluating their reasoning and their intuitions. Perhaps more to the point, such thinkers not only have an insightful knowledge and control of their own thinking (one classic definition of metacognition), they seem to have exceptional versions of what Flavell (1981; also Pinard, 1992) calls "metacognitive experiences." Metacognitive experiences are the emotional concomitants to metacognition that guide one's intuition about what problems are worth pursuing. Meichenbaum (1975) showed that good learners have more positive metacognitive experiences than do poor learners. But it seems from these chapters that great minds have not just positive, but positively sublime metacognitive experiences of the beauty or aesthetic quality of certain ideas. Nobel laureates make much of the depth and beauty of the problems they tackle. In fact, Kuhn (1996) feels that this aesthetic sense is integral to advancing science, since it is the beauty of an idea that can draw people to it. Although, as Kuhn suggests, it may take a lot of expertise in the domain to appreciate the beauty of, say, Einstein's theory of relativity. And (as mentioned in Shavinina) Woodward makes clear that scientific beauty must be tied to proof through experiment.

Still, such intuitions and the metacognitive experiences of beauty they generate are not the result of rational deliberation, which may be what leads Smith to follow Wegner and Wheatley (1999), among others, in considering deliberate choice an illusion.[2] But as the preceding discussion suggests, it might be better to follow Simon (1982) and say that we have only a "bounded rationality" that does not allow us to explicitly consider all options. Thus, our rationality is rooted in a deep emotional intuition that, for Smith, serves to communicate between the conscious and the unconscious mind; a communication that Suzuki (1960/1988) calls "antescientific" (that is, an unconscious intuition that precedes rational science, but is not against it). According to Smith and others, it is by consciously and explicitly articulating an unconscious tacit appreciation of the situation that individuals create their greatest innovations and best solutions to problems.

Persons necessarily engage cognitive, metacognitive, and extracognitive aspects of their performance to accomplish real-world achievements. Extracognitive here refers to the ability to discriminate between good and bad ideas (what Runco calls discretion). Much like Smith, Runco says that intellectual discretion requires *ego strength*, a term he borrows from the psychoanalytic literature to suggest the need for a healthy balance between cognition and (perhaps implicit) emotion. Indeed, Smith reminds us that creativity is not always a joyous experience. New ideas can be unsettling and anxiety provoking, and part of exceptional ability (and even of mundane creativity) is to know when to hold ideas in check that are too threatening, and when to foster ideas as innovative ways of dealing with critical life issues—such as decisions about whether or not to have surgery.

---

[2]As Searle (2000) points out, although there may be illusions of choice, or perception, this does not mean that the idea of choice and perception are illusions.

Individual Creators as Forces of Historical "Internal Development" of a Domain

Runco considers the ability to favor cognitive assimilation over accommodation as key to creativity. But to the end of his career Piaget (1977; Piaget & Garcia, 1983) maintained that these two ideas are dialectically bound together, as Baldwin (1896, 1930) also said long ago. Piaget (1974a, 1974b) would probably have agreed that invention relies on developing personal meaning—what he called *prise de conscience*—but such meaning could only be had in light of deeper understanding of the object—*prise de connaissance*—that develops in tandem. In both cases, it is through dynamically seeking a more complex equilibration of knowledge internal to a domain that our understanding of that domain advances (Piaget, 1977; Piaget & Garcia, 1983)—a point perhaps related to Latour's (1999, 2000) writings on the sociology of science (but see Bloor, 1999 for a strong critique). And to return to Simonton (see also Frege, 1956; Popper, 1994), cultural knowledge is not strictly personal: Although personally understood, the truth of Pythagoras' theorem, or Shakespeare's play *Hamlet*, for example, transcend any particular person's mind.

Transformation of Understanding. The transformation of understanding in a particular field occurs through a dialectic between the current state of knowledge in that field (as well as potentially related fields) and the intuitions and judgement of individuals (or of groups of individuals) working in that field who propose a radical conceptual change to it (e.g., witness Galileo, Lavoisier, and Darwin whose changes generated paradigm shifts for their respective fields). In this sense, creators exercise a "leading control" over their domain by a knowledge transformation that addresses current concerns of their field and remains in accord with the dominant cultural ideology (Ferrari, 2001; Piaget & Garcia, 1983; Ricoeur, 1986), generating a higher equilibration of knowledge within a culturally specific knowledge-space.[3]

All this is to say that creativity may not favor assimilation, as Runco suggests, but it does retain a deeply personal meaning that is also social. Indeed, such meanings necessarily reflect cultural values about acceptable aims for creative endeavors. For an interesting contrast to American views on creativity, consider the Japanese creative term *chindogu* or "un-useless idea." Kenji Kawakami has produced four books of Chindogu items like t-shirts with lettered and numbered grids so you can give precise directions to someone who is scratching your back, or a chopstick mounted fan to cool noodles before you eat them (see the International Chindogu Society

---

[3]*Leading control*, a term taken from martial arts like Aikido, to refer to the ability for a small force to guide a larger force by redirecting its momentum.

Web page for other great examples).[4] Chindogu are invented just for the fun of it, without an eye to practical or potential mass-market value. They are a nice rejoinder to the utilitarianism that threatens many psychological accounts of creativity—pragmatic utility is certainly a core Western value, but so are humor and irony.

As the earlier discussion shows, knowledge development implicates individuals and ideas in dynamic and complex ways. Ideas do not develop in a vacuum but, rather, in a field of cultural and social interaction. There is, in principle, no conflict between institutional and individual perspectives on creativity; in fact, they mutually support each other. Nor does this suppose that fields are progressing toward some set endpoint, just that creativity is necessarily a product of the dynamic historical development of a given field (Lewis, 2000; Piaget & Garcia, 1983).

Another way to advance human flourishing is to promote the ability of individuals to live wisely and well within these sociocultural fields, and it is to this extracognitive aspect of exceptional ability that we now turn.

Flourishing Requires Living Wisely and Well

Knowledge does not exist in the abstract. It is intimately woven into the practical fields of endeavor in which people live and act as members of families, science labs, music schools, or businesses that contain other people—including technicians and administrators who know how to work the tools of that field (Dunbar, 1995; Subotnik, this volume). The question of how best to thrive in complex sociocultural contexts is not an easy one.

For Sternberg such abilities are intimately tied to *tacit knowledge* about the relationships between one's self, others, and the situational context. Tacit knowledge has three main features:

1. it is procedural;
2. it is relevant to valued goals; and
3. it is acquired through practical experience (often with mentoring), and not through logical analysis presented in texts or in class.

Thus, wisdom specifically (and tacit knowledge in general) are tied to activity within a field—to what Nietzsche (1874/1949) calls the *will to power*. Tacit knowledge is crucial to active performance in a field, as opposed to comprehension of a domain of knowledge. Thus tacit knowledge is implicated in what Lakatos (1978) calls *external history*, or Latour (2000) the network of actors, than to internal history of the development of ideas. Tacit

---

[4]The international Chindogu society Web page: http://www.pitt.edu/~ctnst3/chindogu/chin7.html.

knowledge is what stands behind the intuition Shavinina extols in Nobel Laureates, and the phenomenal talent of the teachers and students at Juilliard. Tacit knowledge underlies the intuition exceptional individuals have for a good problem, an intuition that others in their community admire, even adore, because it is a finer sense of how to "play the game" of science or music better than the average member of their community (Bourdieu, 1990). Tacit knowledge has everything to do with what one does—the hours of effort spent on a task, as well as the passions, even enchantment that one experiences and inspires in others.

Nobel Laureates are also drawn to consider the ethical import of how they use their knowledge. Like the Chinese sages described by Li, they imply that a great man must serve humanity. In the case of the Chinese, this view is integral to a Chinese conception of wisdom and personal greatness that descends from Confucius; it is a view found in many ancient cultures, for example in the Aristotelian notion of *phronesis* (i.e., practical wisdom) and in the Sanskrit *Niti*[5]—ancient words to denote practical intelligence that are sensitive to ethical obligations. What all of these ideas share is that of doing what is practically best under the circumstances.

It is this highest and most refined sense of tacit knowledge that Sternberg considers the essence of wisdom. Specifically, it involves tacit knowledge about how to balance the concerns of self and others within particular cultural and institutional contexts. Thus, unlike creativity, wisdom is not always radically innovative, but rather is entrepreneurial; like creativity, however, wisdom is not just in the head, but in how one deals with the conjunction of self, task, and culturally interpreted situations (Csikszentmihalyi, 1997). For Sternberg, wisdom requires balance between the interests of all parties. Thus he is squarely consequentialist—although he seems to follow Hurka (2001) in proposing that this balance must be mediated by intrinsic values that aim at a common good. As he grants, it is not always easy to divine the common good. Ideal problems for Sternberg involve many competing interests and no clear way to resolve them, although one may become more expert and hence wiser in addressing the issues involved. Sternberg suggests that studying these sorts of problems (e.g., hostage ne-

---

[5]English translators struggle to give us a sense of what the term *niti* means. "Niti is a word like some others in Sanskrit, dharma for example, that is impossible to render into English by the use of a single word. It comprises meanings that convey several closely inked ideas. In fact it signifies an attitude and conduct that expresses an whole way of life. The concept of niti would include carrying out duties and obligations, familial and sociopolitical, and the exercise of practical wisdom in affairs public and private: the wisdom not of a saint or a sage but the wisdom that has to govern thinking and conduct of persons who are of the world, and who are in the world. Niti would entail resolute action taken after careful scrutiny and due deliberation. [...]. An all-round and harmonious development of human powers is the basis of niti; obsessions have no part in it, but good sense and good feeling do. To live wisely and well in the truest sense of these two terms—that is niti" (Rajan, 1993, p. xxvii–xviii).

gotiations) can lead one become most wise. These situations do indeed seem to be the kinds of situations studied to measure wisdom empirically, as seen in Baltes' and his associates work on life-planning. For example, clinical psychologists are wiser about problems surrounding life issues (e.g., what to advise a pregnant 14-year-old girl) than are laymen confronted with these everyday dilemmas (Baltes & Smith, 1990; Baltes & Staudinger, 2000; Staudinger & Baltes, 1996). Sternberg notes that wisdom is associated with advice, but we might also add, with wise action (Varella, 1992/1999). Often in practical dilemmas, individuals want advice on what to do, not how to understand a situation. As important, even with the greatest discernment, not all is within our power to know and control.

Ethical theorists like Bernard Williams (1973/1988), have pointed out problems with the consequentialist view of wisdom as seeking an objective common good. Consider Williams' (fictitious) story of Jim who stumbles upon a planned execution of 20 innocent Indians. In honor of his surprising appearance, the executioner, Pedro, offers Jim the chance to save 19 of the Indians if he agrees to shoot 1. Should he do it, for a greater benefit on balance for all stakeholders? One is tempted to answer "yes," but what about Jim's personal integrity? To be obliged to kill someone, even to save the others is an action that goes against our (and his) deep concern for the sanctity of life (Williams, 1973/1988). Surely Jim is not held to have negative responsibility for every atrocity that he fails to prevent; in this case, even if he refuses, isn't the blood of all 20 on Pedro's hands, as their life or death depends on Pedro's actions?

These are not easy questions to answer, and any answer will be specific to the situation. Wisdom, Sternberg reminds us, refers only to highly contextualized situations. Such situations—ones that require wise and deep understanding of the specific circumstances—are typically situations we hope never personally to encounter. If the case of Jim sounds far-fetched, consider the recent case of *Latimer* in Canada, who killed his epileptic disabled daughter, a child in constant pain, unable to take medication to relieve her suffering. Here is the opening of the Supreme Court of Canada ruling:

R. v. Latimer

Neutral citation: 2001 SCC 1.File No.: 26980.
2000: June 14; 2001: January 18.
Present: *McLachlin C.J. and L'Heureux-Dubé, Gonthier, Iacobucci, Major, Binnie and Arbour JJ.*

ON APPEAL FROM THE COURT OF APPEAL FOR SASKATCHEWAN

Constitutional law-Charter of Rights-Cruel and unusual punishment—Accused convicted of second degree murder after killing his severely disabled daughter—Criminal Code providing for mandatory minimum sentence of life imprisonment with no chance

of parole for 10 years—Whether imposition of mandatory minimum sentence for second degree murder constitutes "cruel and unusual punishment" in this case, so that accused should receive constitutional exemption from minimum sentence
—Canadian Charter of Rights and Freedoms, s. 12—Criminal Code, R.S.C. 1985, c. C-46, ss. 235, 745(c).

Criminal law—Defences—Defence of necessity—Accused convicted of second degree murder after killing his severely disabled daughter—Trial judge removing defence of necessity from jury after counsel's closing addresses—Whether jury should have been allowed to consider defence of necessity—Whether timing of trial judge's ruling as to availability of defence rendered accused's trial unfair.
Criminal law—Trial—Jury—Fairness of trial—Jury nullification—Accused convicted of second degree murder following death of his severely disabled daughter—Whether trial unfair because trial judge misled jury into believing it would have some input into appropriate sentence, thereby lessening chance of jury nullification.

The accused was charged with first degree murder following the death of T, his 12-year-old daughter who had a severe form of cerebral palsy. T was quadriplegic and her physical condition rendered her immobile. She was said to have the mental capacity of a four-month-old baby, and could communicate only by means of facial expressions, laughter and crying. T was completely dependent on others for her care. She suffered five to six seizures daily, and it was thought that she experienced a great deal of pain. She had to be spoon-fed, and her lack of nutrients caused weight loss. There was evidence that T could have been fed with a feeding tube into her stomach, an option that would have improved her nutrition and health, and that might also have allowed for more effective pain medication to be administered, but the accused and his wife rejected this option. After learning that the doctors wished to perform additional surgery, which he perceived as mutilation, the accused decided to take his daughter's life. He carried T to his pickup truck, seated her in the cab, and inserted a hose from the truck's exhaust pipe into the cab. T died from the carbon monoxide. The accused at first maintained that T had simply passed away in her sleep, but later confessed to having taken her life. The accused was found guilty of second degree murder and sentenced to life imprisonment without parole eligibility for 10 years; the Court of Appeal upheld the accused's conviction and sentence, but this Court ordered a new trial.

During the second trial defence counsel asked the trial judge for a ruling, in advance of his closing submissions, on whether the jury could consider the defence of necessity. The trial judge told counsel that he would rule on necessity after the closing submissions, and later ruled that the defence was not available. In the course of its deliberations, the jury sent the trial judge a note inquiring, in part, whether it could offer any input into sentencing. The trial judge told the jury it was not to concern itself with the penalty. He added: "it may be that later on, once you have reached a verdict, you—we will have some discussions about that". After the jury returned with a guilty verdict, the trial judge explained the mandatory minimum sentence of life imprisonment, and asked the jury whether it had any recommendation as to whether the ineligibility for parole should exceed the minimum period of 10 years. Some jury members appeared upset, according to the trial judge, and later sent a note

11. EDUCATING SELVES TO BE CREATIVE AND WISE 221

asking him if they could recommend less than the 10-year minimum. The trial judge explained that the Criminal Code provided only for a recommendation over the 10-year minimum, but suggested that the jury could make any recommendation it liked. The jury recommended one year before parole eligibility. The trial judge then granted a constitutional exemption from the mandatory minimum sentence, sentencing the accused to one year of imprisonment and one year on probation. The Court of Appeal affirmed the conviction but reversed the sentence, imposing the mandatory minimum sentence of life imprisonment without parole eligibility for 10 years.

The GLOBE AND MAIL had this to say the next day as their front page story (Kirk Makin, Justice Reporter, Ottawa):

The Supreme Court of Canada Showed no mercy to Robert Latimer yesterday, ruling unanimously that the Saskatewan farmer must serve at least 10 years in prison for the murder of his severely disabled daughter. The Court expressed admiration for Mr. Latimer's devotion to 12-year-old Tracy in the harrowing years she was alive, but it said his decision to kill her was a grave error in judgement that carries undeniable consequences. . . . Struggling to contain his emotions, Mr. Latimer immediately drove to a Saskatoon prison to begin serving the 10 years he must spend behind bars before he will be eligible for parole. Earlier, outside his farmhouse near Wilkie, Sask., Mr. Latimer lashed out at the top court. "This is not a crime . . . I didn't do anything wrong," he said in an emotional but controlled voice.

In another article in the same paper (David Roberts, p.A4) reported that "Mr. Latimer seemed befuddled by his punishment yesterday. But he did not apologize, saying he did not think about prison when he took his child's life. "When you're in a situation like that, you do what's right." . . . Mr. Latimer called the medical procedure that Tracy was facing 'torture' where doctors had recommended removing her femur to relieve her spasms. "To cut the top of her leg off . . . the opportunity for her to even survive that operation wasn't even that great," he said. . . . Questioned what he'll do next, Mr. Latimer said, "Go to jail, I guess."

Is this man wise or evil? To return to my earlier point, deciding how to answer this question cannot be made outside of how we view the value of life, the nature of mercy, and so on. The disabled and their advocacy groups were relieved at the verdict, but some of the jury recommended a lighter sentence than the mandatory 10 year minimum, and were dismayed to discover that their recommendation was disallowed. In fact, the judge's failure to make this minimum sentence clear is what brought the case to the Supreme Court.

What are we to make of this case? Just that sometimes tragedy befalls us and that wisdom then requires us to transcend or to regret or to grieve. In other words, sometimes deep values can conflict, leaving no good choice—but still perhaps better and worse ones, or at least better and worse emotional responses to inevitable choices (Nussbaum, 2001). The case of Jim or the true case of Latimer seems just such cases. For this reason, it is too easy to answer that one can only determine the wise answer to practical dilemmas of grave import from within a system of values. That is certainly true, but as Taylor (1985) says, what is really at stake is often which deep commitments one values more and this requires a "strong evaluation" in which one must articulate what is personally *most* important and why. The community itself necessarily shares in this judgement and the praise or blame that it generates. Such articulation requires second-order desires (meta-emotions), that themselves seem integral to Sternberg's metacomponents (and to metacognition in general, as Shavinina and Runco claim). Meta-emotions provide an extracognitive stance that is much more affectively charged than the problem-solving, truth-oriented perspective favored in cognitive psychology. In fact, it clarifies how metacognition and metacognitive experiences can motivate us to act in light of what, in the highest sense, we value as good or right (Ferrari & Koyama, 2002).

I would like to suggest that our strong evaluations about ethical dilemmas call for a *casuistry* that considers the circumstances very carefully and balances not merely the stakeholders' concerns, but our cultural assessment of the relative weight of our duty, of virtue, and of the probable objective outcome. This position suggests that wisdom requires a higher order "metabalancing" between objective outcomes, individual flourishing, and personal duty, whose wisdom must be judged *ad hominem* (i.e., on the merits of the specific case), not in general. It is only "in the field" of practical judgements about actions that a wise decision can be made (Jonsen & Toulmin, 1988), and such judgement is only intelligible within a particular culture (Taylor, 1985, 1989). In other words, how we judge the relative weight of duty, virtue, and outcome will have everything to do with our culture and the values that we hold in common with others. For example, praise and blame about the use of hallucinogenic drugs will be allocated very differently in the Amazon, where drugs like Ayahuasca are central to religious life and where some users (Shamans and priests) are highly praised as expert guides in interpreting their religious visions (Luna & Amaringo, 1999), and in the United States where they are personally shunned by most, and indeed outlawed.

Wisdom, then, cannot be divorced from culture, and the hermeneutic circle it generates—in Li's words, our approach to understanding of exceptional ability must be *emic*, not *etic*. Put another way, Taylor (1995) suggests wisdom and truth are not determined in a universal or apodictic way (Li's *etic* perspective), as favored by post-positivist views of science, but rather on a case-by-case basis. Culturally specific understanding is framed by an historically constituted worldview, and individuals who inhabit each culture are always positioned with regard to judgements about what is good in that culture.[6] We interpret our world through a cultural lens, constituted historically, as part of a group we value and that we hope is recognized, both politically and morally (Frazer, 1996; Taylor, 1995). This respectful recognition means that when representatives of cultures meet, they deserve to be engaged in dialogue that can potentially transform them in ways that both advance and coordinate their own traditions.

Li eloquently presents this theme in describing the essential differences between American and Chinese conceptions of intelligence and exceptional abilities. The conceptions of Chinese students reflect qualities that are exemplified by Zhuge Liang, considered among the wisest of men in China. Not surprisingly, given our discussion so far, Zhuge Liang was not only an intelligent and creative problem solver, but also a man of great moral stature. Li draws our attention to the fact that although America and China both value intellectual ability and personality traits, the specific configuration that generates long-lasting fame in each country necessarily match the ideals of that sociohistorical setting.

In all cases, we speak from within a social reality that we take to be (quasi)natural until it is challenged. For example, recent theories of biological evolution suggest that race is entirely socially constructed (Appiah, 1996), but many people take race to be a natural category, biologically constitutive of identity. Yet certain races have vanished from America (like my own Italian race—if one grandfather is enough—once considered separate and somewhat inferior) and few think anything of hair color or height, both of which are equally heritable and by which we could classify people if we so desired (Bourdieu, 1990).

Finally, it is not just individuals who are stakeholders in important actions or decisions. Institutions have obligations just as do individuals. The police are there to protect us, and they rely on the courts and government and many other players more powerful than any individual to make sure the system works. Institutions such as the police force and the courts have social responsibilities and those representing them must fulfill those responsibilities; in principle this happens independently of their personal beliefs, but of course not of how people frame the issues (Amsterdam & Bruner, 2000). Some suggest this institutional help is what tipped the balance in favor of George W. Bush over Al Gore in the last U.S. election. Bush had his brother as governor of the pivotal state of Florida and a conservative U.S. Supreme Court who supported their preferred candidate within the

---

[6]This is not to say that we do not share human bodies with a propensity for meaning-making that makes individuals from different cultures very similar in many ways, but it does mean that although we share similar physical make ups and basic psychological capacities, our discernment and what we value and choose to emphasize as good ways of life must reflect our own cultural interpretative lens (Taylor, 1985, 1995).

limits of the law, interpreting ambiguous political situations to his advantage (Amsterdam & Bruner, 2000).

To add to Sternberg, something can be unbalanced—or in Hurka's (2001) sense, disproportionate—and so unwise, not merely because one selfishly considers one's own interests above all else, but sometimes because one considers institutional and not individual interests. Consider the chilling case of the representatives of Ford Motor Company who calculated that it would be cheaper to pay insurance claims for those killed in Ford Pintos than to recall a car model which they knew to have an exploding gas tank under certain kinds of impact.

To sum up, exceptionally high abilities and achievements have been studied in two main ways: through biographical studies of great men and what makes them great—accounts that increasingly go beyond knowledge to consider extracognitive factors such intuitions and work habits—and through studies of the social and cultural settings that foster individual greatness. Within these traditions there are at least two main extracognitive aspects of human flourishing: Creativity and wisdom. Creativity seems more concerned with the internal evolution of knowledge domains, while wisdom seems more tied to judicious practical action. Let us now consider how to integrate these two conceptions of exceptional human flourishing through the notion of selfways or habitus.

Selfways (Habitus)

In his notion of *habitus*, Bourdieu strives to integrate creativity and wisdom, two competing extracognitive aspects of development, into a single term that aims to dissolve the individual/social dichotomy implied by the main traditions of study identified by Shavinina. This idea of habitus has been adopted virtually unchanged by Markus, Mullally, and Kitayama (1997) in their discussion of selfways. So what is a selfway, or habitus? According to Bourdieu:

> The *habitus*... is the active presence of the whole past of which it is the product. [Its] autonomy is that of the past, enacted and acting, which, functioning as accumulated capital, produces history on the basis of history, and so ensures the permanence in change that makes the individual agent a world within the world. The habitus is a spontaneity without consciousness or will, opposed as much to the mechanical necessity of things without history in mechanistic theories as it is to the reflexive freedom of subjects "without inertia" in rationalist theories. (1990, p. 56)

If I understand this rather cryptic paragraph, for Bourdieu (1990, 1996), extracognitive aspects of exceptionally high abilities are best thought of as

11. EDUCATING SELVES TO BE CREATIVE AND WISE

expressions of personal dispositions to pursue certain projects and draw certain distinctions about what is or is not worthwhile. Such dispositions grow out of our entire cultural experience, including our training within particular knowledge domains, and are not merely a reflection of our knowledge or intellectual ability. Habitus or selfways are a product of history and reproduce history through the sense of shared *social reality* that we implicitly and explicitly maintain through our participation in particular cultural and institutional practices. A favorite example of Searle's (1998) is the use of paper money. Paper money actually has no value or function outside of one we agree to socially, a point driven home to me once in Egypt when I was willing to trade Yugoslavian currency at double the banks' rate, but found no one who believed that the currency had any real value. The reality in question is not only material, but also cultural; for example, in situations where it is important to know who to speak to and what to say to get something done, or what is of high quality—some people conduct themselves with distinction and make refined distinctions (they have good taste, or to put it another way, they show a refined tacit knowledge). Individuals with refined tacit knowledge in a domain have a lot of what Bourdieu calls *cultural capital.* The appreciation of important problems by Nobel Laureates is one example of "scientific taste"—analogous to artistic, aesthetic taste shown by "star" Juilliard musicians. Distinction or tacit knowledge provides a basis for Nobel Laureates' or star performers' intuition and sense of direction, noted by Shavinina and Subotnik. In their metacognitive experiences of beauty, the exceptionally well-developed habitus of scientists and musicians show us how much more deeply attuned to their domain and how more refined and richer is their understanding, as compared to most of their contemporaries.

Habitus involves intellect and personality and strives to maintain itself, both implicitly[7] and explicitly. On this view, each individual life (one's personal habitus) is a unique trajectory through a shared social space or field. The arc of that trajectory will depend on cultural capital that is in large part shared with the members of one's group. "Though it is impossible for all (or even two) members of the same class to have had the same experiences in the same order, it is certain that each member of the same class is more likely than any member of another class to have been confronted with the situations most frequent for members of that class" (Bourdieu, 1990, pp. 59–60). Thus it is not surprising, as Simonton notes, that several individuals sharing the same group habitus often independently arrive at the same cre-

---

[7]Implicit habitus is what Bourdieu calls *hexis* (implicit physical expression of habitus through, for example, physical skills such as instrument playing, but also extending to all aspects of the personal self such as posture, mannerisms, and dress. It is these, as the instructors at Juilliard note, that allow us to make an instant impression about people and is one of the reasons auditions are now commonly conducted behind a screen.

ative solutions; these solutions are given precisely by the joint play of the current state of knowledge in a domain and ideological frameworks within which new knowledge is created (Piaget & Garcia, 1983).

Habitus (or selfway) adds depth to Runco's point that for creativity, as for morality, we can identify what Kohlberg calls *preconventional* (naïve), *conventional* (expert), and *postconventional* (innovative) thought. The first and last are associated with creativity and knowledge advancement in different ways. As Simonton suggests, people who are experts in one field, but new to another, often make the greatest contributions to their second field by showing that accepted knowledge in that field has important gaps or alternatives. Those from a different domain—with a different habitus—are more likely to advance knowledge, since they draw different distinctions that can lead them to see things or try things in a different way. Such individuals are most likely to produce what Kuhn (1996) calls *paradigm shifts* that grasp a finer structure of reality, as was the case with Galileo's theory of motion mentioned earlier. On this view, innovation will often involve transposing cultural capital (either ideas, equipment, or methods) from one field to another, or joining fields together that were previously separate. This innovation can be proposed by a single individual, or by research teams who work toward consilience on problem of concern to them all (Dunbar, 1995; Wilson, 1998). And this is as true for producing art as it is for science (Jones & Galiston, 1998; Subotnik, this volume). Individuals who arrive at such exceptional achievements are thus very different from novices or children who have no deep knowledge or cultural capital to draw on.

The ideal social trajectory for a particular personal habitus, produced partly by chance—as Simonton is right to point out—naturally exemplifies what the group habitus considers most creative and wise. Such people have the most cultural capital; that is, they "play the game best," and see the right moves because they (sometimes intuitively) appreciate their beauty, and see stakes or problems as others do not (Bourdieu, 1996).

Which cultural games one becomes more or less an expert at playing is partly a matter of social upbringing, practice, and innate ability (Sternberg, Grigorenko, & Ferrari, 2001). Of course, if we learn to play music from great musicians from a young age, or if as adults we study with the greatest minds in a given knowledge domain, we may develop the habitus needed to excel without even noticing it. This tacit knowledge was shared by both Nobel laureates and musicians who enter Juilliard, because both groups actively sought out the best practitioners in their respective areas of endeavor. As Subotnik emphasizes, the mentor model adopted by Juilliard might be profitably applied to the most talented high school students entering college, like those who win the Westinghouse prize for science.

There is also a sense in which these great minds, like Vernadsky (cited in Shavinina, this volume) strive to "deny death," as Becker (1974) said, by producing something that endures beyond their own mortal lives. Becker quoted Freud as explicitly saying that he wanted to produce something that would endure, and as distressed by the thought that perhaps his work would not last an eternity. For Becker (1974) and Nagel (1986) these concerns are critical to all our lives, and the response of great people is a difference of intensity and not of kind. But the specifics of such concern, once again, is necessarily set in a culture. Individuals in different cultures strive to become a worthy person through articulation of ideal selfways; for example, by becoming an ideal Confucian person (junzi), or by becoming a great scientist or musician. But what is key, following Li, is that the ultimate appeal of such ideals (each of which represents a very different habitus) "may reside in the delicate symbiosis between a sense of self as an agent and a deep social connection" (Li, this volume, p. 201). Great individuals cannot rise above their culture, rather, they are embedded within the values and practices that nurtured them and within which they flourish. The lives and actions of such exemplary (and often idealized) individuals serves as a cultural aspiration, and it is this exemplariness that makes them great leaders or wise men, as was Zhuge Liang in ancient China. We might say that such people embody an ideal habitus or selfway, and inspire and exhort others to follow their example—shaping their intuitions about how to achieve a better world.

As Bourdieu (1990, 1996), (along with Subotnik and many authors in this volume) states, this deep response of the habitus is more than intellectual, it is emotional. Great individuals engender an enthusiastic and passionate response from their audiences. Such individuals, in the most positive sense have an enormous amount of cultural capital that allows them to see farther and respond better to situations than do their rivals, be they political, artistic, or scientific. This ability is perceived by others and by individuals themselves not as intelligence, but as an intuitive perception that is essentially what defines Aristotelian *phronesis*.

Each great leader (or scientist or musician) is a product of their culture (Gardner, 1993, 2002). Mao could not have become president of the United States of America and Kennedy would not have been made president of China. But both in their own countries were pivotal agents of social change, which is no easy thing given the rootedness of human habit and the institutional structures that preserve habits over generations (Bourdieu, 1990); by reaching people emotionally and intellectually—on the level of habitus—they inspired individuals and transformed society. As Shutte and colleagues suggest, in such cases, a match between context, motivational structure, and abilities are key.

Sometimes, we judge great men to be evil despite their great charisma (as with Hitler), or sometimes leaders held a reign of terror (as with Saddam Hussein), but in all cases, our assessment of such individuals is never morally neutral. Although they do not use the term, Nobel laureates and great musicians seem to exemplify and intuitively grasp the Chinese notion of *zuore* (self-perfecting development), striving to become what Li tells us is a *junzi* (a maximally genuine, sincere, and humane human being). And although this concept is specific to China, it is an ideal that America might profitably adopt from its dialogue with Chinese scholars, as it gives depth to Taylor's (1989, 1995) intuitions about self as necessarily orienting toward a culturally-defined good life. For Taylor, the core of our selfway, our habitus, is that which cannot be scrutinized; it remains implicit. The aim is to articulate that selfway in order to orient it toward an ever greater personal and social good. Such articulation is recursive, as Hurka (2001) suggests, and has intrinsic value by upholding perceived virtue and avoiding vice.

Of course, people's habitus can be *out of synch* with the current group habitus even if later groups consider their work genius—as in the case of Galileo, condemned to house arrest for his views. And even more to the point, the tragic suicide of a great tribal man in the face of colonial destruction of his way of life in *Things Fall Apart* (Achebe, 1958). Such stories point to the fact that individuals may experience an absolute conflict between personal understanding and social necessity. In the most difficult and tragic cases, as in the case of Latimer, such people are imprisoned, even killed for their convictions.

IMPLICATIONS FOR EDUCATION

What are the implications of this discussion of creativity, wisdom, and habitus for education? To begin to address this question, I first consider the role of schooling generally, and then consider specific extracognitive ways to foster exceptional abilities.

Role of Schooling

Schools have a variety of aims that sometimes come into conflict and need wise casuistry to balance. Egan (1997) suggests at least 3 principle aims for schooling:[8]

---

[8]For Egan (1997), education toward these aims will be best accomplished differently at different ages, as children learn to appreciate first myth, then romance, then logic, and finally irony.

1. to teach *truths* about the world that are not immediately apparent (e.g., that the earth is a sphere and not a flat surface, as one might initially suppose);
2. to prepare individuals for the *workplace* or for their adult life in society (e.g., reading and math skills, computer literacy, and other general skills, as well as forming good character); and
3. individual *flourishing* (i.e., to live the fullest life possible that expresses one's unique combination of intellectual and personal potential).

Shutte, Solomon, and Gardner, as well as Subotnik are the only authors who mention anything as mundane as helping people get a job and make money. Perhaps this is because the focus is on extracognitive aspects of exceptional ability; a job is necessary but not sufficient to merit discussion in this context. Instead, focus is on how to creatively advance knowledge of objective truths, or on how individuals can flourish wisely. Several recommendations are made for teaching creativity and wisdom.

Fostering Exceptional Abilities Through Developing Extracognitive Skills

Teaching Creativity

Although not emphasized, creativity ultimately seems tied to getting closer to the truth about something (perhaps proposing a new truth that displaces an old one) or to providing (even amusing) insight into the human condition. The techniques used to promote creativity, while not generated through analysis or logic, are necessarily held to standards about truth after the fact. Thus, Runco urges educators to help children develop *tactics* for originality by fostering change in perspectives, use of analogies (perhaps especially local analogies, cf. Dunbar, 1995). He also proposes that children develop borrowing strategies, using ideas from related domains. Runco points out that there is a fine line between nonconformity and deviance, but presumably allows this line to be traced locally. In essence, his advice concerns how to train one's mind effectively, in ways that go beyond a narrow focus on learning current factual knowledge. These concerns are also addressed by Howe (see also Gardner, 1997, 2002; Zimmerman, 2002), and have a long and illustrious history. John Locke (1693/1989) proposed many analogous methods for teaching optimal thinking in his book, *Some Thoughts Concerning Education* perhaps the first modern philosophical book devoted to this topic (see Tully, 1988 for a discussion). In essence, these authors seem to recommend the following:

work hard, think clearly and deeply, be a team player. Standing behind this view is the belief, perhaps the hope, that great people are like us, only more efficient.

Teaching Wisdom

Unlike creativity with its focus on truth, wisdom seems most to concern ideals for human understanding and action—whether our own or (through the advice we give) that of others. How to educate students to foster wisdom is a deep and abiding concern. As Sternberg reminds us, truly exceptional gifts at discerning the import of delicate social situations are not measured by current intelligence tests, or by tests of giftedness. No one cares about the IQ of Martin Luther King, Jr. or Gandhi. Wisdom is not captured by broader theories of intelligence such as Sternberg's triarchic theory or Gardner's theory of multiple intelligence, not even by measures of social or emotional intelligence. Rather wisdom is attributed to individuals who judge rightly or show discernment in complex cultural fields of endeavor. Sternberg argues that educators need to promote giftedness that fosters or expresses wisdom, and he suggests that failure to do this is the part of the reason why, although IQ has risen markedly over the past generations (Flynn, 1987; Neisser, 1997), wisdom (or lack or it) remains very much a constant companion of humankind. Sternberg boldly proposes seven ways to teach wisdom:

1. Provide problems that require wise thinking to solve.
2. Help students think in terms of a common good.
3. Help students think in ways that balance the interests of all stakeholders.
4. Provide past examples of wise thinking and analyze them.
5. Role-model wise thinking for students (a tall order).
6. Help students think dialectically—essentially, show that problems have not right and wrong solutions but better and worse ones that vary according to sociocultural context.[9]
7. Show students you value wise information processing and wise solutions.

Training Character and Habitus

Runco and other authors to this volume suggest that one way to develop wisdom and creativity may be to train character as well as intellect. For ex-

---

[9]Of course, we can also judge the merits of different *ad hominem* solutions, in light of perspicuous contrasts, even if from within our own hermeneutic circle (Taylor, 1995).

ample, students might be helped in *developing ego strength* that allows them to have faith in their intuitions and to manage strong emotional reactions and passions that life can require and evoke from us, along with specific problem-solving tactics, and generalization of solutions to natural problem-solving environments. Such efforts necessarily rely on what Sternberg calls "implicit theories" or folk models of creativity and wisdom that themselves are culturally specified. Indeed, this is integral to the career-training students receive at Juilliard and is probably fostered by all parents and teachers who steer children toward particular domains.

This admirable wish seems very much keeping with Rousseau's proposal that childhood education should bring out each person's unique gifts. Implicit in these suggestions—or perhaps I am reading too much in here—is that to really be creative or wise one should begin early; that childhood is a privileged time of growth and development. But it is well to remember that the idea of childhood is itself is a cultural construction (Kessen, 1979), at least in part, and that for the Chinese among others pursuit of excellence is a lifelong goal. According to Li, they generally believe that high ability is the result of continuous striving for self-perfection (*zuoren*, or becoming a person). Only people with strong personalities are able to be creative or wise leaders, great musicians, or effective community workers. Thus, ego strength must be developed in the depth of a habitus that embodies what is essential for that culture or discipline. Howard Gardner (2002) proposes his own list for developing extraordinary students. He points out that exceptional individuals reflect on their failures, play to their strengths, and compensate for their weaknesses. We see this in the examples of exceptional scholars or businessmen who overcame dyslexia (Fink, 1992, 1998).

At the risk of being a wet blanket, I must confess that much as I support the spirit of these democratic ideas, I am dubious that any purely intellectual methods can really reach students on such a deep level. It is one thing to know what to do and another to have the will to achieve it at the personal cost it entails (Ferrari, 2002; James, 1902). Consider going on a diet to lose weight. Some will fail miserably at such a challenge and others will manage to lose 100 lbs by sheer determined effort. Whatever the difference is between such individuals, I am ready to bet that it lies deeper than their rational assessment of the current situation. Everyone knows that to lose weight one needs to eat a moderate amount of a balanced diet, and exercise—but not everyone manages to implement these goals.

While all of the insights provided by the authors of the volume can, in principle, help "ordinary people" do better, as pointed out by Howe (and by Aristotle long ago) it is one thing to know what to do and another to do it consistently and diligently; this reality is as true of being a good person as it is of developing expertise. The great individuals described by Howe had to pace themselves in their work, and complained of the strain of producing their masterpieces or revolutionary theories. Clearly, not many students—not even those with great potential described by Shutte and Subotnik—will be able to follow such a grueling regimen, although we can always hope. And some students may not consider that this sort of driving work really is a wise way to live a good life that allows for other things they may value—like lying on the beach, or talking with friends.

Personal Cognitive Development

As many authors in this volume emphasize, creativity, wisdom and other forms of high ability are personal achievements—the emphasis being on personal (not individual) identity. Persons are social actors whose strivings are only intelligible when considered within cultural traditions (Ferrari & Mahalingham, 1998; Geertz, 1984; Taylor, 1989). However, Li (also Geertz, 1984) draws an important distinction in every culture between the "naïve theories" of folk belief and the specialized expert knowledge accumulated over centuries of sustained reflection. Thus, for example, acupuncture and Western medical practice are both to be distinguished from naïve ideas on how to stay healthy of "the person on the street" in either culture. When such domains are not assigned or excluded by birth, Shutte and her colleagues suggest that the brightest minds of a culture are drawn to the domains of knowledge for which they feel best matched and are most concerned about. It is to these domains that exceptional individuals contribute by advancing them from within or by creatively overthrowing them in favor of some other conception they judge a better alternative. Such traditions provide ideals that shape their individual disciples (Ricoeur, 1986), as we clearly see in the aspirations of Chinese students reported by Li; in the Juilliard students described by Subotnik; and in the strivings of the students described by Shutte, Solomon, and Gardner. In all these cases, students' ideals about learning and motivational structure matched those of their culture and specific domain of action (e.g., music or community involvement). The students with the best match (and hence the most cultural capital) most successfully strive toward what they consider both a personal and a social good.

Furthermore, students need to match their motivational structure to the structure of the domain, regardless of culture: music is not community work or scientific work so it will need different types of students, and different types of schools to foster exceptional abilities, as Soloman and her associates show. Matching individuals' motivational structure and a domain's reward structures is important to assure that virtually all individuals can sustain commitment to particular cultural fields and acquire the cultural capital they need to excel.

11. EDUCATING SELVES TO BE CREATIVE AND WISE

These considerations suggest that becoming an exceptional person of a particular sort requires developing that sort of selfway (or habitus) through practical activity—not just understanding concepts, no matter how clear and appropriate to the task. As Simonton notes, preparedness for capitalizing on opportunities for creativity is fostered by:

1. an intense fascination with a field (or domain, if we follow Gardner);
2. the expertise to determine what is creative in a given domain;
3. a personality able and disposed to playing with combinations of ideas; and
4. drive and persistence.

All of these are a reflection of a particular sort of selfway that is intimately bound up in social settings. As Subotnik and Shutte, Solomon, and Gardner show, one is heavily influenced by the aspirations of parents and teachers who provide the opportunities, support, and values that shape students' interests, sometime even before they enter school.

Because selfways (and the tacit knowledge or cultural capital they involve) often remain implicit, it may be through a lineage of great teachers that the best students learn how to become great, because these people are able to teach students what Foucault (1994/1997) calls *techniques de soi* (literally, "techniques of self," but might broadly mean a science of selfmaking)—techniques fostered by mentors who themselves achieved a certain selfway. Such techniques of self are part of the tacit knowledge that distinguish those who make it into the elite music schools like Juilliard, or elite universities like Yale or Harvard. And it is fostered in those who attend them.

Because it is so difficult to achieve a professional career in concert performance, elite schools like Juilliard go against the democratic spirit of some of the authors of this volume: only the very best (already well matched to the domain) are able to attend, let alone excel in them. But *elite schools are a prime source for acquiring cultural capital*, not only in developing technical expertise, but even in terms of managing budding careers. As Bourdieu (1996) points out, the deck is stacked in favor of those who have been exposed to the best teachers and who arrive for an audition with a lot of musical capital. The lineage of great musicians and of Nobel scientists described by Subotnick and Shavinina is amazing. Judges holding the auditions for Juilliard say they can sometimes see a teacher's influence as students walk through the door. This same dynamic is seen in Nobel Laureates, as both Subotnick and Shavinina note, with laureates often being trained by previous laureates.

For Bourdieu (1996) this capital is a product of individual social history but is often misrecognized as inborn talent, "the academic taxonomy, a system of principles of vision and division implemented at a practical level, rests on an implicit definition of excellence that, by granting superiority to the qualities socially conferred upon those who are socially dominant, consecrates both their way of being and their state" (p. 37). As Bourdieu (1996) predicts, teachers do not see the skills of students as the result of training or early formative experiences, but as reflecting an internal essence or talent. Howe and other authors (see Ericsson, 2002) follow Bourdieu in saying that we should not underestimate the extent to which dedicated training and masterful teaching contribute to producing "stars" in a particular cultural field.

But Bourdieu may overstate his case. Many exceptional students seek out teachers and peers with talent, and not everyone with good connections is able to acquire the capital needed to be admitted to an elite school. So his thesis should not be used to detract from the acknowledged abilities and skills of these students, or their remarkable achievements; it merely suggests that developing such skills is never divorced from personal and social history. And although Bourdieu (1990, 1996) may insist that such abilities reflect a habitus developed through exposure to appropriate models and institutions, it is heartening to learn that many intellectual giants described by Howe did not even complete their formal schooling, but were systematic in their efforts to learn. Indeed, Howe shows that even without schooling, people who diligently train (sometimes using artifacts like books, rather than direct teachers), persevere in the face of obstacles, and have social skills that bring them help when needed, can rise to greatness. This is clearly seen in historical figures such as Faraday, or Stephenson (who could not even read before age 18). As Howe shows, the principal importance of individual efforts appears to hold true as far back as we can find facts to address this issue.

How can we educate people in ways that transform their selfways, when these selfways are shaped by experiences that go beyond knowledge? I consider this one of the most difficult questions to answer, but one that lies at the heart of extracognitive aspects of high ability. Allow me to close with a suggestion. One way to train selfways is to transform them through educational activities that let individuals engage the world in new ways, actively expressing the advice given by the authors of this volume. Such transformative learning environments already exist, in innovative programs such as the late Ann Brown's (1997) program to *Foster Communities of Learners*, in new online educational environments such as *Knowledge Forum* (Bereiter & Scardamalia, 2000), that require students to construct and debate their own understanding of important science concepts. Another possibility is to use computer simulations and games like *Court Square* (1995–1997) or *Capi-*

talism (1996), that allow students actively to construct practical knowledge of how to excel in business (and similar games exist for tacit learning about science). By engaging in simulated activities with detailed and targeted feedback about how to be successful at them, such activities offer real potential to transform students' selfways in profound and not merely superficial ways. Although these ideas are not new, there are increasing efforts to help teachers incorporate the transformative educational power of these activities into their classrooms (Ferrari, Taylor, & van Lehn, 1999). At an even deeper level, extracurricular activities like sports and art, community service, religious affiliations, and even training in practices like meditation may be needed to effect profound beneficial transformations in students. It is far from clear how to incorporate such concerns into public education as we now know it.

REFERENCES

Achebe, C. (1958). *Things fall apart.* London: Heinemann.
Amsterdam, A., & Bruner, J. (2000). *Minding the law.* New York: Harvard University Press.
Appiah, K. A. (1996). Race, culture, identity: Misunderstood connections. In G. B. Peterson (Ed.), *The tanner lectures on human values* (pp. 51–136). Salt Lake City: University of Utah Press.
Aristotle (~300 B.C./1984). *The complete works of Aristotle* (The revised Oxford translation, Vol. 1) (J. Barnes, Ed.). Princeton, NJ: Princeton University Press.
Baldwin, J. M. (1896). The genius and his environment. *Popular Science Monthly, 49,* 312–320, 522–534.
Baldwin, J. M. (1930). James Mark Baldwin. In C. Murchison (Ed.), *A history of psychology in autobiography.* New York: Russell & Russell.
Baltes, P. B., & Smith, J. (1990). The psychology of wisdom and its ontogenesis. In R. J. Sternberg (Ed.), *Wisdom: Its nature, origins, and development* (pp. 87–120). New York: Cambridge University Press.
Baltes, P. B., & Staudinger, U. M. (2000). Wisdom: A metaheuristic (pragmatic) to orchestrate mind and virtue toward excellence. *American Psychologist, 55*(1), 122–136.
Becker, E. (1974). *The denial of death.* New York: Simon & Schuster.
Bereiter, C., & Scardamalia, M. (2000). Commentary on Part I: Process and product in problem-based learning (PBL) research. In D. H. Evensen & C. E. Hmelo (Eds.), *Problem-based learning: A research perspective on learning interactions* (pp. 185–195). Mahwah, NJ: Lawrence Erlbaum Associates.
Bloor, D. (1999). Anti-Latour. *Studies in History and Philosophy of Science, 30,* 81–112.
Bourdieu, P. (1990). *The logic of practice.* Stanford, CA: Stanford University Press.
Bourdieu, P. (1996). *Mèditations pascaliennes* (Pascalian meditations). Paris: Seuil.
Brown, A. (1997). Transforming schools into communities of thinking and learning about serious matters. *American Psychologist, 52*(4), 399–413.
Case, R. (Ed.). (1991). *The mind's staircase.* Hillsdale, NJ: Lawrence Erlbaum Associates.
Case, R. (1998). The development of conceptual structures. In W. Damon (Series Ed.), D. Kuhn & R. S. Siegler (Vol. Eds.), *Handbook of child psychology, Vol. 2: Cognition, perception, and language* (5th ed., pp. 745–800). New York: Wiley.
Capitalism (1996). Interactive magic. Research Triangle Park, NC.

Court Square (1995–1997). Classroom Inc., NY.

Csikszentmihalyi, M. (1997). *Finding flow: The psychology of engagement with everyday life.* New York: Basic Books.

Dunbar, K. (1995). How scientists really reason: Scientific reasoning in real-world laboratories. In R. J. Sternberg & J. E. Davidson (Eds.), *The nature of insight* (pp. 365–395). Cambridge, MA: The MIT Press.

Eco, U. (1998). *Serendipities: Language and lunacy.* New York: Columbia University Press.

Egan, K. (1997). *The educated mind: How cognitive tools shape our understanding.*

Ericsson, A. (2002). Attaining excellence through deliberate practice: Insights from the study of expert performance. In M. Ferrari (Ed.), *The pursuit of excellence through education* (pp. 21–55). Mahwah, NJ: Lawrence Erlbaum Associates.

Ferrari, M. (2002). Personal and institutional pursuit of excellence. In M. Ferrari (Ed.), *The pursuit of excellence through education* (pp. 195–219). Mahwah, NJ: Lawrence Erlbaum Associates.

Ferrari, M. (2002). (Ed.). *Varieties of Religious Experience: Centennial essays.* Exeter, UK: Imprint Academic. (Also published as a special issue of *Journal of Consciousness Studies*).

Ferrari, M., & Koyama, E. (2002). Meta-emotion and cross-cultural comparison of anger and amae. *Consciousness and Emotion, 3,* 197–211.

Ferrari, M., & Mahalingam, R. (1998). Personal cognitive development and its implications for teaching and learning. *Educational Psychologist, 33,* 35–44.

Ferrari, M., Taylor, R., & VanLehn, K. (1999). Adapting work simulations for school: Preparing students for tomorrow's workplace. *Journal of Educational Computing Research, 21,* 25–53.

Fink, R. P. (1992). Successful dyslexics' alternative pathways for reading: A developmental study (Doctoral dissertation, Harvard Graduate School of Education, 1992). *Dissertation Abstracts International,* F4965.

Fink, R. P. (1998). Literacy development in successful men and women with dyslexia. *Annals of Dyslexia, 48,* 311–346.

Fischer, K. W. (1980). A theory of cognitive development: The control and construction of hierarchies of skills. *Psychological Review, 87,* 447–531.

Fischer, K. W., & Biddell, T. R. (1998). Dynamic development of psychological structures in action and thought. In W. Damon (Ed.), R. M. Lerner (Vol. Ed.), *Handbook of child psychology: Theoretical models of human development* (5th ed., pp. 467–561). New York: Wiley.

Fisher, K. W., & Bidell, T. R. (1998). Dynamic development of psychological structures in action and thought. In W. Damon (Ed.), R. M. Lerner (Vol. Ed.), *Handbook of psychology: Vol. 1. Theoretical models of human development* (5th ed., pp. 467–562). New York: Wiley.

Flavell, J. H. (1981). Cognitive monitoring. In W. P. Dickson (Ed.), *Children's oral communication skills* (pp. 35–60). New York: Academic Press.

Flynn, J. R. (1987). Massive IQ gains in 14 nations: What IQ tests really measure. *Psychological Bulletin, 101*(2), 171–191.

Foucault, M. (1994/1997). Ethics: Subjectivity and truth. In P. Rabinow (Ed.), *The essential works of Michel Foucault 1954–1984, Vol. 1.* New York: The New Press.

Fraser, N. (1996). Social justice in the age of identity politics: Redistribution, recognition, and participation. In G. B. Peterson (1998), *The tanner lectures on human values* (pp. 1–67). Salt Lake City: University of Utah Press.

Frege, G. (1956). The thought: A logical inquiry. *Mind, 65,* 289–311.

Gardner, H. (1993). *Frames of mind* (10th Anniversary edition). New York: Basic Books.

Gardner, H. (1997). *Extraordinary minds: Portraits of four exceptional individuals and an examination of our own extraordinariness.* New York: Basic Books.

Gardner, H. (2002). Learning from extraordinary minds. In M. Ferrari (Ed.), *The pursuit of excellence through education* (pp. 3–20). Mahwah, NJ: Lawrence Erlbaum Associates.

Geertz, C. (1984). "From the native's point of view": On the nature of anthropological understanding. In R. A. Sweder & R. A. Levine (Eds.), *Cultural theory: Essays on mind, self, and emotion* (pp. 123–136). Cambridge, MA: Harvard University Press.

Helmholtz, H. von (1898). An autobiographical sketch (E. Atkinson, Trans.). In *Popular lectures on scientific subjects, second series* (pp. 266–291). New York: Longmans, Green. (Original work published 1891)

Hurka, T. (2001). *Virtue, vice, and value*. New York: Oxford University Press.

James, W. (1902). *The Varieties of Religious Experience: A Study in Human Nature* (Being the Gifford Lectures on Natural Religion Delivered at Edinburgh in 1901–1902). New York and London: Longmans, Green & Co.

Jones, C. A., & Galiston, P. (Eds.). (1998). *Picturing science, producing art*. New York: Routledge.

Jonsen, A. R., & Toulmin, S. (1988). *The abuse of casuistry*. New York: Cambridge University Press.

Kessen, W. (1979). *Psychological development from infancy: Image to intention* (M. H. Bornstein, Ed.). Hillsdale, NJ: Lawrence Erlbaum Associates.

Kuhn, T. S. (1981). A function for thought experiments. In Ian Hacking (Ed.), *Scientific revolutions* (pp. 6–27). New York: Oxford University Press. (Originally published in L'aventure de la science, Mélanges Alexandre Koyré, vol. 2, pp. 307–334, 1964)

Kuhn, T. (1996). *Structure of scientific revolutions* (3rd ed.). Chicago: University of Chicago Press.

Lakatos, I. (1978). *The methodology of scientific research programmes (Philosophical papers, Vol. 1)*. Cambridge; New York: Cambridge University Press.

Latour, B. (1999). For David Bloor . . . and beyond: a reply to David Bloor's 'Anti-Latour.' *Studies in History and Philosophy, 30*, 113–129.

Latour, B. (2000). When things strike back: A possible contribution of "social studies" to the social sciences. *British Journal of Sociology, 51*, 107–123.

Lewis, M. (2000). The promise of dynamic systems approaches for an integrated account of human development. *Child Development, 71*, 36–43.

Locke, J. (1989). *Some thoughts concerning education*. New York: Oxford University Press. (Originally published 1693)

Luna, L. E., & Amaringo, P. (1999). *Ayahuasca visions: The religious iconography of a Peruvian shaman*. Berkeley, CA: North Atlantic Books.

Markus, H. R., Mullally, P. R., & Kitayama, S. (1997). Self-ways: Diversity in ways of cultural participation. In U. Neisser & D. A. Jopling (Eds.), *The conceptual self in context: Culture, experience, self-understanding. The Emory symposia in cognition* (pp. 13–61). New York: Cambridge University Press.

Meichenbaum, D. (1975). Enhancing creativity by modifying what subjects say to themselves. *American Educational Research Journal, 12*(2), 129–145.

Nagel, T. (1986). *The view from nowhere*. New York: Oxford University Press.

Neisser, U. (1997). The roots of self-knowledge: Perceiving self, it, and thou. *Annals of the New York Academy of Sciences, 818*, 19–34.

Nietzsche (1949). *The use and abuse of history* (A. Collins, Trans.). Indianapolis, IN: Bobbs-Merrill. (Original work published 1874)

Nussbaum, M. (2001). *The fragility of goodness: Luck & ethics in Greek tragedy and philosophy*. New York: Cambridge University Press.

Piaget, J. (1974a). *La prise de conscience*. Paris: Presses Universitaires de France.

Piaget, J. (1974b). *Réussir et comprendre*. Paris: Presses Universitaires de France.

Piaget, J. (1977). Etudes d'epistemologie genetique, vol. 35: *Recherches sur l'abstraction reflechissante. I. L'abstraction des relations logico-arithmetiques*. Paris: Presses Universitaires de France.

Piaget, J., & Garcia, R. (1983). *Psychogenesis and the history of science* (H. Feider, Trans.). New York: Columbia University Press.

Pinard, A. (1992). Metaconscience et métacognition (Metaconsciousness and metacognition). *Canadian Psychology, 33,* 27–41.

Popper, K. R. (1994). *Knowledge and the body-mind problem: In defence of interaction* (M. A. Notturno, Ed.). New York: Routledge.

Quételet, A. (1968). *A treatise on man and the development of his faculties.* New York: Franklin. (Reprint of 1842 Edinburgh translation of 1835 French original)

R. V. Latimer. Neutral citation: 2001 SCC 1.File No. 26980. Available online at (http://www.lexum.umontreal.ca/csc-scc/en/rec/html/latimer2.en.html)

Rajan, C. (Trans.). (1993). *The Pancatantra* (by V. Sarma). London, UK: Penguin Books.

Ricoeur, P. (1986). *Lectures on ideology and utopia* (G. H. Taylor, Ed.). New York: Columbia University Press.

Roberts, R. M. (1989). *Serendipity: Accidental discoveries in science.* New York: Wiley.

Searle, J. (2000). Paper presented at Towards a Science of Consciousness conference. Tucson, AZ.

Searle, J. R. (1998). *Mind, language and society: Philosophy in the real world.* New York: Basic Books.

Simon, H. A. (1982). *Models of bounded rationality.* Cambridge, MA: MIT Press.

Staudinger, U. M., & Baltes, P. B. (1996). Interactive minds: A facilitative setting for wisdom-related performance? *Journal of Personality and Social Psychology, 71,* 746–762.

Sternberg, R. J., Grigorenko, E. L., & Ferrari, M. (2002). Fostering intellectual expertise through developing expertise. In M. Ferrari (Ed.), *The pursuit of excellence through education* (pp. 57–83). Mahwah, NJ: Lawrence Erlbaum Associates.

Suzuki, D. T. (1960). *Studies in Zen.* London, UK: Unwin. (Copyright renewed 1988)

Taylor, C. (1985). *Human agency and language: Philosophical papers 1.* New York: Cambridge University Press.

Taylor, C. (1989). *Sources of the self: The making of the modern identity.* Cambridge, MA: Harvard University Press.

Taylor, C. (1995). *Philosophical arguments.* Cambridge, MA: Harvard University Press.

Varela, (1999). *Ethical know-how: Action, wisdom, and cognition.* Stanford, CA: Stanford University Press. (Originally published 1992)

Wegner, D. M., & Wheatley, T. (1999). Apparent mental causation: Sources of the experience of will. *American Psychologist, 54*(7), 480–492.

Williams, B. (1988). Consequentialism and integrity. In S. Scheffler (Ed.), *Consequentialism and its critics* (pp. 20–50). New York: Oxford University Press. (Originally published in 1973)

Wilson, E. O. (1998). *Consilience: The unity of knowledge.* New York: Knopf.

Zimmerman, B. J. (2002). Achieving academic excellence: A self-regulatory perspective. In M. Ferrari (Ed.), *The pursuit of excellence through education* (pp. 85–110). Mahwah, NJ: Lawrence Erlbaum Associates.

Author Index

A

Achebe, C., 228, *235*
Adleman, L. M., 64, *68*
Albert, R. S., 18, *24*, *25*
Allison, P. D., 53, *68*
Almgren, P.-E., 31, *37*
Amabile, T. M., 6, *12*, 190, *204*
Amaringo, P., 222, *237*
Amsterdam, A., 223, 224, *235*
Andrews, M. L., 138, *166*
Appiah, K. A., 223, *235*
Aristotle, 212, *235*
Arnold, K. D., 139, *166*, 190, *204*
Austin, J. H., 65, *68*
Azuma, H., 203, *204*

B

Baldwin, J. M., 216, *235*
Baltes, P. B., 171, 181, *185*, *186*, 219, *235*, *238*
Balthazard, C., 93, *100*
Bamberger, J., 138, *165*
Bandura, A., 120, *135*
Bargh, J. A., 27, *36*
Barker, J., 114, *117*
Barlow, L. W., 53, *68*
Barron, F., 190, *204*, *208*
Basadur, M., 23, *24*
Basseches, J., 182, *185*
Becker, E., 226, 227, *235*
Bempechat, J., 189, *204*
Bennet, W., 54, *68*
Bereiter, C., 234, *235*
Bergson, H., 29, *36*
Berliner, D., 192, 203, *208*
Berry, J. W., 189, *204*, *206*
Beveridge, W. I. B., 66, *68*
Biddell, T. R., 214, *236*
Biggs, J. B., 193, *204*
Blakelock, E., 55, *70*
Bloom, B. S., 120, 122, 123, 131, 134, *134*, 138, 139, *165*, 171, *185*
Bloor, D., 216, *235*
Boden, M. A., 63, 64, *68*
Boodoo, G., 189, *207*
Bouchard, T. J., Jr., 189, *207*
Bourdieu, P., 218, 223, 224, 225, 226, 227, 233, 234, *235*
Bowers, K. S., 93, *100*
Boykin, A. W., 189, *207*
Bradshaw, G. L., 63, *69*
Brannigan, A., 47, *68*
Brody, N., 189, *207*
Bronfenbrenner, U., 190, *204*
Browder, C. S., 7, *12*
Brown, A., 234, *235*
Brown, A. L., 76, 95, *100*
Brown, J. W., 29, *36*
Browne, J., 108, *117*
Bruner, J. S., 92, 96, *100*, 192, *204*, 223, 224, *235*
Burkhardt, F., 108, *117*
Burt, C., 51, 52, *68*

C

Campbell, D. T., 65, *68*
Cannon, W. B., 65, *68*
Cantor, G., 108, *117,*
Cantor, N., 169, *185*
Carlsson, I., 29, 30, 32, 35, *36, 37*
Case, R., 214, *235*
Ceci, S. J., 189, *207*
Chaiklin, S., 74, 83, 84, 87, 91, 93, 94, 96, 97, 98, *101*
Chan, J., 191, *204*
Chao, R. K., 192, *205*
Charles, R., 21, *25*
Chartrand, T. L., 27, *36*
Chase, W., 119, *135*
Chi, M. T. H., 172, *185*
Chubin, D. F., 53, *72*
Cole, J. R., 55, *68*
Cole, S., 55, 59, *68*
Coleman, L. J., 139, *166*
Constant, E. W., II, 44, *68*
Cooper, C., 190, *205*
Covington, M. V., 189, *205*
Cox, C., 5, *12*, 66, 67, *68*
Cramer, P., 27, *36*
Cropper, W. H., 84, *100*
Crozier, W. R., 58, *68*
Crutchfield, R., 67, *68*
Csikszentmihalyi, M., 8, *12*, 83, 84, 98, *100,* 120, 122, *134,* 171, 181, *185,* 189, 190, 203, *205,* 218, *236*

D

Daintith, J., 48, *68*
D'Andrade, R., 192, *205*
Dasen, P. R., 193, *205*
Davidson, J. W., 110, 111, *117*
Davis, R. A., 55, *68*
Darwin, C., 108, 110, *117*
Denner, J., 190, *205*
Dennis, W., 52, 56, 57, 58, 59, 62, *68*
Desmond, A., 108, *117*
Dirac, P. A. M., 84, 85, *100*
DiSessa, A., 192, *205*
Dixon, N. F., 27, *37*
Dobson, D. M., 181, *186*

Drago-Severson, E., 189, *204*
Draguns, J. G., 32, *37*
Dunbar, K., 214, 217, 226, 229, *236*
Duschl, R., 139, *166*
Dweck, C. S., 189, *205*

E

Easton, S. M., 42, *69*
Eccles, J. S., 122, 123, *134*
Eco, U., 213, *236*
Egan, K., 228, *236*
Ehlers, W., 32, *37*
Einstein, A., 76, 77, 90, *100*
Ekvall, G., 34, *37*
Ericsson, A., 234, *236*
Ericsson, K. A., 66, *69,* 76, *100,* 111, *117,* 119, *135*
Eysenck, H. J., 52, 66, 67, *69*

F

Farr, M. J., 172, *185*
Feist, G. J., 55, *69*
Feldhusen, J. F., 7, *12*
Feldman, D. H., 5, 8, *12,* 120, 121, 122, 131, *135,* 189, 203, *205*
Fensham, P., 74, 83, 84, 87, 91, 93, 94, 96, 97, 98, *101*
Ferrari, M. J., 95, *100,* 216, 222, 226, 231, 232, 235, *236, 238*
Fink, R. P., 231, *236*
Finke, R. A., 63, *69*
Fischer, K. W., 214, *236*
Flavell, J. H., 95, *100,* 215, *236*
Fleming, J. S., 190, *205*
Flynn, J. R., 184, *185,* 230, *236*
Forsythe, G. B., 93, *101,* 163, *166,* 171, *186*
Foucault, M., 233, *236*
Fraser, N., 223, *236*
Frege, G., 216, *236*
Frey, D., 75, *100*

G

Gagne, F., 138, *165*
Galiston, P., 226, *237*

AUTHOR INDEX

Galton, F., 4, *12*, 51, *69*
Garcia, R., 212, 216, 217, 226, *237*
Gardner, H., 8, *12*, 90, *101*, 120, 131, *135*, 169, *185*, 189, 190, 192, 203, *205*, 227, 229, 231, *236*,
Gaynor, J. R., 21, *25*
Geertz, C., 232, *237*
Gemelli, A., 30, *37*
Ghiselin, B., 65, *69*, 190, *205*
Glaser, R., 172, *185*
Goldberg, D. E., 64, *69*
Goldsmith, L. T., 189, 203, *205*
Goleman, D., 169, *185*
Goodnow, J. J., 192, *205*
Gottfried, A. E., 190, *205*
Gottfried, A. W., 190, *205*
Greenfield, P. M., 204, *205*
Greenwald, A. G., 27, *37*
Grigorenko, E. L., 93, *101*, 138, 163, *166*, 171, *186*, 226, *238*
Gross, M. U. M., 76, *101*
Grotzer, T. A., 184, *185*
Gruber, H. E., 67, *69*, 90, 98, *101*, *102*, 189, 203, *205*
Guilford, J. P., 66, *69*, 171, *185*, 190, *205*

H

Habicht, J. P., 191, *207*
Hadamard, J., 65, *69*, 73, 90, 92, *100*
Hagstrom, W. O., 50, *69*
Halpern, D. F., 189, *207*
Hamilton, J., 110, *117*
Harkness, S., 192, *205*
Haroutounian, J., 138, *165*
Harris, J. R., 181, *185*
Hayes, J. R., 66, *69*, 111, *117*
Hedlund, 93, *101*, 138, 163, *166*, 171, *186*
Hegel, G. W. F., 182, 183, *185*
Heisenberg, W., 85, 97, *100*
Heller, K. A., 6, *12*
Helmholtz, H. von, 67, *69*, 213, *237*
Hentschel, U., 32, *37*
Hernstein, R., 189, *205*
Hertz, R., 141, *165*
Hewitt, N. M., 139, *166*
Hibbert, C., 114, *177*
Hofer, B. K., 189, 193, *207*

Hoffman, R. R., 172, *185*
Holland, D., 192, *207*
Holland, J. H., 64, *69*
Hollingworth, L. S., 5, *12*
Hollos, M., 192, *206*
Holton, G., 76, *100*, 190, *206*
Horowitz, L. M., 194, *206*
Horvath, J. A., 93, *101*, 163, *166*, 171, *186*
Howe, M. J. A., 7, 8, *12*, 106, 108, 110, 111, 114, 116, *117*, 138, *166*
Huber, J. C., 61, 62, *69*
Hudson, L., 42, *69*
Hui, C. H., 200, *206*
Hung, S. S., 51, *72*
Hurka, T., 218, 224, 228, *237*

I

Imber, J. B., 141, *165*
Irvine, S. H., 189, *206*

J

Jacot, B., 42, *69*
James, W., 29, *37*, 231, *237*
Jarwan, F. A., 7, *12*
Johanson, A., 31, *37*
Johnson, D., 21, *25*
Johnson, G., 31, *37*
Johnson-Laird, P. N., 63, *69*
John-Steiner, V., 76, 90, 91, *101*
Jones, B., 108, 113, *117*
Jones, C. A., 226, *237*
Jonsen, A. R., 222, *237*

K

Kantorovich, A., 65, *69*
Kaplan, N., 190, *206*
Kashimagi, K., 203, *204*
Kassan, L., 160, *166*
Keats, D., 193, 196, *206*
Kessen, W., 231, *237*
Kholodnaya, M. A., 88, 99, *101*
Kihlstrom, J. F., 169, *185*
Kingsbury, H., 138, *165*
Kirson, D., 194, *207*
Kitayama, S., 203, *206*, 224, *237*

Klein, R. E., 191, *207*
Koestler, A., 44, *69*
Kogan, J., 138, *165*
Kohlberg, L., 179, *185*, 199, *206*
Koyama, E., 222, *236*
Koza, J. R., 64, *69*
Krampe, R. T., 111, *117*
Krammpe, R. T., 119, *135*
Krebs, H., 88, *101*
Kroeber, A. L., 41, 44, 45, 47, *69*
Kragh, U., 30, 31, *37*
Krauze, T. K., 53, *68*
Kuhn, T. S., 86, 87, *101*, 190, *206*, 212, 213, 215, 226, *237*
Külpe, O., 29, *37*

L

Labouvie-Vief, G., 182, *185*
Lai, C.-Y., 197, 198n, 199, 200, 201, *208*
Lakatos, I., 212, 217, *237*
Lamb, D., 42, *69*
Langley, P., 63, *69*, 71
Laskin, E., 131, *135*
Latimer, R. V., 219, 220, 221, *237*
Latour, B., 212, 216, 217, *237*
Lazarus, R. S., 18n, *24*
Lee, W. O., 197, 199, 200, 202, *206*
Lehman, H. C., 56, 57, 58, *69*
Lehwald, G., 7, *12*
Leites, N. S., 5, *12*
LeVine, R. A., 188, 192, *206*
Lewis, M., 217, *237*
Li, J., 190, 192, 194, 197, 198, 199, 200, 202, 203, *206*
Li, L.-J., 198, *208*
Libet, B., 28, *37*
Lilja, A., 32, 33, *37*
Liu, Z., 198, *206*
Locke, J., 229, *237*
Loehlin, J. C., 189, *207*
Long, J. S., 53, *68*
Lorenz, K., 86, *101*
Lotka, A. J., 52, *69*
Lowenstein, E., 194, *206*
Lubart, T. I., 8, *13*, 52, 66, 72
Luna, L. E., 222, *237*
Luria, A. R., 192, *206*
Lykken, D. T., 52, *70*

Lynn, R., 189, *206*

M

Mach, E., 65, 66, *70*
MacKinnon, D. W., 6, *12*
Maercker, A., 181, *185*
Magen, N., 192, 203, *208*
Mahalingam, R., 232, *236*
Mahapatra, M., 203, *207*
Malmström, P., 32, 33, *37*
Markus, H. J., 203, *206*, 224, *237*
Martindale, C., 66, *70*
Martinez-Pons, M., 120, *135*
Marton, F., 74, 83, 84, 87, 91, 93, 94, 96, 97, 98, *101*
Maurer, K., 139, *166*
Mayer, J. D., 169, *186*
McClelland, D. C., 191, *206*
McCrae, R. R., 66, *70*
McCurdy, H. G., 8, *12*
McMorris, M. N., 86, *101*
Meacham, J., 178, *185*
Mednick, S. A., 66, *70*
Meichenbaum, D., 215, *237*
Mencius, 199, *207*
Merton, R. K., 41, 46, 47, 49, 53, *70*
Miller, A. I., 81, 86, *101*
Miller, A. L., 64, *70*
Miller, J. G., 203, *207*
Mitchell, S., 48, *68*
Moles, A., 56, *70*
Moore, D. G., 110, 111, *117*
Moore, J., 108, *117*
Mullally, P. R., 224, *237*
Munroe, R. H., 191, 192, *207*
Munroe, R. L., 191, 192, *207*
Murray, C., 189, *205*

N

Nagel, T., 227, *237*
Ne'eman, Y., 65, *69*
Neisser, U., 184, *185*, 189, *207*, 230, *237*
Nemirovsky, R., 90, *101*
Nerlove, S. B., 191, *207*
Nicholls, J. G., 189, *207*
Nietzsche, 217, *237*
Nussbaum, M., 222, *237*

O

Ochse, R., 86, 87, 90, 92, *101*
O'Connor, C., 194, *207*
Oden, M. H., 5, *13*
Ogbu, J. U., 189, *207*
Ogburn, W. K., 45, 46, *70*
Okagaki, L., 177, *186*, 193, 203, *207*
Olmstead, A., 138, *165*
Olson, D. R., 189, *207*

P

Parad, H. W., 194, *206*
Parker, K., 93, *100*
Pascual-Leone, J., 182, *185*
Patinkin, D., 42, 43, *70*
Perkins, D. N., 184, *185*, 189, 192, *207*
Perleth, C., 7, *12*
Perloff, R., 189, *207*
Persson, R. S., 138, 141, 146, *165*, *166*
Piaget, J., 20, *24*, 212, 216, 217, 226, *237*
Piirto, J., 138, *166*
Pinard, A., 215, *238*
Pinker, S., 189, *207*
Planck, M., 90, *101*
Platz, A., 55, *70*
Plucker, J., 23, 24, *24*
Poincaré, H., 65, 67, *70*, 74, *101*
Polanyi, M., 171, *186*
Policastro, E., 90, 92, 93, *101*
Popper, K. R., 216, *238*
Powell, K., 120, *135*
Price, D., 45, 46, 47, 48, 52, *70*
Prinz, J. J., 53, *68*
Proctor, R. A., 63, *70*

Q

Qin, Y., 63, *70*
Quételet, A., 54n, 56, 59, *70*, 214, *238*
Quinn, N., 192, *207*

R

Rahn, H., 6, *12*
Rajan, C., 218, *238*
Randel, B., 189, 193, *207*
Raskin, E. A., 60, *70*
Rathunde, K., 120, 121, 122, *134*, 190, 203, *205*
Ravid, D., 192, 203, *208*
Redner, S., 54n, *70*
Regher, G., 93, *100*
Renzulli, J. S., 6, *12*, 18, *24*, 170, *186*
Ricoeur, P., 216, 232, *238*
Riegel, K. F., 182, *186*
Ringle, J., 121, *135*
Risemberg, R., 126, *135*
Roberts, J. M., 191, *207*
Roberts, R. M., 65, *70*, 213, *238*
Robinson, D. N., 171, *186*
Robsin, C., 141, *166*
Roe, A., 5, *12*, *13*, 66, 67, *70*
Romney, A. K., 192, *207*
Rosenblueth, A., 74, *101*
Rothenberg, A., 63, 66, *70*, 72, 85, 86, 88, *101*
Rovai, E., 51, *72*
Runco, M. A., 17, 18, 21, 23, 24, *24*, 25
Rushton, J. P., 189, *207*
Russell, B., 115, *117*
Ryhammar, L., 35, *37*

S

Salford, L. G., 32, 33, *37*
Salovey, P., 169, *186*
Sand, B. L., 138, *166*
Sander, C. F., 30, *37*
Scardamalia, M., 234, *235*
Schiefele, U., 122, 123, *134*
Schmidt, C. P., 138, *166*
Schmookler, J., 42, 44, 45, 46, *70*
Schwartz, J., 194, *207*
Searle, J. R., 215, 225, *238*
Selman, E., 139, *166*
Serpell, R., 192, 193, 203, *207*
Seymour, E., 139, *166*
Shadish, W. R., Jr., 54n, *70*
Shapiro, G., 65, *70*
Shaver, P., 194, *207*
Shavinina, L. V., 99, *101*
Shockley, W., 52, *71*
Shrager, J., 63, *71*
Shuter-Dyson, R., 138, *166*
Shweder, R. A., 192, 203, *207*

Simon, H., 119, *135*
Simon, H. A., 53, 63, *69, 70, 71,* 76, *100,* 213, 215, *238*
Simonton, D. K., 8, *13,* 42, 45, 46, 47, 48, 49, 50, 51, 52, 53, 54n, 55, 56, 57, 58, 59, 60, 61, 62, 63, 64, 65, 66, *71,* 72, 90, 93, *101,* 189, *207*
Singer, D. G., 20, *25*
Singer, J., 20, *25*
Skinner, B. F., 67, *72*
Sloboda, J. A., 110, 111, *117,* 138, *166*
Smiles, S., 105, 113, *117*
Smith, J., 119, *135,* 181, *185, 186,* 219, *235*
Smith, G. J. W., 29, 30, 31, 32, 33, 35, *37*
Smith, S., 108, *117*
Smith, S. M., 63, *69*
Snook, S. A., 93, *101,* 163, *166,* 171, *186*
Sobel, R. S., 63, *72*
Solomon, B., 120, *135*
Soriano, L. J., 181, *186*
Sosniak, L., 138, *166*
Spearman, C. E., 189, *207*
Staudinger, U. M., 171, 181, *185, 186,* 219, *235, 238*
Steiner, C. L., 139, 160, *166*
Stent, G. S., 48, *72*
Sternberg, R. J., 8, *13,* 52, 64, 66, *72,* 93, 95, 99, *100, 101,* 138, 163, *166,* 169, 171, 176, 177, 181, 182, *186,* 189, 192, 193, 196, 199, 203, *207, 208,* 226, *238*
Stevenson, H. W., 189, 193, *207, 208*
Stewart, J. A., 53, *68*
Stigler, J. W., 189, 193, *208*
Stipek, D. J., 189, *208*
Storr, A., 190, *208*
Strauss, S., 192, 203, *208*
Strykowski, B. F., 51, *72*
Suárez-Orozco, C., 191, *208*
Suárez-Orozco, M., 191, *208*
Subotnik, R. F., 138, 139, 140, 160, *166*
Suler, J. R., 66, *72*
Sullivan, M. A., 192, *207*
Summers, E., 160, *166*
Super, C. M., 192, 193, 203, *205, 208*
Suzuki, D. T., 215, *238*
Svensson, B., 32, *37*

T

Tannenbaum, A. J., 6, *13*
Taylor, C., 222, 223, 228, 230n, 232, *238*
Taylor, C. W., 190, *208*
Taylor, R., 235, *236*
Terman, L. M., 4, 5, *13,* 51, 72, 189, *208*
Tesch-Römer, C., 111, *117,* 119, *135*
Thomas, D., 45, 46, *70*
Tootill, E., 48, *68*
Torrance, E. P., 22, *25,* 190, *208*
Toulmin, S., 222, *237*
Triandis, H., 200, *206*
Trygg, L., 32, *37*
Tu, W. M., 197, 199, 200, 201, *208*
Turner, S. P., 53, *72*
Tweney, R. D., 64, 67, *72*

U

Urbina, S., 189, *207*

V

VanLehn, K., 235, *236*
Varela, 219, *238*
Vega, L., 23, *24*
Vernadsky, V. I., 77, 78, 79, *101*
Vernon, P. E., 189, *208*

W

Wachs, T. D., 190, *208*
Wagner, R. K., 93, *101,* 163, *166,* 171, 177, *186*
Walberg, H. J., 51, *72*
Wallace, D. B., *102*
Wallach, M. A., 17, *25*
Wang, Q., 198, *208*
Wanner, R. A., 47, *68*
Ward, T. B., 63, *69*
Wasser, A., 160, *166*
Watts, I., 112, *117*
Wechsler, J., 86, 96, *102*
Wegner, D. M., 28, *37,* 215, *238*
Weisberg, R., 113, *117*
Weisberg, R. W., 60, *72*
Werner, H., *37*
Wertheimer, M., 73, *102*

AUTHOR INDEX

Whalent, S., 120, 121, 122, *134*
Wheatly, T., 28, *37*
White, L., 42, *72*
Whitehead, A. N., 29, *37*
Wiener, N., 74, *101*
Wigfield, A., 122, 123, *134*
Williams, B., 219, *238*
Williams, L. P., 108, 111, 113, 115, *117*
Williams, W. M., 93, *101*, 163, *166*, 171, *186*
Wilson, E. O., 226, *238*
Wilson, M., 89, 90, 92, 97, 98, *102*
Wing, C., 17, *25*
Winner, E., 120, 121, 131, *135*, 138, *166*, 189, 203, *208*
Wober, M., 193, 203, *208*
Woodward, C. E., 84, 86, 88, 89, *102*
Wright, J. C., 194, *206*
Wu, S.-P., 197, 198n, 199, 200, 201, *208*
Wu, Z., 193, 196, *208*

Y

Yang, K. S., 199, 200, 202, *208*
Yang, S.-Y., 192, 193, 196, 199, 203, *208*
Yarbrough, C., 191, *207*
Yu, A. B., 199, 200, 202, *208*
Yue, X.-D., 187, 194, 197, 198, 199, 200, 203, *206*, *208*

Z

Zajonc, R., 18n, *25*
Zhang, H., 193, 196, *208*
Zhang, W.-G., 198, *208*
Zimmerman, B. J., 120, 121, 126, *135*, 229, *238*
Zuckerman, H., 44, 72, 82, 83, 87, 89, *102*, 138, *166*
Zythow, J. M., 63, *69*

Subject Index

A

Accommodation, 19
Assimilation, 19

B

Balance theory, 172–176

C

Career age, 56–57
Chance, 39–67, 212–213
Cognitive development, 18–19, 232–235
Control, 30
Creative functioning, 33–36
Creative output, 50–62
Creative potential, 57
Creative process, 57–65
Creativity, 9–10, 17–24, 32–36, 40, 211–235
   judgement, 213–215
   personal creativity, 18–24
      cognition, 18–19
      developmental trends, 21–22
   unconscious processes, 27–36
Creators, 43, 49–67
   serendipity, 65

D

Development, 18–19, 21–22, 139–140, 143, 182–183, 232–235
Diligence, 110–114

E

Education, 228–229
   creativity, 229–230
Ego strength, 215, 231
Equal-odds rule, 55–56
Essentials of learning attitude, 195
Excellence, 187–204
   Chinese, 193–202
Exceptional achievements, 3, 105–116
   extracognitive facets, 3–12
Exceptional adults, 5
Expertise, 119–121, 211
External history, 217
Extracognitive phenomenon, 18, 73–100, 197, 211
   creativity, 17–24
   in adolescents, 80–82
   in nobel laureates, 82–93
   metacognition, 95–96

G

Geniuses, 105–117
   diligence, 110–114
   extracognitive factors, 107, 110–117
   perseverance, 114–115
   social capabilities, 115–116
Giftedness, *see also* High ability, 11, 73, 77, 80, 169
   wisdom, 169–185, 230

H

Habitus, 224–228, 230–231

cultural capital, 225
social reality, 225
High ability, 3, 9–11, 17, 73, 187–204, 211
cultural differences, 191–193
Human civilization, 3

I

Ideas, 42–43, 212
Internal history, 212
Intuition, 74, 91–93
IQ, 51–52, 214

J

Judgement, 213–215
Julliard, 137–165

L

Lotka Law, 52

M

Metacognition, 95–96, 214, 215
Monotonic benefits assumption, 120
Motivation, 120
Multiples, 41–42, 45–51
identical, 43–44

P

Perceptgenetic theory, 28–30, 32–33
anxiety, 30
Perseverance, 114–115, 126–127
Personality traits, 3–8
Phronesis, 218
Price Law, 56
Principle of accumulative advantage, 52–53

S

Selfways, *see* Habitus

Serendipity, 65
Social capabilities, 115–116
Social factors, 4, 8–9
macro-social forces, 8
micro-social factors, 8
Sociocultural determinism, 41–42, 46, 50
Sociocultural factors, *see* Social factors
Specific, 74
Stochastic, 42, 48, 62

T

Talent, *see also* Giftedness, 119–134
expertise, 119–121
mastery, 129–131
motivation, 120
perseverance, 126–127
study, 122–124
Talent development, 139–140, 143
The Julliard School, 137–165
stars, 152–157
underachievers, 157–160
Tacit knowledge, 217–218, 225–226
external history, 217

U

Unconscious processes, 27–36

W

Wisdom, 169–185, 230
balance theory, 172–176
development, 182–183
measuring, 180–181
metacomponents, 176–178
R. vs. Latimer, 219–221
values, 178–179

Z

Zeitgeist, 41, 44
Zhuge Liang, 187–188, 190–191, 197, 201